THE
Print
Shop
Deluxe
IDEA BOOK

Sherry Kinkoph

alpha
books

A Division of Macmillan Computer Publishing

201 W. 103rd Street, Indianapolis, Indiana 46290 USA

To my nephew, Jacob Cannon, a future Print Shop Deluxe aficionado—or at least he will be whenever he learns to read this book.

International Standard Book Number: 1-56761-492-2

Library of Congress Catalog Card Number: 94-70828

96 95   8 7 6 5 4

Interpretation of the printing code: the rightmost number of the first series of numbers is the year of the book's printing; the rightmost number of the second series of numbers is the number of the book's printing. For example, a printing code of 94-1 shows that the first printing of the book occurred in 1994.

Printed in the United States of America

Acknowledgments

Special thanks to Seta Frantz and Herb Feltner for trying all of the projects in this book, and to San Dee Phillips and Michelle Shaw for sorting through them.

Publisher

Marie Butler-Knight

Managing Editor

Elizabeth Keaffaber

Product Development Manager

Faithe Wempen

Acquisitions Manager

Barry Pruett

Senior Development Editor

Seta Frantz

Production Editors

Michelle Shaw and Audra Gable

Copy Editor

San Dee Phillips

Cover Designer

Karen Ruggles

Designer

Barbara Webster

Indexer

Johnna Van Hoose

Production Team

Gary Adair, Dan Caparo, Brad Chinn, Kim Cofer, Lisa Daugherty, Jennifer Eberhardt, Mark Enochs, Beth Rago, Bobbi Satterfield, Kris Simmons, Carol Stamile, Robert Wolf

Special thanks to C. Herbert Feltner for ensuring the technical accuracy of this book.

Contents

What Is The Print Shop Deluxe?

The Print Shop Deluxe is a desktop publishing program that turns you and your computer into a creative manufacturer of greeting cards, banners, signs and flyers, letterhead, calendars, and more. In essence, it allows you to become a designer, copywriter, and layout artist—all rolled into one. Best of all, it's incredibly simple to use and tons of fun.

So where did this program come from? The Print Shop Deluxe has a long history of development. In 1984, Broderbund Software created the original Print Shop, which became a phenomenally popular program among adults and children. Just as the name implied, the program allowed you to create all kinds of materials normally associated with a printing company. It was fun to use and turned your computer into a virtual stationery store. In 1989, Broderbund updated this program as The New Print Shop, an improved version with higher-resolution graphics, more flexibility, and better printing quality. The popular program became even easier to use. Broderbund also created add-on pieces that furthered the program's capabilities.

In 1992, Broderbund introduced The Print Shop Deluxe, with an improved graphical interface that featured even greater flexibility. In The Print Shop Deluxe, you will find crisper and full-color scalable graphics and more detailed layouts for each project type; scalable fonts and special effects make the design potential almost limitless. Broderbund has also created several Print Shop Deluxe Graphics Collections that feature more art: Business Graphics, Sampler Graphics, Comic Characters, Amazing Animals, Celebrations, and Sports Graphics—among others. The Print Shop Deluxe is available now on Windows, DOS, and Macintosh platforms.

What Can You Do with The Print Shop Deluxe?

Start by asking yourself a few questions. Have you ever wanted to create your own greeting cards? Have you ever needed to make a poster or flyer for a sale or an upcoming event? Have you ever wanted to design your own banners to hang up at parties? With The Print Shop Deluxe, you can do all these things and more, right on your own computer. The Print Shop Deluxe programs are for people who are tired of buying the same old generic stuff at the store. With the software, you can personalize, tailor, and design your own stationery, calendars, signs, advertising, useful computer crafts, and more.

This book will show you hundreds of ideas you can use around the home, office, or school. There are projects for families and professionals, and even projects just for kids. You'll learn how to make sale flyers, real estate signs, labels, newsletters, recipe cards, book markers, restaurant menus, and garage sale signs, to name just a few. If you have The Print Shop Deluxe on your computer, whether it's for Windows, DOS, or the Macintosh, you can complete any of the project ideas in this book!

How to Use This Book

The first section of the book contains projects divided into the following 13 categories. This includes an explanation on how to read the project steps. Among the projects themselves, you'll find ideas ranging from business and school projects to home and craft projects.

- How to Build a Project
- Cards
- Letterhead & Stationery
- Signs & Flyers
- Banners
- Calendars
- Parties, Holidays, & Other Celebrations
- Business Projects
- School Projects
- Home Projects
- Club & Organization Projects
- Craft Projects
- Kid Stuff

The next section of the book covers the basics of getting in and out of the program, such as how to navigate the various menus and tips for printing. Here you'll learn how to modify graphics, import your own art, and create your own special effects.

Finally, at the end of the book, check out the tables of available typestyles and all the Print Shop Deluxe graphics. We sincerely believe you'll find this book to be the most comprehensive guide to The Print Shop Deluxe program.

Using a little imagination, combined with the power of your computer, you'll be amazed at the variety of creations available at your fingertips. However, don't take our word for it; turn the page and find out for yourself.

How to Build a Project

It's a good idea to read this short section before starting into the projects. You'll learn how to use the project pages, and how to read the numbered steps detailing each project. If you're unfamiliar with the Print Shop Deluxe program (PSD for short), turn to Section Two for detailed instructions on using the software. There, you'll find help for working with text, graphics, and more. If you'd like to see what fonts and art are available on PSD, you'll find them cataloged in the back of the book.

What Kinds of Projects You'll Find

The projects are divided into 12 parts: Cards; Letterhead & Stationery; Signs & Flyers; Banners; Calendars; Parties, Holidays, & Other Celebrations; Business Projects; School Projects; Home Projects; Club & Organization Projects; Craft Projects; and Kid Stuff.

At the beginning of each of the project categories, you'll find "parts pages." These pages will show you the menu sequences, where applicable, for completing each type of project, and provide any special tips for working with that particular project type. The menus pictured on the parts pages are from PSD-Windows. If you're working with DOS or Mac versions, you'll find extra (and necessary) information for your particular program, too.

> *DOS, Windows, Mac?* If you're new to the world of computers, running across the terms *DOS*, *Windows*, and *Macintosh* (or Mac for short) may throw you for a loop. However, don't panic. DOS stands for *disk operating system*: a program that provides the most basic instructions your computer needs to operate. DOS is the "boss" of your computer system.
>
> Windows is a program that runs on top of your computer's DOS system and gives everything a friendly, visual approach. Windows is a *graphical user interface* that lets you choose commands by using menus or icons. (*Icons* are little pictures.)
>
> Mac is a different type of computer altogether. It's made by Apple Computers, Inc. Mac, like Windows, is a graphical user interface that allows you to command the computer through a visual display of menus and icons. However, Mac has its own kind of operating system that differs from DOS.

On the rest of the pages, you'll find various project ideas, one project idea per page. Each project page will contain a title of the idea, a picture of the project, and numbered steps to help you create the project. All of the projects shown were created using the basic PSD program (not the extra add-on graphics libraries, or the Print Shop Deluxe Companion).

In addition to these items, you'll also come across tips, other ideas for using the project, and important information about the Print Shop programs. Be sure to read these; they'll help you create professional-looking projects, give you suggestions for modifying existing projects, and help spark new ideas.

What Do You Need to Get Started?

Other than a creative spirit, the first tangible item you need to get started is a copy of PSD up and running on your computer. The second thing you need is a printer to print out your projects. A mouse is very nice, too. You'll use it to build all of your projects. Aside from these things, there's not much else to worry about.

Starting the Program

To begin, the PSD program must be installed on your computer's *hard disk drive* (the internal storage device that stores and runs your software). If you haven't yet installed the program, see Appendix A at the back of this book for instructions.

To start PSD, follow the instructions listed for your specific type of software:

PSD-Windows

1. From the Windows Program Manager screen, double-click on the **The Print Shop Deluxe Program Group** icon.

2. Double-click on the **Print Shop Deluxe** icon.

> ***What's a Double-Click?*** A double-click is two quick taps or presses of the left mouse button. A regular click is just one tap.

PSD-DOS

1. At the DOS prompt, change to the drive and directory where you installed the program. For example, this will probably be C:PSDELUXE. At the C:\> prompt, type **PSDELUXE** and press **Enter**.

2. Type **PSD** and then press **Enter**.

PSD-Mac

1. From the Macintosh main screen, double-click on the **PSDeluxe** folder.

2. Double-click on the **Print Shop Deluxe** icon.

A Project Example

Take a look at the instruction steps in the following project. Each step consists of concise bulleted ministeps that will lead you through each aspect of building the project.

1. Project: Choose Banner. • Choose Vertical.

Click here.→

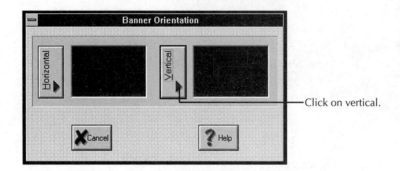

Click on vertical.

   Each project step begins with the Main menu screen. Step 1 always tells you which menu items to choose as you start each project. According to step 1 above, you would choose the Banner project type, then choose the appropriate paper orientation.

2. Backdrop: Choose Ogre. • Click OK.

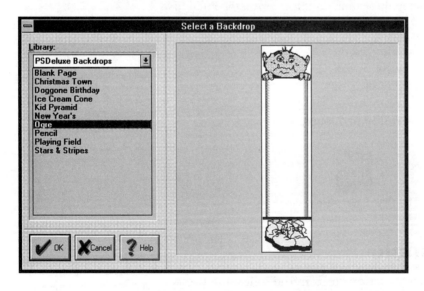

   Step 2 specifies which backdrop art to use. In this example, you would select the backdrop art titled "Ogre."

3. Layout: Choose Ogre 5. • Click OK.

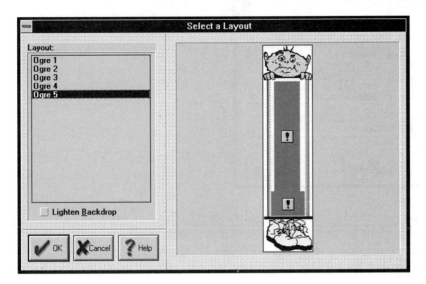

Step 3 specifies a layout design to use for the project.

4. Fill in Headline block 1: Double-click block. • Font: Subway.
    • Type your child's name. • Click OK.

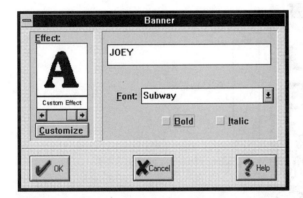

Step 4 tells you how to edit a headline block. You would select the headline block, then change the font to Subway. Then you would type in a name.

5. Fill in Headline block 2: Double-click block. • Font: NewZurica.
    • Style: Bold. • Type: GROWTH CHART. • Click OK.

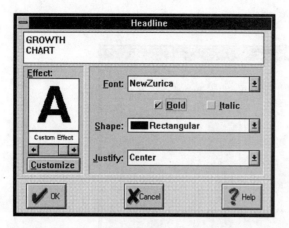

Step 5 instructs you how to edit another headline block, this time changing the font and style. Other editing examples will include text size, color, positioning, and more. Figure 1.1 shows you what the finished project looks like.

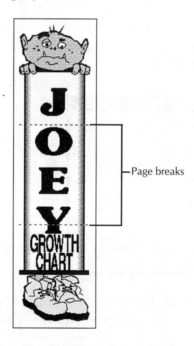

Figure 1.1
A finished project completed with PSD-Windows.

You won't find numbered steps for saving or printing when you finish the project idea. Those steps are always the same, and you'll find them in Section Two if you're not sure how to do them.

Now You're Ready to Begin

It's a good idea to thumb through all the ideas shown in the project section of the book. You'll find examples of each kind of project you can make using Print Shop Deluxe, as well as ideas for building other types of projects. Of course, there just isn't enough room to tell you about everything you can build with the program. However, the projects you see will surely inspire you to try innovative ideas of your own!

The wonderful thing about the PSD program is that you find yourself *being* very creative, even if you don't consider yourself a creative person. This program makes it easy to invent projects. You can modify every idea in this book to suit your needs. We've included ideas that range from simple to challenging. Experiment, explore, and exhaust all possibilities. No matter what version of the PSD you have, Windows, DOS, or Mac, you can create your own variations of the projects shown.

Good luck—and have fun!

Cards

You can use card projects for a variety of occasions: invitations, greetings, stationery, congratulations, customer service responses, announcements, holidays, and much more. Follow the basic steps shown to create any card project.

- Birthday
- Belated Birthday
- Valentine's Day
- Mother's Day
- Father's Day
- Holiday Cut-Out
- Sympathy
- Wedding
- Anniversary
- New Baby
- Open House
- Announcement
- Graduation
- Just Moved
- Party Invitation
- Thank-You
- Family Reunion
- Friendship
- Customer Service Response
- Baby Shower
- Notecard

PSD-Windows steps:

1. Select Greeting Card from the Project menu screen.

2. Select the project orientation.

3. Choose a backdrop graphic design, and click OK.

4. Choose a layout design, and click OK.

5. Use the Tool Palette and pull-down menus to fill in each layout element.

6. Select the Project menu; then select Inside of Card. Repeat steps 3–5.

7. Optional: Select the Project menu; then select Back of Card. Repeat steps 4–5.

8. Pull down the File menu, and select Save. In the File Save As dialog box, type in a file name, and click OK.

9. Pull down the File menu, and select Print. In the Print dialog box, choose any printing option, and click OK.

Windows Shortcut

Instead of pulling down the Project menu to move to the inside of the card, click on the Navigation button. Located in the lower right corner of your window, this button has two directional arrows to take you to each side of your card project.

All of the instructions for individual card projects in this book are Windows steps. However, if you're using PSD-DOS or PSD-Mac, you can create the exact same projects. For the most part, your steps will be the same. There may be some slight differences in the instructions.

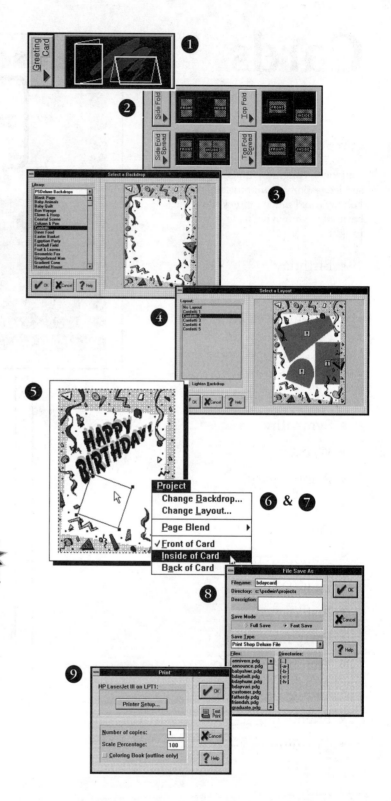

PSD-DOS steps:

1. Select Greeting Card from the Project menu.

2. Select Create a new project.

3. Select the project orientation.

4. Choose Select a Backdrop from the menu list. Choose a backdrop design and click Done.

5. Choose Select a Layout from the menu list. Choose a layout design.

6. Choose Fill In or Edit from the menu list. Fill in each layout element.

7. Choose Go to Inside of Card; repeat steps 4–6.

8. Optional: Select Go to Back of Card; repeat steps 5–6.

9. Choose Save from the menu list. Type in a file name and any description of the project; then choose the Save File command.

10. Choose Print from the menu list and select the Print command.

If you're using PSD-DOS, your project steps will differ slightly. Unlike the Windows steps in which you click OK to complete a task, click Done (where applicable) when you finish with each project step. Instead of using a Tool Palette or pull-down menus to fill in layout elements, use a menu list and dialog boxes. Line Justify denotes horizontal justification, and Placement denotes vertical justification—so look for those commands to control positioning.

When creating your own layout, use the Add New Elements command to insert the various layout elements. If you ever become confused about using a menu or dialog box, look at the bottom of your screen for brief instructions telling you what to do.

PSD-Mac steps:

1. Select Greeting Card from the Project menu screen.

2. Select the project orientation.

3. Choose a backdrop graphic design, and click OK.

4. Choose a layout design, and click OK.

5. Use the Tool Palette and pull-down menus to fill in each layout element.

6. Select the Project menu; then select Inside of Card. Repeat steps 3–5.

7. Optional: Select the Project menu; then select Back of Card. Repeat steps 4–5.

8. Pull down the File menu, and select Save. In the Save dialog box, type in a file name, and click Save.

9. Pull down the File menu, and select Print. In the Print dialog box, choose any printing option, and click Print.

Your PSD-Mac project steps will vary slightly. Unlike PSD-Windows and PSD-DOS users, use the Text menu to select fonts, sizes, and justification. Like the Windows steps, double-click a text block to select it. Once selected, you can start typing in text, or pull down the Text menu and change text options. When finished typing, just click outside the block. Justification denotes horizontal justification, and Placement denotes vertical justification—so look for those commands on the Text menu to control positioning.

Mac Short-cut

Instead of pulling down the Project menu to move to the inside of the card, click on the Navigation menu. Located in the lower left corner of your window, this menu displays three options to take you to each side of your card project.

Folding the Card Project

PSD prints out your card project so that you can easily fold it. Fold the page in half from top to bottom (short edge to short edge); then fold in half again (see the illustration).

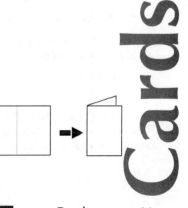

Birthday

You can create birthday cards for adults, children, work associates, family, and others. This project is an example of a humorous card.

1. Project: Choose Greeting Card.
   • Click Side Fold.

2. Backdrop: Choose Blank Page.
   • Click OK.

3. Layout: Choose No Layout.
   • Click OK.

4. Click on New Object tool.
   • Choose Column Graphic.
   • Move graphic to left side of card.
   • Resize to fill entire vertical space. • Double-click graphic.
   • Choose Space Ships. • Click OK.

5. Click on New Object tool.
   • Choose Text. • Move block to upper right corner of card.
   • Double-click text block. • Font: Boulder. • Font Size: Medium.
   • Justification Horizontal: Center.
   • Justification Vertical: Center.
   • Type: In a Galaxy, light years away . . . You were born . . . (line 3 should be blank). • Click OK.
   • Resize the text block to fit in text.

6. Click on New Object tool.
   • Choose Square Graphic. • Move graphic to bottom right corner of remaining space. • Double-click graphic. • Choose Spaceship.
   • Click OK. • Resize to fill remaining empty space.

7. Select Inside of Card.

8. Backdrop: Choose Blank Page.
   • Click OK.

9. Layout: Choose No Layout.
   • Click OK.

10. Click on New Object tool.
    • Choose Column Graphic.
    • Double-click graphic. • Choose

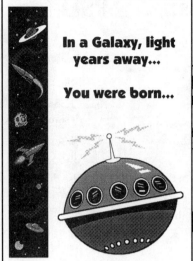

Space Ships. • Click OK. • Click on Rotate tool. • Rotate graphic (90 degrees). • Click on Pointer tool.
• Move graphic to top of card.
• Resize to fill the space.

11. Click on New Object tool.
    • Choose Text. • Move the block below Column Graphic. • Double-click text block. • Font: Jester.
    • Font Size: Medium.
    • Justification Horizontal: Center.
    • Justification Vertical: Center.
    • Type: Those light years catch up to you pretty fast, huh! • Click OK.
    • Move and resize text block to fit text.

12. Click on New Object tool.
    • Choose Text. • Move the block below first text block. • Double-click text block. • Font: Boulder.
    • Font Size: Large. • Justification Horizontal: Center. • Justification Vertical: Center. • Type: HAPPY BIRTHDAY! • Click OK. • Move and resize text block to fit text.

Variation

There's even more "out-of-this-world" art to use! You'll find a UFO backdrop design when you open the Backdrop dialog box. Try using this art for the inside of your card along with Layout UFO2. Then fill a headline block with "HAPPY BIRTHDAY!" and a text block with the same inside greeting shown in step 11. Print your project on colored paper for added pizzazz!

Belated Birthday

For missed birthday salutations, here's a belated birthday project that's sure to put you back in good graces!

1. Project: Choose Greeting Card.
   • Click Side Fold.

2. Backdrop: Choose Blank Page.
   • Click OK.

3. Layout: Choose No Layout.
   • Click OK.

4. Click on New Object tool. • Choose Square Graphic. • Resize to fill lower two thirds of card. • Double-click graphic. • Choose Football. • Click OK.

5. Click on New Object tool. • Choose Headline. • Move block to upper portion of card. • Double-click headline block. • Font: Bazooka. • Type: OOPS! • Shape: Double Arch Up. • Click OK. • Resize the block to fill remaining space.

6. Select Inside of Card.

7. Backdrop: Choose Football Field. • Click OK.

8. Layout: Choose Football Field 2. • Click OK.

9. Fill in first text block: Double-click block. • Font: Bazooka. • Font Size: Medium Large. • Justification Horizontal: Center. • Justification Vertical: Center. • Type: I FUMBLED ON YOUR BIRTHDAY! • Click OK.

10. Fill in second text block: Double-click block. • Font: NewZurica. • Style: Bold. • Font Size: Small. • Justification Horizontal: Center. • Justification Vertical: Center. • Type: Hope you had a great day! • Click OK.

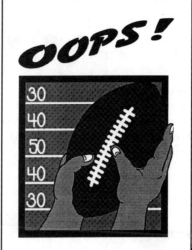

Variation

Another spin-off of this idea is to use the football-oriented column and row graphics. Use the Football Player column graphic on the cover of the card, and the Football Players row graphic on the inside of the card. You can still use the same greeting from the project steps above, or create a new one.

Valentine's Day

Valentine's Day presents many possibilities in card making. You can design personal cards for friends, loved ones, and children. Use the opportunity to be creative, serious, or funny. Here's a simple Valentine's Day card using a row graphic border.

1. Project: Choose Greeting Card.
   • Click Side Fold.

2. Backdrop: Choose Blank Page.
   • Click OK.

3. Layout: Choose No Layout.
   • Click OK.

4. Click on New Object tool.
   • Choose Row Graphic. • Double-click graphic. • Choose Cupids.
   • Click OK. • Move graphic to top of card. • Resize to fill space as shown in above example.

5. Repeat step 4 and add another row graphic, this time placing it at the bottom of the card. • Resize to fill space as shown in example.

6. Follow step 4 to add yet another of the same row graphic. • Click on Rotate tool. • Rotate the graphic 90 degrees. • Click on Pointer tool.
   • Resize and move graphic to the left side of the card, forming a border with the other two graphics.

7. Repeat step 6, except this time rotate the graphic 90 degrees in the other direction. • Resize and move graphic to the right side of the card, completing a border of Cupids. • You may have to move all four graphics around to make a border.

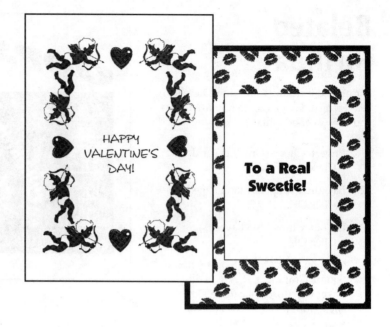

8. Click on New Object tool.
   • Choose Text. • Resize block to fit in the middle of the Cupid border.
   • Double-click text block. • Font: Scribble. • Font Size: Medium.
   • Justification Horizontal: Center.
   • Justification Vertical: Center.
   • Type: HAPPY VALENTINE'S DAY! • Click OK.

9. Select Inside of Card.

10. Backdrop: Choose Lips! Lips!.
    • Click OK.

11. Layout: Choose Greeting Card 4.
    • Click OK.

12. Fill in border: Double-click border.
    • Choose Eight Point. • Click OK.

13. Fill in text block: Double-click block. • Font: Boulder. • Font Size: Medium. • Justification Horizontal: Center. • Justification Vertical: Center. • Type: To a Real Sweetie! • Click OK. • Click on Frame Tool. • Choose Thin Line.
    • Use the Color Palette to change the background behind the text to the color white.

Design Tip

Valentine cards are great for gluing on extra effects. Using a clear-drying glue and try adding glitter, bows, dried flowers, lace, and other decorative touches to make a special keepsake.

Copy and Paste

If you're using Windows or Mac, you can use the Copy and Paste commands from the Edit menu to do steps 5–7. Then use the Flip command on the Tool Palette to do step 7 and put the last column in place.

Mother's Day

Mother's Day is one of the most popular days of the year to give a card. Here's your chance to personalize a Mother's Day card to really say what you're thinking. This particular project is a good example of keeping a theme in your card design. The front uses the Butterflies backdrop, and the inside uses the Wildflowers square graphic. Both complement each other very well.

1. Project: Choose Greeting Card.
   • Click Top Fold.

2. Backdrop: Choose Butterflies.
   • Click OK.

3. Layout: Choose Greeting Card 7.
   • Click OK.

4. Fill in border: Double-click border.
   • Choose Eight Point. • Click OK.

5. Fill in bottom Headline block: Double-click block. • Font: Paramount. • Shape: Rectangle. • Type: Happy Mother's Day!. • Click OK. (Don't edit top headline block or square graphic, just leave them blank or delete them.)

6. Select Inside of Card.

7. Backdrop: Choose Blank Page.
   • Click OK.

8. Layout: Choose No Layout.
   • Click OK.

9. Click on New Object tool. • Choose Border. • Double-click Border. • Choose Eight Point. • Click OK.

10. Click on New Object tool. • Choose Square Graphic. • Double-click graphic. • Choose Wildflowers. • Click OK. • Move block to lower left corner; resize to fill space as shown in example above.

11. Click on New Object tool. • Choose Text. • Resize block to fit in upper right portion of card. • Double-click block. • Font: Paramount. • Font Size: Small. • Justification Horizontal: Center. • Justification Vertical: Center. • Type: Moms like you are rather rare, Giving all your love and care, So on this day we want to share, Our appreciation to one so fair. • Click OK.

Design Tip

Unless you're using a color printer, don't forget to add color to your greeting cards. Use colored pencils, markers, or watercolors to bring your cards to life.

Father's Day

Don't forget to give Dad a personalized card on Father's Day. This project emphasizes the fishing graphic motif.

1. Project: Choose Greeting Card.
   • Click Side Fold Spread.

2. Backdrop: Choose Blank Page.
   • Click OK.

3. Layout: Choose No Layout.
   • Click OK.

4. Click on New Object tool.
   • Choose Border. • Double-click Border. • Choose Four Point.
   • Click OK.

5. Click on New Object tool.
   • Choose Headline. • Double-click headline block. • Font: Jester.
   • Style: Bold. • Shape: Arc Up.
   • Customize: Effect 11; scroll the scroll box until you reach effect 11 on the Customize bar. • Type: Sit back and relax, Dad. • Click OK.

6. Click on New Object tool.
   • Choose Square Graphic.
   • Double-click graphic. • Choose Adirondack Chair. • Click OK.
   • Resize graphic to fill remaining space in card.

7. Select Inside of Card.

8. Backdrop: Choose Fishing.
   • Click OK.

9. Layout: Choose No Layout.
   • Click OK.

10. Click on New Object tool.
    • Choose Headline. • Double-click headline block. • Font: Jester.
    • Style: Bold. • Type: It's Father's Day! • Click OK. • Move block to top and resize to fill space.

11. Click on New Object tool.
    • Choose Text. • Double-click text block. • Font: Jester. • Font Size: Small. • Style: Bold. • Justification Horizontal: Center. • Justification Vertical: Center. • Type: So take it easy, enjoy the day, Do a little fishing down on the bay, Catch a little guppy if you may, Then tell us how much it really did weigh!
    • Click OK. • Resize block to fit in lower left corner, as shown in example.

Variation

If you have the Amazing Animals graphics library (a collection of more PSD art) loaded on your computer, you can use the various fish cartoon drawings to illustrate the front of your card design. Check out all of the water "life," and be creative!

Holiday Cut-Out

Here's a project idea for a Christmas card using a cut-out technique, which lets you see through the cover of the card to the inside.

1. Project: Choose Greeting Card.
   • Click Top Fold.

2. Backdrop: Choose Tree & Presents.
   • Click OK.

3. Layout: Choose No Layout.
   • Click OK.

4. Click on New Object tool. • Choose Square Graphic. • Double-click graphic. • Choose Thought Bubble. • Click OK. • Move block to upper right corner of card. • Resize block to fill space.

5. Select Inside of Card.

6. Backdrop: Choose Blank Page.
   • Click OK.

7. Layout: Choose No Layout.
   • Click OK.

8. Click on New Object tool. • Choose Square Graphic. • Repeat to add two more square graphics. • Move and line up each graphic to make a vertical column on the left side of the card. • Double-click top square graphic. • Choose Holly. • Select Apply to All Squares. • Click OK. • Click on Rotate tool. • Rotate each graphic 45 degrees.

9. Click on New Object tool. • Choose Text. • Double-click block. • Font: Boulder. • Size: Small.
   • Justification Horizontal: Center.
   • Justification Vertical: Center.
   • Type: Hmmm, did I remember to deck the halls yet? • Click OK.
   • Move block to middle right side of card, resizing as necessary to fit.
   • Use the Color controls to set the

background color to a light gray color and shade 30%.

10. Click on New Object tool.
    • Choose Text. • Double-click block. • Font: Jester. • Size: Medium. • Justification Horizontal: Center. • Justification Vertical: Center. • Type: Hope you find time to have a Merry Christmas! • Click OK. • Move block beneath first text block and resize to fit.

11. Print and fold card. • Use scissors or Xacto knife to cut out thought bubble shape through both layers of paper. When complete, cut-out should reveal Text block 1 from inside of card when folded (this may take some experimenting).

Measure Up

You can quickly check the placement of the cutaway text by holding the printed, folded card up to a light source. If the text block appears behind the Thought Bubble art, follow step 11. If not, go back to PSD and move the block to fit.

Design Tip

There are many great ideas you can explore for designing cards with cut-outs and other special effects. Give your cards scalloped edging that you can trim with scissors. Or try your hand at making a partial card cover that lets you see half of the inside of the card. You can also create a tri-fold design and other effects. Don't let yourself be limited to the standard print-it-out and fold-it-up format. A good place to look for special effects ideas is your local card shop.

Sympathy

For a simple, yet elegant sympathy card, follow the steps in this project idea.

1. Project: Choose Greeting Card.
   • Click Top Fold.

2. Backdrop: Choose Stained Glass.
   • Click OK.

3. Layout: Choose Stained Glass 1.
   • Click OK.

4. Fill in the text block. Double-click text block. • Font: Signature.
   • Font Size: Medium Large.
   • Justification Horizontal: Center.
   • Justification Vertical: Center.
   • Type: Sincerest Sympathies.
   • Click OK.

5. Select Inside of Card.

6. Backdrop: Choose Blank Page.
   • Click OK.

7. Layout: Choose No Layout.
   • Click OK.

8. Click on New Object tool.
   • Choose Border. • Double-click Border. • Choose Joined Lines.
   • Select Wide Border. • Click OK.
   • Use the Color controls to set Behind Object to the color green.

9. Click on New Object tool.
   • Choose Text. • Size to fit inside of border. • Double-click text block. • Font: Signature. • Font Size: Medium Large. • Justification Horizontal: Center. • Justification Vertical: Center. • Type: Our condolences to you and your family • Click OK. • Click on Frame tool. • Add a Thin Line frame. • Use the Color controls to set the Frame to a purple color and Behind Text to a shade of purple (10–20% screen).

Design Tip

When using Script fonts, such as the Signature font used in this project, remember this simple design rule: never use all capital letters with a script font. Script fonts look like cursive handwriting, which appears in upper- and lowercase letters.

Wedding

For an informal card to mail or enclose with a wedding gift, try this project idea.

1. Project: Choose Greeting Card.
   • Click Top Fold Spread.

2. Backdrop: Choose Blank Page.
   • Click OK.

3. Layout: Choose No Layout.
   • Click OK.

4. Click on New Object tool. • Choose Border. • Double-click border. • Choose Thick Border. • Click OK. • Use the Color Palette to change the Border to another color. (If you have a color printer, choose green. If you have a monochrome printer, choose dark gray.)

5. Click on New Object tool. • Choose Square Graphic. • Double-click square graphic. • Choose Swans. • Click OK. • Resize graphic to fill space, as shown in example. • Use the Color controls to change color of graphic to gray or green, 30% shading.

6. Select Inside of Card.

7. Backdrop: Choose Doves & Mint.
   • Click OK.

8. Layout: Choose Doves & Mint 3.
   • Click OK.

9. Fill in top Headline block: Double-click block. • Font: Sherwood. • Shape: Arc Up. • Type: Congratulations! • Click OK.

10. Fill in text block: Double-click block. • Font: Calligrapher. • Font Size: Small. • Justification Horizontal: Center. • Justification Vertical: Center. • Type: May you have a blessed marriage, One that's sure to grow, Full of warmth and happiness, And love that makes you glow. • Click OK.

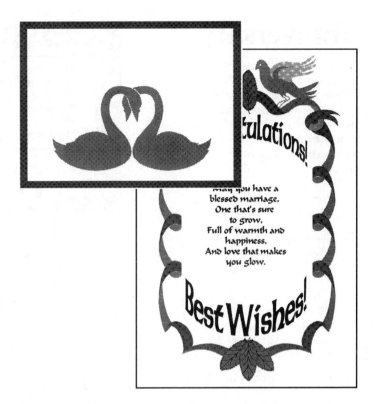

11. Fill in bottom Headline block: Double-click block. • Font: Sherwood. • Shape: Arc Down. • Type: Best Wishes! • Click OK.

Design Tip

If you're using poems or prose in your card text, be sure to separate the stanzas where necessary. To add blank lines between text, just press the Enter key while in the Edit Text dialog box. To indent text, press the Spacebar 3–5 times before starting your sentence. The indent will show up best if you justify the text to the left of the block.

Shading Your Art

This project let you experiment with shading a layout element (you set a square graphic at 30% gray in step 5). You can use the shading controls (also called screening) to create all kinds of special effects in your PSD projects. Don't hesitate to experiment with various shades or screens and colors. Just remember, the true test of how they will look occurs when you print the project out on paper.

Anniversary

Of course, you can create all kinds of anniversary cards using Print Shop Deluxe. However, did you ever think of making an anniversary card for your business or shop? Here's a project idea for a business anniversary card that not only celebrates an anniversary, but promotes a sale as well.

1. Project: Choose Greeting Card.
   • Click Side Fold Spread.

2. Backdrop: Choose Confetti.
   • Click OK.

3. Layout: Choose Confetti 4.
   • Click OK.

4. Fill in mini-border (located in upper middle of project): Double-click mini-border. • Choose Celtic. • Click OK.

5. Fill in Text block 1 (inside mini-border): Double-click block. • Font: Calligrapher. • Font Size: Medium. • Justification Horizontal: Center. • Justification Vertical: Center. • Type: D. Hardy Jewelers is proud to announce our 75th anniversary! (substitute your company name and anniversary year). • Click OK.

6. Fill in Text block 2: Double-click block. • Font: Signature. • Font Size: choose Other. • Type in 20-point. • Click OK. • Justification Horizontal: Center. • Justification Vertical: Center. • Type: Join us in Celebrating! • Click OK.

7. Select Inside of Card.

8. Backdrop: Choose Hourglass.
   • Click OK.

9. Layout: Choose Hourglass 5.
   • Click OK.

10. Remove Border: Click border.
    • Click on Delete tool.

11. Fill in Headline block 1: Double-click block. • Font: Standout.
    • Type: ANNIVERSARY SALE!
    • Click OK.

12. Fill in Headline block 2 (in the hourglass): Double-click block.
    • Font: NewZurica. • Type: 75 Years (substitute your anniversary years). • Click OK.

13. Fill in Text block 1: Resize block to take up small space at top of card.
    • Double-click text block. • Font: NewZurica. • Style: Bold. • Font Size: Small. • Type: Special Anniversary Savings for all our valued Customers! (or your business message). • Click OK.

14. Fill in Text block 2: Resize block to take up remaining depth space.
    • Double-click text block. • Font: NewZurica. • Style: Bold. • Font Size: Small. • Type savings message, date, and time of anniversary open house.
    • Click OK.

Variation

Looking for other "anniversary" backdrops? Try using the Watch & Confetti backdrop available for top-fold spread projects. For a simple wedding anniversary, use the Candy Box backdrop art available for top-fold projects.

New Baby

Welcome new arrivals to the family with a personally designed card.

1. Project: Choose Greeting Card.
   • Click Top Fold.

2. Backdrop: Choose Baby Things.
   • Click OK.

3. Layout: Choose Baby Things 5.
   • Click OK.

4. Fill in Headline 1 (in rattle): Double-click block. • Font: Jester.
   • Type: New Baby. • Click OK.

5. Fill in Headline 2 (top right): Double-click block. • Font: Jester.
   • Shape: Arc Up. • Type: Congratulations! • Click OK.
   • Resize headline to fill space as shown.

6. Fill in Headline 3 (bottom right): Double-click block. • Font: Jester.
   • Shape: Bottom Arch. • Type: It's a Boy! (or Girl, as appropriate).
   • Click OK. • Resize headline to fill space as shown.

7. Remove Border: Click border.
   • Click on Delete tool.

8. Select Inside of Card.

9. Backdrop: Choose Blank Page.
   • Click OK.

10. Layout: Choose Greeting Card 9.
    • Click OK.

11. Fill in Border: Click border. • Click on Delete tool. • Delete Border.

12. Fill in Square graphic block 1 (top): Double-click graphic. • Choose Teddy. • Select Apply to All Squares. • Click OK.

13. Fill in Headline block: Double-click block. • Font: Heather. • Type: Can't wait to see him! (or Can't wait to see her!) • Click OK.

14. Click on New Object tool.
    • Choose Horizontal Ruled Line.
    • Double-click on Horizontal Ruled Line. • Choose Baby Pins.
    • Click OK. • Move line to top of card; resize to fit across entire length.

15. Repeat step 14, this time moving the ruled line to the bottom of the card.

16. Click on New Object tool.
    • Choose Vertical Ruled Line.
    • Double-click on Vertical Ruled Line. • Choose Baby Pins. • Click OK. • Move line to left of card; resize to fit vertical space between horizontal ruled lines.

17. Repeat step 16, this time moving the vertical line to the right side of the card.

Copy and Paste

If you're using Windows or Mac, you can use the Copy and Paste commands from the Edit menu to do steps 15 and 17.

Variation

Here's a cute Baby Announcment card idea using a side-fold orientation with Baby Animals backdrop art, and layout 5. When you're filling in the message on the front of the card, type "There's a new kid on the block!" in Scribble font. On the inside of the card, choose the same backdrop and layout again, this time adding information about the baby, birth date, birth weight, and so on.

Open House

Open House invitations are useful for new home owners, real estate showings, new businesses, clubs, and more. These project steps show you how to make an open house invitation for a school open house.

1. Project: Choose Greeting Card.
   • Click Side Fold Spread.

2. Backdrop: Choose Blank Page.
   • Click OK.

3. Layout: Choose No Layout.
   • Click OK.

4. Click on New Object tool.
   • Choose Row Graphic. • Double-click row graphic. • Choose ABC 123. • Click OK. • Move graphic to top of card and resize to fill space.

5. Repeat step 4, this time placing the graphic at the bottom of the card.

6. Repeat step 4 again, but rotate the graphic. • Click on Rotate tool.
   • Rotate the graphic until it's in a vertical position. • Click on Pointer tool. • Move the graphic to the left side of the card. • Resize graphic to fit between the other two graphics, forming a border.

7. Repeat step 4 one last time, but rotate the graphic in the other direction. • Click on Rotate tool.
   • Rotate the graphic into a vertical position. • Click on Pointer tool.
   • Move the graphic to the right side of the card. • Resize graphic to fit between the other two graphics, completing the border.

8. Click on New Object tool.
   • Choose Text. • Move block to center of card, inside row border.
   • Double-click text block. • Font: Heather. • Font Size: Medium.
   • Justification Horizontal: Center.
   • Justification Vertical: Center.
   • Type: PTO Open House. • Click OK. • Resize block to fit text.

PTO Open House

Willard Elementary School PTO proudly presents

Fall Open House
Thursday, October 6 from 6:00 to 9:00 p.m.

Refreshments available in the Main Lobby

Discussion Groups begin at 7:00 p.m. in the Auditorium

School tours every hour PTO sign up in the Cafeteria

9. Select Inside of Card.

10. Backdrop: Choose Blank Page.
    • Click OK.

11. Layout: Choose No Layout.
    • Click OK.

12. Click on New Object tool.
    • Choose Row Graphic. • Double-click row graphic. • Choose ABC 123. • Click OK. • Move block to top of card. • Resize graphic to fit all the way across the spread.

13. Click on New Object tool.
    • Choose Text. • Resize text block to fit below row graphic on left side of card spread. • Double-click text block. • Font: Heather. • Font Size: Medium to Small (varies between lines of text).
    • Justification Horizontal: Center.
    • Justification Vertical: Center.
    • Type your school name and open house information, including date and time. • Click OK.

14. Repeat step 13 for the right side of the card, typing in your open house information.

Design Tip

Yes, you can use any of the row or column graphics to create your own borders, thanks to the handy Rotate command! You can also create borders out of the Ruled line art, too. Just be creative!

Copy and Paste

If you're using Windows or Mac, you can use the Copy and Paste commands from the Edit menu to duplicate blocks.

Announcement

Announcement cards are useful for a range of projects, whether you're advertising special sales promotions to valued clients or updating family and friends on a recent marriage. The steps featured on this page will help you create a semiformal wedding announcement.

1. Project: Choose Greeting Card.
   • Click Top Fold.

2. Backdrop: Choose Blank Page.
   • Click OK.

3. Layout: Choose Greeting Card 25.
   • Click OK.

4. Fill in Border: Double-click border.
   • Choose Spring. • Select Wide Border. • Click OK.

5. Fill in text block: Double-click block. • Font: Calligrapher. • Font Size: Small. • Justification Horizontal: Center. • Justification Vertical: Center. • Type: Mr. and Mrs. (*name of the parents*) proudly announce the marriage of their daughter (*name of the daughter*) to (*name of the groom*). • Click OK.

6. Select Inside of Card.

7. Backdrop: Choose Blank Page.
   • Click OK.

8. Layout: Choose Greeting Card 25.
   • Click OK.

9. Fill in Border: Double-click border.
   • Choose Spring. • Select Wide Border. • Click OK.

10. Fill in text block: Double-click block. • Font: Calligrapher. • Font Size: Small. • Justification Horizontal: Center. • Justification Vertical: Center. • Type: Please join them in a reception celebrating this occasion Saturday, October 16, nineteen hundred and ninety-five at

half past 3 o'clock at their home, 108 Delancey Street, Millville, Pennsylvania (using your own dates, time, and place).
• Click OK.

Design Tip

When dealing with formal and semiformal events, keep your card designs crisp and simple. Use elegant borders and fonts, but don't clutter your project with too much artwork. The main focus of an announcement card is the announcement, not the art!

Graduation

Parents, grandparents, family, friends, school faculty, and businesses will all find designing a graduation card a simple project to complete, especially if you follow these steps.

1. Project: Choose Greeting Card.
   • Click Side Fold Spread.

2. Backdrop: Choose Blank Page.
   • Click OK.

3. Layout: Choose Greeting Card 25.
   • Click OK.

4. Remove bottom Headline: Click block. • Click on Delete tool.

5. Fill in Border: Double-click border.
   • Choose Diamond Corners.
   • Click OK.

6. Fill in square graphic: Resize square graphic to fill space, as shown in illustration. • Double-click graphic. • Choose Graduation. • Click OK.

7. Fill in Headline: Resize block to fill space, as shown in illustration.
   • Double-click headline block.
   • Font: Paramount. • Style: Bold.
   • Shape: Double Arch Up. • Type: Congratulations! • Click OK.

8. Select Inside of Card.

9. Backdrop: Choose Graduation Caps. • Click OK.

10. Layout: Choose Graduation Caps 4. • Click OK.

11. Fill in text block: Double-click block. • Font: Paramount. • Style: Bold. • Font Size: Small.
    • Justification Vertical: Center.
    • Justification Horizontal: Center.
    • Type: Best Wishes to you in all your future endeavors! • Click OK.

12. Fill in Headline: Double-click block. • Font: Paramount. • Shape: Perspective Left. • Customize: Effect 1. (Move the customize scroll bar to the left to find effect 1— normal-looking type.) • Type: You Finally Made It! • Click OK.

Variation

Planning on sending a money gift to a recent graduate? Design your own pocket card that allows you to slip in dollar bills. Base your design on the inside of the card where the bottom inside edge folds up about a third of the way. Glue the edges down to form a pocket.

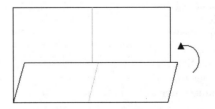

Set It Sideways!

You don't always have to set headlines and text blocks horizontally. Use the Rotate command to set text vertically, too. This will create some interesting designs for you. Experiment for the best effects!

Just Moved

Whether you've moved your family or your business, you can design a card to alert everyone to your change of address. The following steps show you how to make a "Just Moved" card.

1. Project: Choose Greeting Card.
   • Click Top Fold.

2. Backdrop: Choose Blank Page.
   • Click OK.

3. Layout: Choose No Layout.
   • Click OK.

4. Click on New Object tool. • Choose Square Graphic. • Double-click graphic. • Choose PSDeluxe Initial Caps. • Choose Victorian. • Click OK. • Resize block to fill card parameters, as shown in project example.

5. Click on New Object tool. • Choose Text. • Move block to middle of square graphic circle. • Resize to fill inside space. • Double-click text block. • Font: Calligrapher. • Font Size: Medium Large. • Justification Horizontal: Center. • Justification Vertical: Center. • Type: We've Moved! • Click OK.

6. Select Inside of Card.

7. Backdrop: Choose Blank Page.
   • Click OK.

8. Layout: Choose Greeting Card 25.
   • Click OK.

9. Fill in Border: Double-click border.
   • Choose Blue Check. • Click OK.

10. Fill in text block: Double-click block. • Font: Calligrapher. • Font Size: Medium. • Justification Horizontal: Center. • Justification Vertical: Center. • Type: Here's our new address: (press Enter to leave an empty line, and then type your name and address). • Click OK.

Variation

Is your business relocating? Create a "We Moved" announcement to send to your customers. Using a top-fold spread orientation, design a card front with a simple border, headline, text block with company name, and a small graphic. On the inside, use Fireworks backdrop and layout 4 to create a new location address and sales information.

Party Invitation

PSD is perfect for creating your own party invitations to birthday parties, cookouts, New Year's Eve parties, holiday gatherings, dinner parties, office parties, school parties, and much more. The instructions shown on this page are for a classic children's birthday party invitation, with traditional clown art.

1. Project: Choose Greeting Card.
   • Click Top Fold Spread.

2. Backdrop: Choose Clown with Card. • Click OK.

3. Layout: Choose Clown with Card 1. • Click OK.

4. Fill in text block: Double-click block. • Font: Subway. • Font Size: Medium Large. • Type: IT'S A PARTY! • Click OK.

5. Select Inside of Card.

6. Backdrop: Choose Clown & Confetti. • Click OK.

7. Layout: Choose Clown & Confetti 4. • Click OK.

8. Fill in Headline: Double-click block. • Font: NewZurica. • Type: You're Invited! • Click OK.

9. Fill in Text block 1 (left): Double-click block. • Font: Jester. • Style: Bold. • Font Size: Medium. • Type: Jacob Cannon is turning 6! (substitute your child's name). • Click OK. • Resize block to fit text, if necessary.

10. Fill in Text block 2: Double-click block. • Font: Subway. • Font Size: Medium. • Type: Come to Jacob's Birthday Party, Friday, Dec. 3 from 3–5! (substitute your child's name, date, and time of party). • Click OK.

Variation

Dinosaurs are still the craze for children's parties. PSD has some dinosaur art that you can use to create a neat party invitation. The Amazing Animals graphic library also has three additional dinosaurs to choose from: Brontosaurus, Dimetrodon, and Pterodactyl.

Thank-You

Need to thank someone for a job well done? Need to extend special thanks to a friend or customer? Thank-you cards are useful around the home, school, or office. These steps create a business thank-you card project that you can send to customers.

1. Project: Choose Greeting Card.
   • Click Side Fold Spread.

2. Backdrop: Choose Gradient Cone.
   • Click OK.

3. Layout: Choose No Layout.
   • Click OK.

4. Click on New Object tool. • Choose Headline. • Move block to top of card, as shown in example.
   • Double-click headline block.
   • Font: Moderne. • Type: THANKS! • Click OK.

5. Click on New Object tool. • Choose Text. • Move text block to bottom of card. • Double-click text block.
   • Font: Moderne. • Font Size: Small. • Justification Horizontal: Center. • Justification Vertical: Center. • Type: on behalf of Johnson Electricians, Inc. (substitute your company name). • Click OK.
   • Resize block to fit text, if necessary.

6. Select Inside of Card.

7. Backdrop: Choose Gradient.
   • Click OK.

8. Layout: Choose Gradient 5.
   • Click OK.

9. Fill in Headline: Double-click block.
   • Font: Moderne. • Type: Your business means a lot to us! • Set Custom Effect: Effect 1, normal type. • Click OK. • Resize Headline block to fit below protruding backdrop art.

10. Fill in Text block 1 (left): Double-click block. • Font: Moderne.
    • Font Size: Small. • Justification Horizontal: Center. • Justification Vertical: Center. • Type: Thanks for putting your trust in our company. Quality is our number one concern, and we want to make our customers the happiest customers around. We hope our service was more than satisfactory. • Click OK.

11. Fill in Text block 2 (right): Double-click block. • Font: Moderne.
    • Font Size: Small for the paragraph, Medium for the phone number. • Justification Horizontal: Left. • Justification Vertical: Center. • Type: If there are any suggestions or questions concerning Johnson Electricians, please give us a call and we'll respond right away! Thanks again. 777-0000 (substitute your company name) • Click OK.

Family Reunion

Family reunions can be formal or fun. Try the following steps for a fun reunion picnic invitation with a Fourth of July theme.

1. Project: Choose Greeting Card.
   • Click Top Fold.

2. Backdrop: Choose Kids. • Click OK.

3. Layout: Choose Kids 4. • Click OK.

4. Fill in Headline: Double-click block.
   • Font: Bazooka. • Type: SMITH FAMILY REUNION (substitute your family name). • Click OK.

5. Fill in text block: Double-click block.
   • Font: Jester. • Font Size: Medium.
   • Justification Horizontal: Center.
   • Justification Vertical: Center.
   • Type: The Event You've All Been Waiting For! • Click OK.

6. Using the Color controls, set the Page Background color to red.
   • Shade at 20%.

7. Select Inside of Card.

8. Backdrop: Choose Blank Page.
   • Click OK.

9. Layout: Choose Greeting Card 7.
   • Click OK.

10. Remove Square graphic: Click graphic. • Click on Delete tool.

11. Remove bottom Headline: Click block. • Click on Delete tool.

12. Fill in Border: Double-click border.
    • Choose Stars & Stripes.
    • Click OK.

13. Fill in Headline: Double-click block. • Font: Jester. • Type: Time for Our Annual Reunion Picnic!
    • Click OK. • You may have to resize block to fill space, as shown in example.

14. Click on New Object tool.
    • Choose Text. • Move block beneath Headline block. • Resize to fill remaining space. • Double-click text block. • Using different fonts, as shown in illustration, type in your reunion details. • Click OK.

Design Tip

Experiment with using different font sizes for your text. You can control sizes for words, sentences, or entire paragraphs. Highlight or select the word or words you want to change; then set a new font size.

Friendship

While you can certainly go to any card store and find dozens of all-occasion cards, there's something satisfying about designing one from the heart. This project idea lets you design a light-hearted friendship card.

1. Project: Choose Greeting Card.
   • Click Side Fold.

2. Backdrop: Choose Sheep in Field.
   • Click OK.

3. Layout: Choose Sheep in Field 5.
   • Click OK.

4. Remove all blocks in layout except the last block, tilted in bottom right corner: Click each block, one at a time. • Then click on Delete tool.

5. Fill in remaining text block (bottom right corner): Double-click block.
   • Font: Jester. • Font Size: Small.
   • Justification Horizontal: Center.
   • Justification Vertical: Center.
   • Type: I Can Always Count on Ewe! • Click OK.

6. Select Inside of Card.

7. Backdrop: Choose Blank Page.
   • Click OK.

8. Layout: Choose Greeting Card 4.
   • Click OK.

9. Fill in Border: Double-click border.
   • Choose Blue Check. • Select Wide Border. • Click OK.

10. Fill in text block: Double-click block. • Font: Jester. • Font Size: Medium. • Style: Bold.
    • Justification Horizontal: Center.
    • Justification Vertical: Center.
    • Type: Thanks for being such a good friend! • Click OK.

Variation

Personalize your friendship card by adding a text block that fits inside the top cloud of this backdrop. Then add your friend's name, using the same font found in step 5.

Customer Service Response

Many businesses use customer response cards to evaluate their service. This proj-ect idea offers a professional-looking card you can distribute to all of your clients.

1. Project: Choose Greeting Card.
   • Click Top Fold Spread.

2. Backdrop: Choose Blank Page.
   • Click OK.

3. Layout: Choose No Layout.
   • Click OK.

4. Click on New Object tool.
   • Choose Border. • Double-click border. • Choose Diamond Corners. • Click OK.

5. Click on New Object tool.
   • Choose Text. • Double-click text block. • Font: NewZurica. • Font Size: Medium. • Style: Bold. • Justification Horizontal: Center. • Type name of company. • Click OK. • Move block to upper portion of card. • Resize to fit text.

6. Click on New Object tool. • Choose Square Graphic. • Double-click graphic block. • Choose Lily Ornament. • Click OK. • Move graphic below text block.

7. Click on New Object tool.
   • Choose Text. • Double-click block. • Font: Boulder. • Font Size: Medium • Justification Horizontal: Center. • Justification Vertical: Center. • Type: CUSTOMER RESPONSE CARD. • Click OK.
   • Move block below square graphic. • Resize to fit text.

8. Select Inside of Card.

9. Backdrop: Choose Blank Page.
   • Click OK.

10. Layout: Choose No Layout.
    • Click OK.

11. Click on New Object tool.
    • Choose Text. • Move text block to top of card spread. • Double-click text block. • Font: NewZurica. • Font Size: 14 (select Other, type 14, and then click OK). • Justification Horizontal: Left. • Justification Vertical: Top. • Type: We appreciate your business! Please take a few moments and fill out this customer response card to let us know how we can serve you better. • Click OK. • Resize block to fit at very top of card.

12. Click on New Object tool.
    • Choose Text. • Resize block to fit entire middle section of card, leaving room for a small text block at the bottom. • Double-click text block. • Font: NewZurica. • Font Size: 12 (select Other, type 12, and click OK). • Justification Horizontal: Left. • Justification Vertical: Top. • Type your company questionnaire. (Use the questions in the project example to help you.) • To make lines for responses, just hold down the Shift key while pressing the Hyphen key. • Click OK.

13. Click on New Object tool
    • Choose Text. • Move text block to bottom of card.
    • Double-click text block. • Font: NewZurica.
    • Font Size: 12 (select Other, type 12, and click OK).
    • Justification Horizontal: Left. • Justification Vertical: Center.
    • Type: Thank you for your feedback. (Then add text explaining how to return the card.) • Click OK. • Resize text block to fit at very bottom of card.

Leland Lawnscape Company

CUSTOMER RESPONSE CARD

We appreciate your business! Please take a few moments and fill out this customer response card to let us know how we can serve you better.

1. Did we respond in a prompt and considerate fashion?

2. Was the crew friendly and helpful?

3. Are you pleased with the results of our lawn care service?

4. Will you use our lawn care service again?

5. Would you recommend our business to others?

6. How would you rate our overall service on a scale of 1-10 (1 being poor and 10 being excellent)?

7. How would you rate the quality of the plants delivered (if applicable)?

8. Has our landscaping improved the look of your lawn (where applicable)?

9. Do you feel our prices are competitive and adequate for the services you received?

10. How can we improve our lawn care services?

Thank you for your feedback. Please return this card in the enclosed postage-paid envelope or drop it off at our office. Let us know if we can be of further assistance to you and your lawn care needs. Call 000-0000.

Baby Shower

Shower invitations for babies or brides are simple to make using these PSD steps.

1. Project: Choose Greeting Card.
   • Click Side Fold.

2. Backdrop: Choose Baby Quilt.
   • Click OK.

3. Layout: Choose Greeting Card 10.
   • Click OK.

4. Remove Border: Click border.
   • Click on Delete tool.

5. Fill in Headline block: Double-click block. • Font: NewZurica. • Type: It's time for . . . • Click OK.

6. Fill in text block: Double-click block. • Font: Boulder. • Font Size: Large. • Type: A Baby Shower! • Click OK. • Resize block to fit text.

7. Select Inside of Card.

8. Backdrop: Choose Baby Quilt.
   • Click OK.

9. Layout: Choose No Layout.
   • Click OK.

10. Click on New Object tool. • Choose Text. • Resize block to fill entire card. • Double-click text block. • Font: NewZurica. • Font Size: Medium. • Style: Bold. • Justification Horizontal: Center. • Justification Vertical: Center. • Type: Join us for a Baby Shower for (add name of person, date, time, address, and phone number). • Click OK.

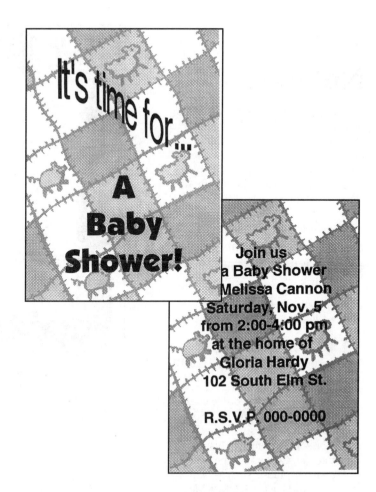

Can You See It?

If you're having trouble seeing the text printed on top of the Baby Quilt backdrop art, try making the backdrop lighter. There's a check box option in the Layout dialog box that lets you lighten the design. Another alternative to illegible type is to try setting a bolder font.

Coordinate!

Use the Baby Quilt design in your Baby Shower card and coordinate it with Baby Shower decorations. Make place mats, place cards, and other decorative party materials using the project ideas in other sections of this book.

Notecard

You can use the notecards you design on Print Shop Deluxe the same way as those you purchase in a card shop. Place graphics and borders on the fronts of the cards, and leave the insides blank for personal messages. Follow these steps to see how.

1. Project: Choose Greeting Card.
    • Click Side Fold.

2. Backdrop: Choose Fruit & Leaves.
    • Click OK.

3. Layout: Choose No Layout.
    • Click OK.

4. Select Back of Card.

5. Layout: Choose Greeting Card 3.
    • Click OK.

6. Fill in text block: Double-click block. • Font: Chaucer. • Font Size: Small. • Justification Horizontal: Center. • Justification Vertical: Center. • Type your name or phrase, such as Nancy's Notecards. • Click OK. • Move block down, almost touching row graphic below.

7. Fill in row graphic: Double-click row graphic. • Choose Chickens. • Click OK.

Nancy's Notecards

Variation

Create a similar card with a top-fold orientation. Follow these steps after selecting a Blank Page backdrop and No Layout:

1. Click on New Object tool.
    • Choose Column Graphic.
    • Double-click graphic. • Choose Southwest Strip. • Click OK.
    • Click on Rotate tool. • Rotate 90 degrees, turning the block into a

row graphic. • Move block to bottom of card and resize to fill space.

2. Click on New Object tool.
    • Choose Headline. • Double-click block. • Font: Calligrapher.
    • Shape: Double Arch Up. • Type: A Note from Nancy (substitute your name). • Click OK. • Resize block to fill space. • Use the Color Palette to give the Page background a color and shading.

3. Add another rotated Southwest Strip to the back of the notecard to complete your design.

Gift Idea

Print out 8–10 copies of your personally designed notecards. Match them with envelopes, package them in a pretty box, and you have a perfect gift to give!

Letterhead & Stationery

Letterhead and stationery designed with Print Shop Deluxe are useful for businesses, schools, clubs, and home. You'll find many uses: special sales letters, correspondence to customers, holiday letterhead, one-page family newsletters, or even school progress reports. Follow the basic steps shown for creating any letterhead project.

- Letterhead
- Memo
- Notepad
- Forms
- Message Pads
- File Labels
- Business Cards
- Logos

PARTY TIME

Specialists in Party Rental Equipment and Supplies!

Sharon Parker
908 Sunset Lane
Fishers, IN 49034

Dear Ms. Parker:

Thank you for your order placed with us last week. We are happy to learn of your previous patronage and find out about your satisfaction with our equipment and our customer service personnel. We hope you will be as equally satisfied with your upcoming carnival event. In case our customer service personnel did not mention this, I'd like to make you aware of our new Dunk Tank and SuperSonic Popcorn machine. Both pieces rent for $25.00 and come with all the necessary cords and supplies (10 lb.s popcorn included). Please let us know if you would like to use these items at your upcoming carnival.

We are also expecting a new Cotton Candy machine due to arrive anytime now. It also rents for $25.00 and includes all the ingredients necessary to produce 100 cotton candy treats. If you would like, I can put that on hold for you as well.

Thank you again for your repeat business. We look forward to serving you and hope you will let us know of anything else we can do to make your carnival a success!

Sincerely,

Dean Hardy,
Manager

PARTY TIME COMPANY
1092 West Main Street, Kewanee, IL 00000, (000) 000-0000

PSD-Windows steps:

1. Select Letterhead from the Project menu screen.

2. Select the project orientation.

3. Choose a backdrop graphic design, and click OK.

4. Choose a layout design, and click OK.

5. Use the Tool Palette and pull-down menus to fill in each layout element.

6. Pull down the File menu, and select Save. In the File Save As dialog box, type in a file name, and click OK.

7. Pull down the File menu, and select Print. In the Print dialog box, choose any printing options, and click OK.

How Big Is Letterhead?

Letterhead projects come in two sizes: Single Page and Notepad. Regular letterhead, called Single Page, is standard 8 1/2-by-11-inch paper size. Notepad projects print out at 5 1/2-by-8 1/2-inch size. Because of their smaller size, notepad projects print two to a page.

All of the instructions for individual letterhead and stationery projects in this book are Windows steps. However, if you're using PSD-DOS or PSD-Mac, you can create the exact same projects. For the most part, your steps will be the same. There may be some slight differences in the instructions.

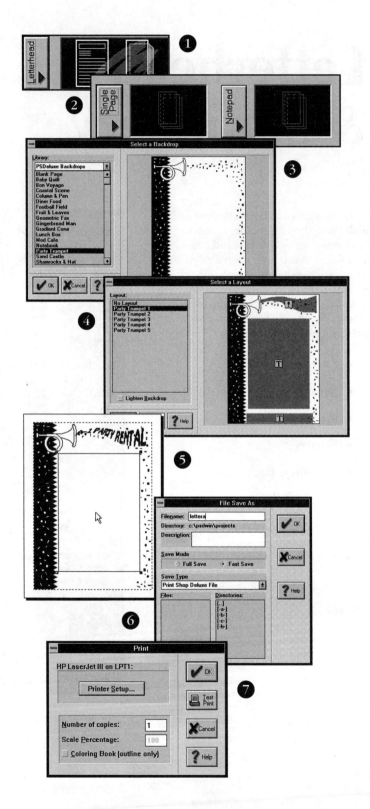

PSD-DOS steps:

1. Select Letterhead from the Project menu.

2. Select Create a new project.

3. Select the project orientation.

4. Choose Select a Backdrop from the menu list. Choose a backdrop design, and click Done.

5. Choose Select a Layout from the menu list. Choose a layout design.

6. Choose Fill In or Edit from the menu list. Fill in each layout element and click Done.

7. Choose Save from the menu list. Type in a file name and a description; choose the Save File command.

8. Choose Print from the menu list, and select Print.

If you're using PSD-DOS, your project steps will differ slightly. For starters, PSD calls your regular size letterhead project orientation, appropriately, Regular instead of Single Page (like PSD-Windows). Instead of clicking OK when a task is complete as you do in Windows, you click Done (where applicable) when finished with each project step. Instead of using a Tool Palette or pull-down menus to fill in layout elements, you use a menu list and dialog boxes. Line Justify denotes horizontal justification, and Placement denotes vertical justification—so look for those commands to control positioning.

When creating your own layout, use the Add New Elements command to insert the various layout elements. If you ever become confused about using a menu or dialog box, look at the bottom of your screen for brief instructions telling you what to do.

PSD-Mac steps:

1. Select Letterhead from the Project menu screen.

2. Select the project orientation.

3. Choose a backdrop graphic design, and click OK.

4. Choose a layout design, and click OK.

5. Use the Tool Palette and pull-down menus to fill in each layout element.

6. Pull down the File menu, and select Save. In the Save dialog box, type in a file name, and click Save.

7. Pull down the File menu, and select Print. In the Print dialog box, choose any printing options, and click Print.

Your PSD-Mac project steps will vary ever so slightly. Unlike PSD-Windows and PSD-DOS users, you use the Text menu to select fonts, sizes, and justification. As in the Windows steps, you double-click a text block to select it. Once selected, you can start typing in text, or pull down the Text menu and change text options. When finished typing, just click outside the block. Justification denotes horizontal justification, and Placement denotes vertical justification—so look for those commands on the Text menu to control positioning.

Letterhead

Letterhead is essential for any professional correspondence: for business, school, community organizations, or clubs. Letterhead is also useful for personal correspondence, for adults and children. The following example shows how to create a professional business letterhead.

1. Project: Choose Letterhead.
   • Choose Single Page.

2. Backdrop: Choose Blank Page.
   • Click OK.

3. Layout: Choose Letterhead 37.
   • Click OK.

4. Fill in Square graphic (upper left corner): Double-click graphic block.
   • Choose Paintbrush. • Click OK.
   • Move graphic to the left and resize slightly.

5. Fill in Row graphic: Double-click graphic block. • Choose Ink Swash.
   • Click OK. • Move graphic to bottom of letterhead. • Resize to fill space, as shown in example. • Use the Color controls to change the graphic object color to purple.

6. Fill in Text block 2 (bottom block in layout): Resize block to fit above the newly moved row graphic from step 5. • Double-click text block.
   • Font: Stylus. • Font Size: Medium. • Justification Horizontal: Center. • Justification Vertical: Top.
   • Style: Bold. • Type: You can count on us—we're the Professionals! Click OK. • Use the Color controls to change Behind Text to yellow. • Pull down Object menu and select Order. • Select Send to Back.

7. Fill in Text block 1 (found in middle of project): Move text block to top of project, resizing to fit beside square graphic at top, as shown in example. • Double-click text block.
   • Font: Stylus. • Style: Bold. • Font

Size: 40-point (choose Other, type 40, and click OK). • Justification Horizontal: Center. • Justification Vertical: Center. • Type: Professional Painters, Inc. • Press Enter to move to second line.
• Font: NewZurica. • Font Size: 14-point (choose Other, type 14, and click OK). • Type business address and phone number on second line.
• Click OK.

8. Click on New Object tool. • Choose Text. • Move block to bottom of letterhead, below row graphic.
   • Resize to fit. • Double-click text block. • Font: Signature. • Font Size: Small. • Justification Horizontal: Center. • Justification Vertical: Bottom. • Type: over 75 years of experience. • Click OK. • Use the Color controls to set Behind Text to yellow.
   • Pull down the Object menu. • Select Order.
   • Select Send to Back.

We Need Order

The Order command used in this project controls the layering of layout elements. Use it to place text on top of graphics, to overlap blocks, and to create special effects.

Memo

Memos are fun and easy to make using the letterhead project type. You can design all kinds of memos for the office or school. Here's a stylistic memo designed from scratch, using an initial cap graphic.

1. Project: Choose Letterhead.
    • Choose Single Page.

2. Backdrop: Choose Blank Page.
    • Click OK.

3. Layout: Choose No Layout.
    • Click OK.

4. Click on New Object tool.
    • Choose Square Graphic. • Move graphic to upper left corner of letterhead. • Double-click graphic block. • Change library to PSDeluxe Initial Caps. • Choose Pattern. • Click OK. • Resize block as shown in example. • Click on Frame tool. • Choose Drop Shadow. • Use the Color controls to set a 40% shade for graphic.

5. Click on New Object tool.
    • Choose Text. • Move block next to square graphic. • Double-click text block. • Font: NewZurica.
    • Style: Bold. • Style: Shadow.
    • Font Size: 64-point (choose Other, type 64, and click OK).
    • Justification Horizontal: Full.
    • Justification Vertical: Top.
    • Type: E M O. • Click OK. • Use the Color controls to change the text color to blue.

6. Click on New Object tool.
    • Choose Horizontal Ruled Line.
    • Move Horizontal Ruled Line block beneath text block. • Resize to fit, as shown in example.
    • Double-click block. • Choose Traditional. • Click OK.

7. Click on New Object tool.
    • Choose Text. • Double-click block. • Font: Chaucer. • Font Size: 62-point (choose Other, type 62, and click OK). • Justification Horizontal: Center. • Justification Vertical: Top. • Style: Shadow.
    • Type: M. • Click OK. • Use Color controls to set text color to blue. • Resize and move block so the letter M sits mostly inside the open white square of the initial cap graphic set in step 4.

It's a Masthead

A masthead is a block of text or art, or a combination of both, that appears at the top of a page. Mastheads usually appear at the top of newsletters, letterheads, and other communication materials. You can create mastheads, similar to the one designed for this project, and include them on envelopes, brochures, or even transfer the design onto a T-shirt!

Notepad

Notepad projects make wonderful ways to communicate with a handwritten message. Or you can type your message right along with your design. Remember, these projects print two to a page, so try to economize! Here's a simple notepad designed from scratch for school use.

1. Project: Choose Letterhead.
   • Choose Notepad.

2. Backdrop: Choose Blank Page.
   • Click OK.

3. Layout: Choose No Layout.
   • Click OK.

4. Click on New Object tool.
   • Choose Row Graphic. • Double-click graphic. • Choose ABC 123.
   • Click OK. • Move graphic to top of project. • Resize to fill space as shown in example.

5. Click on New Object tool.
   • Choose Headline. • Move block to bottom of project. • Double-click block. • Font: Boulder. • Shape: Bottom Arch. • Justification: Center. • Customize: Effect 8.
   • Type: From the Desk of PRINCIPAL HUGHES (substitute your staff member's name). • Click OK.

Design Tip

Take your finished notepad design to a professional printer who can make actual notepads. This is a great office gift idea!

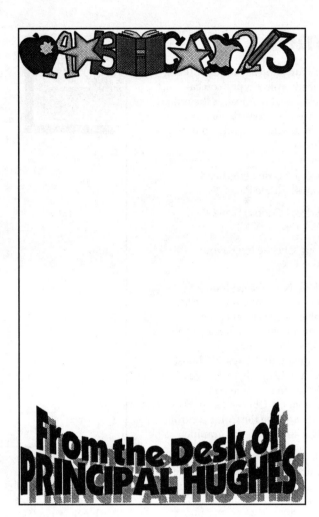

Variation

How about an environmentally concerned notepad? In a blank notepad screen, add a square graphic and two headline graphics. Use the World square graphic and resize it to fit in the upper right corner of the project. Resize both headlines to fit around the "world." Set the font in Boulder, and use the Top Arch and Bottom Arch for the headline shapes. Then add a text block that encompasses the other three blocks, and give it a colored background. Have it printed on recycled paper.

Forms

You can design all sorts of forms using the Print Shop programs: business forms, record-keeping forms, school report sheets, inventory forms, and much more. The following project steps create an invoice.

1. Project: Choose Letterhead.
   • Choose Single Page.

2. Backdrop: Choose Blank Page.
   • Click OK.

3. Layout: Choose Letterhead 12.
   • Click OK.

4. Fill in square graphic: Double-click graphic. • Choose Tennis. • Click OK. • Move block to the left as shown in project example.

5. Fill in ruled line: Double-click block. • Choose Scotch.
   • Click OK.

6. Fill in text block: Double-click block. • Font: NewZurica. • Font Size: 12-point. • Justification Horizontal: Left. • Justification Vertical: Top. • Type in your company invoice information.
   • Hold down the Shift key and press the Hyphen key to make lines to write on. • Click OK.
   • Click on Frame tool. • Select Thick Line. • Depending upon how complicated your form is, this block may take some experimenting to create the look you want. (In this example, use the Spacebar to space out words, and the hyphen key to create lines.)

7. Click on New Object tool.
   • Choose Headline. • Move block to top of project. • Resize block to stretch across top of letterhead, as shown in example. • Double-click block. • Font: Boulder. • Shape: Top Arch. • Justification: Center.
   • Type: A-1 SPORTS SUPPLY.
   • Click OK.

8. Click on New Object tool.
   • Choose Text. • Move block below headline. • Resize block to fit between headline block and ruled line block. • Double-click block. • Font: Moderne. • Font Size: Medium. • Justification Horizontal: Center. • Justification Vertical: Top. • Type in company address and phone number.
   • Click OK.

Variation

Use your PSD program to make all kinds of business forms, such as travel logs, mileage reports, expense reports, purchase order forms, packing lists, and more. Turn to the Business Projects section of this book for other great ideas.

A-1 SPORTS SUPPLY

8098 South Williams Street
Vandalia, IL 00000
(000) 000-0000

INVOICE NUMBER _____ Date _____ Contact _____

Order Number   Quantity   Price   Total

Customer: Total:
                                       Tax:
                                       Discount:
                                       Final Total:

Message Pads

The notepad orientation of the letter-head projects allows you to design numerous projects for written messages. Here's a clever design idea to make a message pad to place by the phone at home.

1. Project: Choose Letterhead.
   • Choose Notepad.

2. Backdrop: Choose Blank Page.
   • Click OK.

3. Layout: Choose No Layout.
   • Click OK.

4. Click on New Object tool.
   • Choose Square Graphic.
   • Double-click graphic. • Choose Speech Bubble. • Click OK.
   • Move graphic to top of Notepad.
   • Resize to fill space, as shown in project example.

5. Click on New Object tool.
   • Choose Square Graphic.
   • Double-click graphic. • Choose Owl. • Click OK. • Move graphic to lower left corner. • Resize to fill space as shown in project example.

6. Click on New Object tool.
   • Choose Headline. • Enlarge block to fit headline, as shown in example. • Double-click headline block. • Font: Bazooka. • Shape: Rectangular. • Type: HEY! • Click OK. • Click on Rotate tool.
   • Rotate block 90 degrees. • You may have to resize block to fit.

7. Click on New Object tool.
   • Choose Text. • Enlarge block to fit text, as shown in example.
   • Double-click headline block.
   • Font: NewZurica. • Font Size: Small. • Justification Horizontal: Center. • Justification Vertical: Center. • Type: THERE'S A MESSAGE FOR YOU. • Click OK.

• Click on Rotate tool. • Rotate block 90 degrees. • You may have to resize block to fit.

More Messages

Design your own holiday message pads for home or office. Use holiday art, and add a holiday message. You can also make matching holiday letterhead for correspondence with family and friends. Remember, these make great gift ideas!

File Labels

Use the Print Shop programs to make labels for many uses: book labels, CD and VCR tape labels, lunch box labels, gardening labels, food labels, envelope labels, and more. Follow the steps in this project idea to make file labels for the office. By using the notepad orientation, you will be able to print out two sets of labels per page.

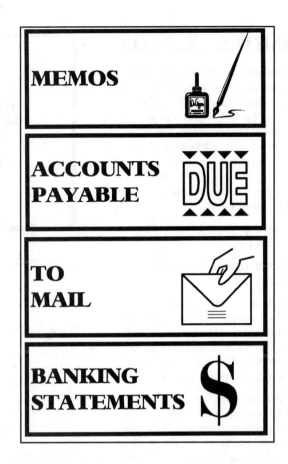

1. Project: Choose Letterhead.
   • Choose Notepad.

2. Backdrop: Choose Blank Page.
   • Click OK.

3. Layout: Choose No Layout.
   • Click OK.

4. Click on New Object tool. • Choose Text. • Move block to top of project. • Resize to fill top ¼ of area. • Double-click text block. • Font: Heather. • Font Size: Medium Large. • Justification Horizontal: Left. • Justification Vertical: Center. • Type: MEMOS. • Click OK. • Click on Frame tool. • Choose Thick Line.

5. Repeat step 4, substituting new text as shown in example. • Move block to top of project, below first text block. • Resize to fill next ¼ of area.

6. Repeat step 4, substituting new text as shown in example. • Move block to middle of project, below second text block. • Resize to fill ¼ of area, as shown in project example.

7. Repeat step 4, substituting new text, as shown in example.• Move block to bottom of project, below third text block. • Resize to fill last remaining ¼ of area.

8. Click on New Object tool.
   • Choose Square Graphic.
   • Double-click graphic. • Choose Ink & Pen. • Click OK. • Move graphic to fit inside first text block, on right side. • Resize if necessary.

9. Repeat step 8, substituting new graphic. • Choose PSDeluxe Calendar Icons. • Choose Due.

10. Repeat step 8, substituting new graphic • Choose Mail (Calendar Icons).

11. Repeat step 8, substituting new graphic. • Choose Money (Calendar Icons).

Variation

Follow the same steps above to make name tags for parties, conventions, or club gatherings. Instead of typing in file labels, type in names. Design a logo to place on the right side of each tag.

Business Cards

You can make a nearly infinite variety of business cards (in both conventional and large sizes) using the Print Shop programs. Here are steps for making a conventional business card. You may have to experiment a few times to get the size just right.

1. Project: Choose Letterhead.
   • Choose Notepad.

2. Backdrop: Choose Blank Page.
   • Click OK.

3. Layout: Choose No Layout.
   • Click OK.

4. Click on New Object tool.
   • Choose Mini-border. • Fit mini-border in middle of page, sizing the border as shown in example.
   • Double-click Border. • Choose Double Diamond. • Click OK.

5. Click on New Object tool.
   • Choose Square Graphic.
   • Double-click graphic. • Choose Happy Tooth. • Click OK. • Move block inside Mini-border, on left side of space. • Resize to fill space, as needed.

6. Click on New Object tool.
   • Choose Text. • Double-click block. • Font: NewZurica. • Font Size: 10-point (choose Other, type 10, and click OK). • Justification Horizontal: Center. • Justification Vertical: Center. • Type business name, address, and phone number. • Make first line of text bold. • Click OK. • Move text block inside mini-border and place on right side. • Resize to fill space, as necessary.

Lavern Williams, DDS
906 East Fay Street
Vickston, NM 00000
(000) 000-0000

Design Tip

You can create business cards using the letterhead or greeting-card project type. Just find a graphic you like, and add text with name, address, and phone number. Size everything to business card proportions. Take your printout to a professional printer to have a set of conventional business cards with your design printed!

Logos

With the design capabilities available on your computer, you can create logos for use on letterheads, business cards, envelopes, brochures, flyers, newsletters, and more. Match a graphic with your company name, and experiment with different editing commands to combine the two elements. This project example shows a logo at the top of a letterhead. Design elements, such as the ruled line, keep the logo theme throughout the project.

1. Project: Choose Letterhead.
   • Choose Single Page.

2. Backdrop: Choose Blank Page.
   • Click OK.

3. Layout: Choose No Layout.
   • Click OK.

4. Click on New Object tool. • Choose Headline. • Double-click headline block. • Font: NewZurica. • Shape: Top Arch. • Type: Luv & Hugs Preschool. • Click on Customize button. • Under Shadow options, select Drop Shadow. • Change Shadow color to light blue. • Click OK. • Click OK again. • Move block to top of page. • Resize to fill space as shown in example.

5. Click on New Object tool. • Choose Square Graphic. • Double-click graphic. • Choose Teddy. • Click OK. • Move graphic directly below headline, overlapping the two blocks. • Pull down Object menu. • Select Order. • Select Send to Back.

6. Click on New Object tool. • Choose Horizontal Ruled Line. • Double-click Horizontal Ruled Line block. • Choose Paper Links. • Click OK. • Move line under square graphic, slightly overlapping graphic. • Resize to fill horizontal width of page. • Pull down Object menu. • Select Order. • Choose Send to Back.

706 Main Street, Fishers, IN 00000
(000) 000-0000

7. Click on New Object tool.
   • Choose Horizontal Ruled Line.
   • Double-click Horizontal Ruled Line block. • Choose Paper Links.
   • Click OK. • Move line to bottom of page, as shown in example.
   • Resize to fill horizontal width of page.

8. Click on New Object tool.
   • Choose Text. • Double-click text block. • Font: Paramount. • Font Size: Medium. • Justification Horizontal: Center. • Justification Vertical: Center. • Type business address and phone number.
   • Click OK. • Move block to very bottom of page, as shown in example. • Resize block to fit text.

Design Tip

To make a simple logo out of headline block and a square graphic, just select the art and type you want to use, and then experiment overlapping the blocks to form a logo.

Signs & Flyers

Signs and flyers are useful in a variety of ways: announcing sales, new businesses, or special events; showing directions; identifying lost and found items; providing real estate notices; and more. Follow the basic steps shown for creating any letterhead project.

- Garage Sale
- Promotional
- Directional
- Help Wanted
- Lost & Found
- Message
- New Business
- Sale
- Real Estate
- Event
- Election
- Door
- Science Fair

PSD-Windows steps:

1. Select Sign from the Project menu screen.

2. Select the project orientation.

3. Choose a backdrop graphic design, and click OK.

4. Choose a layout design, and click OK.

5. Use the Tool Palette and pull-down menus to fill in each layout element.

6. Pull down the File menu, and select Save. In the File Save As dialog box, type in a file name, and click OK.

7. Pull down the File menu, and select Print. In the Print dialog box, choose any printing options, and click OK.

All of the instructions for individual sign and flyer projects in this book are Windows steps. However, if you're using PSD-DOS or PSD-Mac, you can create the exact same projects. For the most part, your steps will be the same. There may be some slight differences in the instructions.

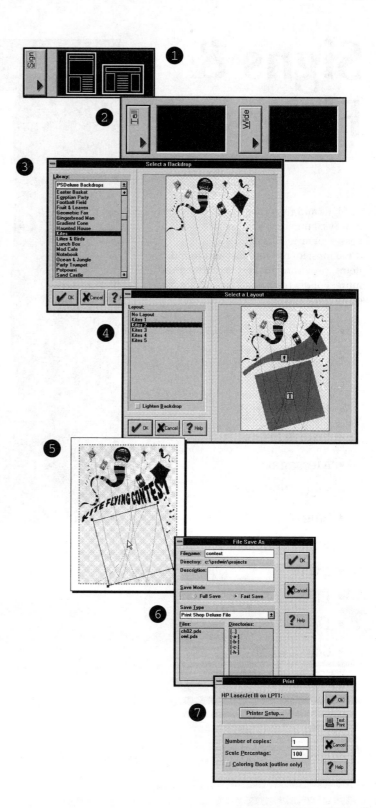

PSD-DOS steps:

1. Select Sign from the Project menu.

2. Select Create a new project.

3. Select the project orientation.

4. Choose Select a Backdrop from the menu list. Choose a backdrop design, and click Done.

5. Choose Select a Layout from the menu list. Choose a layout design.

6. Choose Fill In or Edit from the menu list. Fill in each layout element. Press Esc when done.

7. Choose Save from the menu list. Type in a file name, a description, and then choose Save File.

8. Choose Print from the menu list, and select Print.

If you're using PSD-DOS, your project steps differ slightly. Instead of clicking OK when a task is complete as you do in Windows, you click Done (where applicable) when finished with each project step. Instead of using a Tool Palette or pull-down menus to fill in layout elements, you use a menu list and dialog boxes. Line Justify denotes horizontal justification, and Placement denotes vertical justification; so look for those commands to control positioning.

When creating your own layout, use the Add New Elements command to insert the various layout elements. If you ever become confused about using a menu or dialog box, look at the bottom of your screen for brief instructions telling you what to do.

PSD-Mac steps:

1. Select Sign from the Project menu screen.

2. Select the project orientation.

3. Choose a backdrop graphic design, and click OK.

4. Choose a layout design, and click OK.

5. Use the Tool Palette and pull-down menus to fill in each layout element.

6. Pull down the File menu, and select Save. In the Save dialog box, type in a file name, and click Save.

7. Pull down the File menu, and select Print. In the Print dialog box, choose any printing options, and click Print.

Your PSD-Mac project steps will vary slightly. Unlike PSD-Windows and PSD-DOS users, you use the Text menu to select fonts, sizes, and justification. As in the Windows steps, you double-click a text block to select it. Once selected, you can start typing in text, or pull down the Text menu and change text options. When finished typing, just click outside the block. Justification denotes horizontal justification, and Placement denotes vertical justification; so look for those commands on the Text menu to control positioning.

Signs & Flyers

Garage Sale

If you're having a garage sale, then you need to advertise. You can create a sign that clearly states the sale and date. Combine that crucial information with details about what's for sale and you can create a great sign to post around the neighborhood.

1. Project: Choose Sign. • Choose Tall.

2. Backdrop: Blank Page. • Click OK.

3. Layout: Choose No Layout. • Click OK.

4. Click on New Object tool. • Choose Border. • Double-click border. • Choose Blue Check. • Click OK.

5. Click on New Object tool. • Choose Headline. • Double-click headline block. • Font: NewZurica. • Shape: Rectangular. • Click Customize button. • Under Fill, select Blend Down. • Click OK. • Type: GARAGE SALE! • Click OK. • Move headline to top of sign, resizing to fill space as shown.

6. Click on New Object tool. • Choose Text. • Double-click text block. • Font: Boulder. • Font Size: Medium Large. • Justification Horizontal: Center. • Justification Vertical: Center. • Type your address. • Click OK. • Move block below headline, resizing to fit.

7. Click on New Object tool. • Choose Square Graphic. • Double-click graphic. • Choose Sale. • Click OK. • Move block to center of sign, resizing as shown.

8. Click on New Object tool. • Choose Text. • Move block to left of square graphic. • Double-click text block. • Font: Boulder. • Font Size: Medium. • Justification Horizontal: Center. • Justification Vertical: Center. • Type: BABY CLOTHES. • Click OK. • Resize block to fit text, as needed. • Click on Rotate tool. • Rotate block 25 degrees.

9. Repeat step 8, placing block left of square graphic. • Type: DISHES. • Click on Rotate tool and rotate the block about -25 degrees. • Move block as shown in example and resize to fill space.

10. Repeat step 8, placing block below first text block. Type: APPLIANCES. • Click on Rotate tool and rotate block about -25 degrees. • Move and resize block to fit text.

11. Repeat step 8 again, placing block to the right of the square graphic. Type: FURNITURE. • Click on Rotate tool and rotate the block about 25 degrees. • Move and resize block to fit.

12. Click on New Object tool. • Choose Text. • Move Text block to bottom of sign, resizing to fill remaining space. • Double-click block. • Font: Boulder. • Font Size: 42-point (choose Other, type 42, and click OK). • Justification Horizontal: Center. • Justification Vertical: Center. • Type date and time of garage sale. • Click OK.

Design Tip

If you're going to post your sign outdoors in inclement weather, be sure to laminate or cover the sign in clear plastic wrap to keep the ink from running. For sturdier signs, glue, staple, or tape the printout to heavy cardboard.

Promotional

Promotional signs are an attractive way to bring attention to special items or services you have to offer. The following sign project is for a restaurant.

1. Project: Choose Sign. • Choose Tall.

2. Backdrop: Choose Mod Cafe.
   • Click OK.

3. Layout: Choose Mod Cafe 1.
   • Click OK.

4. Fill in Headline: Double-click block.
   • Font: Jester. • Type: TODAY'S SPECIAL. • Click OK.

5. Fill in Text block 1: Double-click block. • Font: Jester. • Font Size: Medium. • Justification Horizontal: Center. • Justification Vertical: Center. • Type your restaurant's daily specials. • Click OK.

6. Fill in Text block 2: Double-click block. • Font: Palatia. • Style: Bold. • Font Size: Medium. • Justification Horizontal: Center. • Justification Vertical: Center. • Type your restaurant's children's special (or other specials available).
   • Underline first line. • Click OK.

Variation

Try these other available restaurant-and-food-related graphics: Backdrop: Diner Food; Square graphics: Burger, Cherry Pie, Lunch, Restaurant Icon; Row graphics: Orange Slices, Today's Special; and Column graphics: Mod Cafe Cups, Restaurant Table, Waiter.

Here's a variation of the project idea shown:

1. Instead of selecting a backdrop and layout, design your own. Add a row graphic to top of sign. Use Today's Special art.

2. Add a column graphic to left side of page. Use Waiter. Resize as large as you can.

3. Add a text block in remaining space detailing the daily specials. Set inside a thin line frame and a light gray background color, shaded at 40%.

Directional

Print Shop Deluxe is perfect for creating quick directional signs for special events. Here's a simple idea for a school directional sign.

1. Project: Choose Sign. • Choose Wide.

2. Backdrop: Choose Blank Page. • Click OK.

3. Layout: Choose No Layout. • Click OK.

4. Click on New Object tool. • Choose Border. • Double-click border. • Choose Diamond Corners. • Select Wide Border. • Click OK.

5. Click on New Object tool. • Choose Headline. • Move block to top of sign; resize to fill entire space as shown in example. • Double-click headline block. • Font: NewZurica. • Style: Bold. • Shape: Rectangular. • Justification: Center. • Type: REGISTRATION ROOM 25 (substitute your room number). • Click OK.

6. Click on New Object tool. • Choose Horizontal Ruled Line. • Double-click line. • Choose Scotch. • Click OK. • Move line below headline block, resizing to fill page width, as shown in example.

PSD Windows Tip

If you have other Windows graphic programs, you have another resource for art. You can create original artwork, or use clip art from other programs and paste them into your PSD projects. Simply copy the design from the other graphics program into the Windows Clipboard. (Anytime you cut, copy, or paste text or art, it goes into a temporary holding area, called the Clipboard.) After art has been placed in the Clipboard, exit the program and return to PSD-Windows. Once you've opened the PSD project file you want, pull down the Edit menu and Paste the art into your project from the Clipboard. You'll then be able to scale, stretch, and modify it using PSD commands.

Variation

Here's another idea for a directional sign. Design a simple layout with just a square graphic and a text block. Use the Calendar Icon square graphic Exclamation, and rotate it so that it becomes an arrow pointing in the desired direction. Resize the square graphic as large as possible. Add a text block beside it, indicating where to go.

Help Wanted

Here's a handy project idea for posting a Help Wanted sign on a window or a bulletin board. Use these steps to create this sign.

1. Project: Choose Sign. • Choose Wide.

2. Backdrop: Choose Blank Page. • Click OK.

3. Layout: Choose Sign 13. • Click OK.

4. Fill in Border: Double-click border. • Choose Autumn Leaves. • Click OK.

5. Fill in Headline: Double-click block. • Font: Boulder. • Click on Customize button. • Shadow: Drop Shadow. • Position: Lower Right. • Click OK. • Type: HELP WANTED. • Click OK.

6. Fill in Text block: Double-click block. • Font: Paramount. • Style: Bold. • Font Size: 50-point (choose Other, type 50, and click OK). • Justification Horizontal: Center. • Justification Vertical: Bottom. • Type brief hiring details. • Click OK.

HELP WANTED
Now Hiring Part-Time
Secretary
8-5, Mon-Fri
Some Evenings
APPLY WITHIN

Variation

For a wide sign variation of the same project idea, set up a simple layout with two square graphics, a headline, and a text block. Set the square graphics in the upper corners, filling them with Pushpin art. Place a headline block between the square graphics and add a large text block beneath that contains all of your hiring details.

Design Tip

Make your sign sturdier by attaching it to stiffer posterboard or cardboard. If you're placing your sign in a window, use paper that won't glare and font sizes that you can easily read from a distance.

Signs & Flyers

Lost & Found

The Print Shop programs can help you create a lost and found sign that no one will ignore. Try this project.

1. Project: Choose Sign. • Choose Tall.

2. Backdrop: Choose Blank Page. • Click OK.

3. Layout: Choose Sign 27. • Click OK.

4. Fill in Headline: Double-click block. • Font: Boulder. • Click on Customize button. • Choose Drop Shadow. • Click OK. • Type: LOST. • Click OK.

5. Fill in Square graphic: Double-click graphic block. • Choose Lovable Pup. • Click OK. • Click on Frame tool. • Choose Thick Line.

6. Fill in Text block: Double-click block. • Font: Boulder. • Font Size: Medium. • Justification Horizontal: Center. • Justification Vertical: Center. • Type a brief description of the missing pet and the number to call. • Click OK.

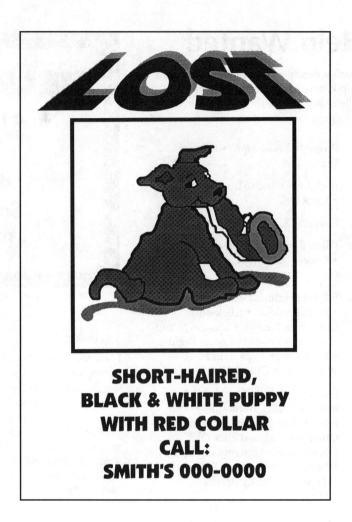

Design Tip

If you're posting a lost and found sign around the neighborhood, it might be a good idea to attach it to sturdy cardboard or posterboard. If you're expecting inclement weather, seal your sign in plastic or have it laminated. Remember to keep your font sizes legible so you can read it from a distance.

Variation

Here's a perfect sign for kids who lose hats, scarves, and gloves at school. Create a tall sign using the Winter Child backdrop and layout Winter Child 3. Headline should read "LOST & FOUND," and the text block should describe the lost item of the week.

Message

Families on the go find it helpful to post reminder signs around the house for particular chores or errands—especially for those chores and errands that they repeat frequently. This project idea helps you create a reminder message that you can hang on the refrigerator, post on a door, or place on a table.

1. Project: Choose Sign. • Choose Wide.

2. Backdrop: Choose Blank Page. • Click OK.

3. Layout: Choose Sign 14. • Click OK.

4. Fill in Border: Double-click border. • Choose Geo. • Click OK.

5. Fill in Square graphic: Double-click graphic. • Choose Elephant Forgets. • Click OK. • Resize graphic slightly.

6. Fill in Text block: Double-click block. • Font: Boulder. • Font Size: Large. • Justification Horizontal: Center. • Justification Vertical: Center. • Type: DON'T FORGET! • Press Enter to start new line. • Change Font: Paramount. • Style: Bold. • Font Size: Medium Large. • Type message on next two lines. • Click OK. • Resize block if necessary.

Variation

Make a No Smoking sign for the office. Create a simple, effective no smoking sign using the No Smoking square graphic, or making your own with the International No square graphic.

1. Create a wide sign; use the Film Loop border.

2. Add a text block to fill the inside space; select Boulder typestyle and type "SMOKING."

3. Add the International No square graphic, and resize to fit over the text block.

4. Edit the Colors of the graphic, and shade at 50% Red.

5. Edit the Order, and choose Send to Back.

Design Tip

In the variation tip, you learn how to use the International No square graphic. However, that's not the only way to use it. Combine it with various other graphics to form funny or serious warnings. This square graphic also makes great buttons that you can wear around the office, at clubs, or kids' parties.

New Business

Flyers are always very helpful for marketing a new business. The following project idea is for a Grand Opening flyer for a travel agency; you can distribute it on car windshields, bulletin boards, and mailboxes.

1. Project: Choose Sign. • Choose Tall.

2. Backdrop: Choose Coastal Scene. • Click OK.

3. Layout: Choose Coastal Scene 5. • Click OK.

4. Fill in Headline: Double-click block. • Font: Palatia. • Style: Bold. • Shape: Arc Up. • Click on Customize button. • Under Shadow Effect, choose Silhouette. • Under Color, set Text to white and Shadow to black. • Click OK. • Type: Travis Travel Agency (or name of your company). • Click OK.

5. Click on New Object tool. • Choose Text. • Move block directly below headline. • Resize as shown in example. • Double-click text block. • Font: NewZurica. • Font Size: Extra Small. • Justification Horizontal: Center. • Justification Vertical: Top. • Type name of owners. • Press Enter to move to new line. • Change Font: Signature. • Type years of experience. • Click OK.

6. Fill in middle Text block: Double-click block. • Font: Jester. • Font Size: 28-point (choose Other, type: 28, and click OK). • Type: GRAND OPENING! Stop in for a Visit! Register to Win a Trip to Hawaii!. • Click OK. • Resize block to fit beside palm tree. • Click on Frame tool. • Choose Thin Line.

7. Fill in bottom Text block: Double-click block. • Font: Moderne. • Font Size: Small. • Type: Let us help you

plan your dream vacation!. • Click OK. • Move block to lower right corner. • Click on Frame tool. • Choose Drop Shadow.

8. Click on New Object tool. • Choose Text: Double-click block. • Font: Boulder. • Font Size: Small. • Justification Horizontal: Center. • Justification Vertical: Top. • Type in address and phone number of new business. • Click OK. • Move block to lower left corner, resize as necessary.

Design Tip

Copy your flyers onto colored paper for greater impact. You can also use a vertical tri-fold to turn your flyer into an instant mailer! The blank side of the flyer should appear on the outside. Just staple or tape the folded flyer closed, and add a mailing address.

Sale

Use flyers to promote sales for businesses, neighborhoods, and more. The project below is an example of a school sale flyer.

1. Project: Choose Sign. • Choose Tall.

2. Backdrop: Choose Gingerbread Man. • Click OK.

3. Layout: Choose Gingerbread Man 5. • Click OK.

4. Fill in Headline: Double-click block. • Font: Boulder. • Click on Customize button. • Under Shadow Effect, choose Drop Shadow. • Position: Lower Right. • Under Colors, set Text to black and Shadow to light gray. • Click OK. • Type: BAKE SALE!. • Click OK.

5. Fill in Text block 1 (below headline): Double-click block. • Font: Moderne. • Font Size: 28-point (choose Other, type 28, and click OK). • Justification Horizontal: Center. • Justification Vertical: Center. • Type details about sale (date, time, and place). • Choose Extra Small size for last two lines. • Click OK. • Click on Frame tool. • Choose None.

6. Fill in Text block 2: Move block to fit beside gingerbread man. • Double-click text block. • Font: Boulder. • Font Size: 28-point (choose Other, type 28, and click OK). • Justification Horizontal: Center. • Justification Vertical: Center. • Type: PIES! CAKES! COOKIES! BREADS! BROWNIES! And More! • Click OK. • Use the Color controls to select Yellow for Behind the Text.

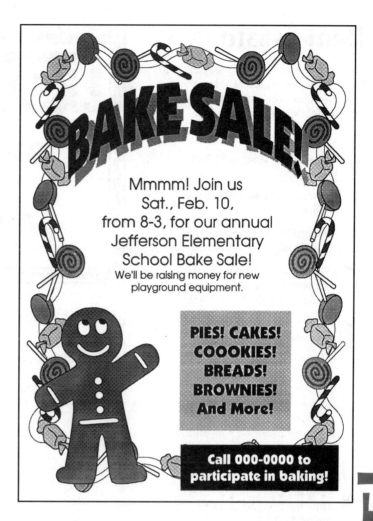

7. Click on New Object tool. • Choose Text block. • Move block to bottom right corner, as shown in example. • Double-click text block. • Font: Boulder. • Font Size: Small. • Justification Horizontal: Center. • Justification Vertical: Center. • Type phone number to be called. • Click OK. • Use the Color controls to choose white for Text and black for Behind Text.

Design Tip

Does your flyer need some color? Have the kids in your school help color the signs with crayons, markers, or paint! This is a great way to get kids to participate. This is also a good idea for clubs and organizations.

Real Estate

You can use sale signs for the home in a variety of ways: selling cars, lawn equipment, or even real estate. The project idea below is for a sign that you can post in a yard or in a window.

1. Project: Choose Sign. • Choose Wide.

2. Backdrop: Choose Blank Page. • Click OK.

3. Layout: Choose Sign 13. • Click OK.

4. Fill in Border: Double-click border. • Choose Diamond Corners. • Select Wide Border. • Click OK.

5. Edit Headline: Click block. • Click on Delete tool.

6. Click on New Object tool. • Choose Text. • Double-click block. • Font: Subway. • Font Size: 120-point (choose Other, type 120, and click OK). • Justification Horizontal: Center. • Justification Vertical: Center. • Type: FOR SALE. • Click OK. • Resize block to fit text as shown in example. • Use the Color controls to set white for Text and black for Behind Text.

7. Fill in Text block (bottom block): Double-click block. • Font: Subway. • Font Size: Large. • Justification Horizontal: Center. • Justification Vertical: Center. • Type: BY OWNER call 000-0000. • Click OK.

Design Tip

Be sure to mount your sign onto sturdier cardboard or posterboard. If the weather is damp or rainy, laminate or wrap your sign in plastic to keep the ink from running.

Event

You can create event flyers for home, school, community, or office. Follow these steps to make an event flyer for school.

1. Project: Choose Sign. • Choose Tall.

2. Backdrop: Choose Football Field. • Click OK.

3. Layout: Choose Football Field 3. • Click OK.

4. Fill in Text block: Resize block to make room for headline block at top. • Double-click text block. • Font: Jester. • Font Size: Medium. • Justification Horizontal: Center. • Justification Vertical: Center. • Type event message, date, and time. • Click OK.

5. Fill in bottom Headline block: Resize block as large as possible across bottom of sign. • Double-click headline block. • Shape: Pennant Right. • Font: Bazooka. • Click on Customize button. • Under Shadow Effect, choose Drop Shadow. • Under Colors, set Text to black and Shadow to light gray. • Click OK. • Type your team's name. • Click OK.

6. Click on New Object tool. • Choose Headline. • Move block to top of sign. • Resize as large as possible to fill space. • Double-click headline block. • Font: Boulder. • Shape: Double Arch Up. • Click on Customize button. • Under Shadow Effect, choose Drop Shadow. • Under Colors, set Shadow to light gray. • Click OK. • Type: TEAM RALLY! • Click OK.

Variation

Make your own Community Event Flyers! You can make all sorts of flyers for special activities around your town. Here's an idea for a Halloween pumpkin-carving contest:

1. Select a tall sign, layout 13.

2. Use the Jolly Pumpkins Row graphics at the top and bottom.

3. Type the event details in Jester, 30-point. Resize the Text block to make room for a Column graphic on the right.

4. Add a column graphic: Halloween Candy.

Signs & Flyers

Election

Signs can help your campaign for an election at school, your neighborhood, or community. Here's a simple election sign idea that's a winner!

1. Project: Choose Sign. • Choose Tall.

2. Backdrop: Choose Blank Page. • Click OK.

3. Layout: Choose Sign 19. • Click OK.

4. Fill in Border: Double-click border. • Choose Stars & Stripes. • Click OK.

5. Fill in Headline block: Double-click block. • Font: Boulder. • Click on Customize button. • Under Shadow Effect, choose Block Shadow. • Under Colors, set Shadow to gray shaded at 40%. • Click OK. • Type: VOTE. • Click OK.

6. Fill in Text block: Double-click block. • Font: Tubular. • Font Size: 120-point (choose Other, type 120, and click OK). • Justification Horizontal: Center. • Justification Vertical: Center. • Style: Shadow. • Type your candidate's name. • Press Enter to start a new line. • Change Font: StageCoach. • Font Size: 44-point (choose Other, type 44, and click OK). • Type the office the candidate is running for in the election. • Click OK.

Design Tip

Have your election signs printed on red and blue paper for a patriotic feel. Or add color to ordinary white paper using markers or paint to fill in the border or letters.

Variation

For a wide version of a patriotic sign, choose the American Flag backdrop. Add a simple headline, using Heather font, and rotate it so it sits at the far right side of the page.

Door

Here's an idea for a door sign for a child's room. The Print Shop programs allow you to create numerous sign ideas to post on doors at home, at school, or in the office.

1. Project: Choose Sign. • Choose Tall.

2. Backdrop: Choose Volcano.
    • Click OK.

3. Layout: Choose Volcano 5.
    • Click OK.

4. Fill in Text block: Double-click block. • Font: Boulder. • Font Size: Large. • Justification Horizontal: Full. • Justification Vertical: Center. • Type: DANGER! • Press Enter to start a new line. • Font: Bazooka. • Font Size: Medium. • Type: ROOM MAY EXPLODE! • Click OK.

5. Fill in Headline block: Double-click block. • Font: Subway. • Type: KEEP OUT! • Click OK.

Variation

Make a simple door sign for honeymooners following these steps:

1. Use a wide sign orientation.

2. Add a square graphic, and choose Swans. Resize the graphic as large as possible.

3. Add a headline block above the graphic, using Heather font and Arc Up shape.

Design Tip

To hang your door sign, attach a piece of yarn to the back or punch a hole in the top and add a reinforcement ring. Then hang the sign on a doorknob. If that's not satisfactory, the old tape-it-up technique will also work just fine. Let kids color in their own door signs with crayons, markers, or paint. (Makes a good rainy day project!)

Science Fair

Help make your child's science-fair project a big success with easy-to-read signs, created with the Print Shop programs. Follow these steps:

1. Project: Choose Sign. • Choose Wide.

2. Backdrop: Choose Blank Page. • Click OK.

3. Layout: Choose Sign 2. • Click OK.

4. Fill in Headline block: Double-click block. • Font: NewZurica. • Click on Customize button. • Under Shadow Effect, choose Block Shadow. • Click OK. • Type the science project's title. • Click OK.

5. Fill in Text block 1: Double-click block. • Font: Tribune. • Font Size: Medium. • Justification Horizontal: Left. • Justification Vertical: Top. • Type a brief introduction to your project. • Click OK.

6. Fill in Text block 2: Double-click block. • Font: Tribune. • Font Size: 30-point (choose Other, type 30, and click OK). • Justification Horizontal: Right. • Justification Vertical: Top. • Type your project information. • Click OK. • Click on Frame tool. • Choose Drop Shadow.

7. Fill in Square graphics: Double-click on first graphic block. • Choose World. • Select Apply to All Squares. • Click OK.

WORLD WATER SUPPLY-2000

In the year 2000 the world's water supply will not have changed significantly since the earth began.

Why? Because the earth recycles its water naturally. Follow the steps in this science project to see how...

Design Tip

Complement your science project booth with a matching banner project. Follow the banner steps under the Banners/Science Fair project in the next project section of this book.

Banners

For those occasions requiring a really big sign, banner projects are just the thing. Banners are simple to create, print and hang. They come in handy for party decorations, big sale events, science fair projects, team rallies, and much more. With PSD, you'll be able to create horizontal banners and vertical banners to fulfill all your banner needs.

- Garage Sale
- Election
- Sports
- Party
- Store Sale
- Science Fair
- Finish Line
- Contest Event

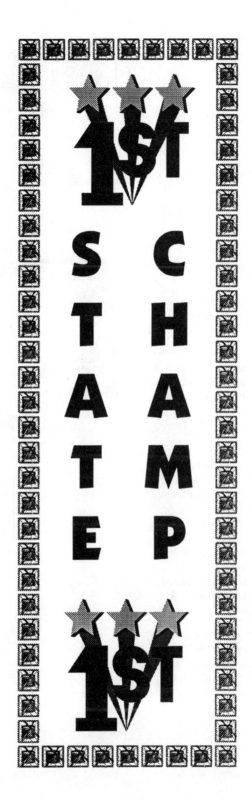

PSD-Windows steps:

1. Select Banner from the Project menu screen.

2. Select the project orientation.

3. Choose a backdrop graphic design, and click OK.

4. Choose a layout design, and click OK.

5. Use the Tool Palette and pull-down menus to fill in each layout element.

6. Pull down the File menu, and select Save. In the File Save As dialog box, type in a file name, and click OK.

7. Pull down the File menu, and select Print. In the Print dialog box, choose any printing options, and click OK.

When creating banner projects, remember a few things. Banners can be big. That means there isn't much room for lots of text and graphics. Banner text works a lot like headline blocks; horizontal banners can have up to two lines of text, and vertical banners can have one line of text. However, unlike headlines, banner text does not get squeezed to fit into the space. Instead, the more letters and words you type, the longer the banner.

You can also increase banner length using the Adjust Length option from the Project menu. Leading Space can add inches to the front end of your banner; and Trailing Space can add inches to the back end of your banner.

Since banners are so big, you won't always be able to see the whole project on your screen. Use the scrolling functions (scroll bars) to view the different parts of your banner. Use the + or - keys on your keyboard's numeric keypad to scroll. If you use continuous-feed paper to print your banners, all you have to do is hang them up after printing them out. If you use a laser or inkjet printer, assemble your printed banner pages with tape to turn them into a banner for hanging.

All of the instructions for individual banner projects in this book are Windows steps. However, if you're using PSD-DOS or PSD-Mac, you can create the exact same projects. For the most part, your steps will be the same. There may be some slight differences in the instructions.

PSD-DOS steps:

1. Select Banner from the Project menu.

2. Select Create a new project.

3. Select the project orientation.

4. Choose Select a Backdrop from the menu list. Choose a backdrop design, and click Done.

5. Choose Select a Layout from the menu list. Choose a layout design.

6. Choose Fill In or Edit from the menu list. Fill in each layout element.

7. Choose Save from the menu list. Type in a file name, a description, then choose Save File.

8. Choose Print from the menu list, and select Print.

If you're using PSD-DOS, your project steps will differ slightly. Instead of clicking OK when a task is complete as you do in Windows, you click Done (where applicable) when finished with each project step. Instead of using a Tool Palette or pull-down menus to fill in layout elements, you use a menu list and

dialog boxes. Line Justify denotes horizontal justification, and Placement denotes vertical justification; so look for those commands to control positioning.

When creating your own layout, use the Add New Elements command to insert the various layout elements. If you ever become confused about using a menu or dialog box, look at the bottom of your screen for brief instructions telling you what to do.

PSD-Mac steps:

1. Select Banner from the Project menu screen.

2. Select the project orientation.

3. Choose a backdrop graphic design, and click OK.

4. Choose a layout design, and click OK.

5. Use the Tool Palette and pull-down menus to fill in each layout element.

6. Pull down the File menu, and select Save. In the Save dialog box, type in a file name, and click Save.

7. Pull down the File menu, and select Print. In the Print dialog box, choose any printing options, and click Print.

Your PSD-Mac project steps will vary slightly. Unlike PSD-Windows and PSD-DOS users, you use the Text menu to select fonts, sizes, and justification. As in the Windows steps, you click on a text block to select it. Once selected, you can start typing in text, or pull down the Text menu and change text options. When finished typing, just click outside the block. Justification denotes horizontal justification, and Placement denotes vertical justification; so look for those commands on the Text menu to control positioning.

Garage Sale

A big banner can draw a lot of attention to a neighborhood sale. The following project idea will help you create a simple, yet attractive, garage sale banner.

1. Project: Choose Banner. • Choose Horizontal.

2. Backdrop: Choose Blank Page. • Click OK.

3. Layout: Choose Banner 28. • Click OK.

4. Click on New Object tool. • Choose Border. • Double-click Border. • Choose Blue Check. • Click OK.

5. Fill in Headline block: Double-click block. • Font: Boulder. • Click on Customize. • Shadow: Drop Shadow. • Type: GARAGE SALE. • Click OK.

6. Edit graphic block: Click block. • Click on Delete tool.

7. Click on New Object tool. • Choose Text. • Resize block to fill bottom of banner and move into place. • Double-click block. • Font: Paramount. • Style: Bold. • Font Size: Small. • Justification Horizontal: Full. • Justification Vertical: Center. • Type the dates and times of the garage sale. • Click OK.

GARAGE SALE
FRI & SAT 9-5

Banner Tip

If you use string or wire to hang your banner, it's a good idea to reinforce the banner in the corners from which it will hang. This is especially true for banners displayed outside on windy days. Before punching holes for the string or wire, try reinforcing the back of the banner with heavy-duty tape. It is also a good idea to add weights to the bottom of the banner to keep it from flapping.

Election

Banners are great political-campaigning aids for school, local, or national elections. Use these steps to create a patriotic-looking banner.

1. Project: Choose Banner. • Choose Horizontal.

2. Backdrop: Choose Blank Page. • Click OK.

3. Layout: Choose Banner 2. • Click OK.

4. Fill in Border: Double-click border. • Choose Stars & Stripes. • Click OK.

5. Fill in Square graphic: Double-click graphic. • Choose PSDeluxe Calendar Icons library. • Choose Flag • Choose Apply to All Squares. • Click OK.

6. Fill in Headline block: Double-click block. • Font: Boulder. • Font Size: Large/Small. • Click Customize on button. • Choose Shadow: Drop Shadow. • Click OK. • Type the name of the person running for election and the position she is running for. • Click OK.

Design Tip

Need more than two lines of text in your horizontal banner? Modify your banner layout to include a text block that fits another line.

Variation

Prefer a vertical election banner? Choose a Vertical orientation with the Stars & Stripes backdrop and Stars & Stripes Layout 1. After filling in the Headline block with candidate's name, add a text block to the top of the banner with the word "VOTE." Change Behind Text color to blue, 40% shading.

Banners

Sports

What better way to root for your school's team or favorite sports star than with a large banner! Drape banners inside gymnasiums and school hallways, wave them from bleacher stands, or tape them to team buses and lockers. The project idea on this page illustrates how to create a vertical banner.

1. Project: Choose Banner. • Choose Vertical.

2. Backdrop: Choose Blank Page. • Click OK.

3. Layout: Choose Banner 3. • Click OK.

4. Fill in Headline block: Double-click block. • Font: Tribune. • Style: Bold. • Click on Customize button. • Shadow Effect: Drop Shadow. • Position: Upper Left. • Click OK. • Type your team's name. • Click OK.

5. Fill in Column graphic: Double-click block. • Choose Football Player. • Click OK.

6. Pull down the Project menu. • Choose Change Backdrop. • Choose Playing Field. • Click OK.

Design Tip

You can cut out or trim banner projects to make flags or pennants. Just attach your banner to a lightweight balsa stick or wooden rod; wave it to cheer on your favorite team!

Variation

To make a horizontal banner with a similar theme, use Banner Layout 1. Use Football Square graphic in the first graphic block. Use 1st Square graphic in the second graphic block. Shade both graphic blocks at 40%. Make sure both blocks fill as much space as necessary. Set the entire page background in the color green, shaded at 40%. Add a headline (same as preceding step 4) and print your banner!

Party

Large banners make excellent party decorations for home, school, or business. Use these steps to create a simple birthday banner.

1. Project: Choose Banner. • Choose Horizontal.

2. Backdrop: Choose Blank Page. • Click OK.

3. Layout: Choose Banner 22. • Click OK.

4. Fill in Headline block: Double-click block. • Font: NewZurica. • Click on Customize button. • Choose Shadow Effect: Drop Shadow. • Position: Lower Right. • Click OK. • Type: HAPPY BIRTHDAY! • Click OK.

5. Fill in Square graphic block: Double-click graphic. • Choose Birthday Cake. • Select Apply to All Squares. • Click OK.

6. Edit Row graphic. • Click graphic. • Click on Delete tool.

7. Click on New Object tool. • Choose Text. • Move block below headline. • Resize to fill remaining space. • Double-click text block. • Font: Paramount. • Font Size: Small. • Justification Horizontal: Full. • Justification Vertical: Center. • Type the name of the birthday person. • Click OK.

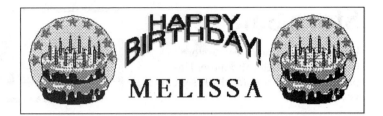

Variation

Make a 3-D Banner to give added punch to your party banners by attaching extra graphics, streamers, or balloons. To add 3-D graphics, print out extra copies of graphics (such as the Firecracker square graphic) to use on your banner. Cut out the shape of the graphic. Take a narrow strip of paper and fold it accordion-style. Attach the graphic shape to one end of the strip. Attach the other end of the strip to the banner. Try using different lengths of paper strips to create your 3-D art. Once you attach the 3-D graphics, you should have a banner with art that springs off!

Banners

Store Sale

Use banners to advertise new store items, sales, services, and more. This project idea makes an ideal sale sign for your business.

1. Project: Choose Banner. • Choose Horizontal.

2. Backdrop: Choose Blank Page. • Click OK.

3. Layout: Choose Banner 1. • Click OK.

4. Fill in Border: Double-click border frame. • Choose Triangle. • Click OK.

5. Fill in Headline: Double-click block. • Font: Subway. • Size: Large/Small. • Type your sales feature. • Click OK.

6. Fill in Square graphic block 1 (left): Double-click block. • Choose Sale. • Click OK. • Rotate block as shown in example (about 25 degrees). • Resize block to fill space between text and border.

7. Fill in Square graphic block 2 (right): Double-click block. • Choose Sale. • Click OK. • Rotate block as shown in example (about 325 degrees). • Resize block to fill space between text and border.

Variation

Is your school, church, or club having a fund-raiser? Use banners to advertise and decorate. Layouts, such as Number 11, make great use of art, border, and text.

Design Tip

Need a sturdier banner? Attach your banner projects to posterboard or other stiff cardboard products to add plenty of support.

Science Fair

You can use banners to make signs for school fairs and exhibits. The following example is an incredibly simple banner for a science-fair project. The Chef backdrop is perfect for a science project with steps like those in a recipe. Additional banners can demonstrate the various steps and results involved with the project.

1. Project: Choose Banner.
   • Choose Horizontal.

2. Backdrop: Choose Chef. • Click OK.

3. Layout: Choose Chef 2. • Click OK.

4. Fill in Headline: Double-click block.
   • Font: Jester. • Type your banner project's title. • Click OK.

Other Ideas

Use PSD banners for professional trade shows and business presentations. With the crisp graphics and text, you can create quality banners that are sure to draw attention to your booth!

Variation

Here's an idea for making another kind of science fair banner. This one focuses on electricity. Using a horizontal orientation and Banner Layout 1, add a column graphic. Use the Lightning Bolt art. Rotate the graphic so that it becomes completely horizontal. Resize the graphic to fill the entire banner. Set the art in another color, such as yellow. Set your headline so that it overlaps; give it a special effect treatment.

Banners

Finish Line

If your community, school, or business sponsors a marathon or fun-run race, you'll need a finish line. Banners make excellent finish lines! Follow these steps to create a simple finish line.

1. Project: Choose Banner. • Choose Horizontal.

2. Backdrop: Choose Blank Page. • Click OK.

3. Layout: Choose Banner 13. • Click OK.

4. Fill in Border: Double-click border. • Choose Stars & Stripes. • Click OK.

5. Click on New Object tool. • Choose Text. • Double-click block. • Font: Subway. • Font Size: Medium. • Justification Horizontal: Full. • Justification Vertical: Center. • Type: FINISH LINE. • Click OK. • Resize block to fill entire space inside border.

Design Tip

To make longer finish-line banners, don't forget to use the Adjust Length commands to add inches to the front and back ends of your banner project.

FINISH LINE

Variation

Another good use of banners, similar to the Finish Line project, is for grand openings of stores, restaurants, and other businesses. To create a simple grand opening sign for a restaurant, especially for a ribbon-cutting ceremony, try this idea. Use the horizontal orientation and Banner Layout 1. Use the Burger square graphic in both graphic blocks, rotating them slightly. In the main Headline block, set the words "GRAND OPENING" in Boulder font. Add two more headlines in a Top Arch shape to fit above each square graphic. Use the name of the restaurant in these blocks.

Another Idea

You can use your banner to hang above the finish line, or you can have the winner break through the banner as he or she crosses the finish line!

Contest Event

Use Print Shop Deluxe to create great banners for community, school, or business contests. This project idea is for a pie-eating contest at a community fair. Follow these steps.

1. Project: Choose Banner. • Choose Horizontal.

2. Backdrop: Choose Art Deco. • Click OK.

3. Layout: Choose Art Deco 5. • Click OK.

4. Fill in Square graphic block: Double-click block. • Choose Cherry Pie. • Click OK. • Resize block to fill space on left side of banner. • Click on Flip tool. • Choose Horizontal.

5. Fill in Headline block: Double-click block. • Font: Boulder. • Font Size: Small/Large. • Click Customize button. • Choose Shadow: Block Shadow. • Click OK. • Type: PIE-EATING CONTEST. • Click OK.

What Else Can I Do?

Here are some other contest banner ideas: spelling bee, game booths for the school fair, sales contests at the office, prize give-aways to bring in customers, birthday parties, family reunion and picnic activities, and athletic events.

Variation

What about school fairs or community carnivals? You'll need banners for game booths. Here's an easy idea. Use the Penguin column graphic in a vertical banner, resizing the graphic so that it fills the entire space inside the banner. Add a headline block for the name of the game booth, such as RING TOSS, and another headline block with the price of the game.

Banners

Calendars

With the versatile PSD calendars, you can make numerous projects for your home, office, school, or community. Create your own yearly, monthly, weekly, or daily calendars to keep for yourself or give away.

- Yearly
- Monthly
- Weekly
- Daily
- Event
- Team
- Wedding Planner
- Vacation Schedules
- Advent

Calendars

In putting together a calendar project, you'll find a few extra steps at the beginning of the procedure. Dialog boxes appear for you to enter a specific year and month, and to choose a week, day, or times. Once you choose those elements, you may then go on to choose a backdrop and layout. With all PSD programs, each calendar project automatically assigns a year, month, or week title as a headline or text block. For example, when creating a yearly calendar, PSD automatically displays the year you choose. You can modify these blocks at any time, but they're handy to use as is and can save you a step in designing your calendar.

When working with calendar projects, you must always choose a layout as you begin your project. You can modify headline, graphics, and text blocks, but the calendar block itself has limited editing commands, unless you are using PSD version 1.2. For example, you cannot reposition or scale a calendar block as you can other layout elements. However, if you use version 1.2, you can.

Follow the basic steps shown for creating any calendar project.

PSD-Windows steps:

1. Select Calendar from the Project menu screen.

2. Select the calendar type (Yearly, Monthly, Weekly, Daily).

3. Select the project orientation (Tall or Wide).

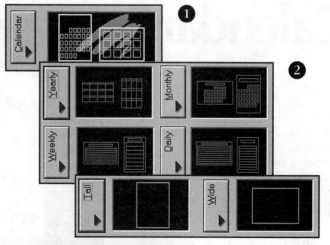

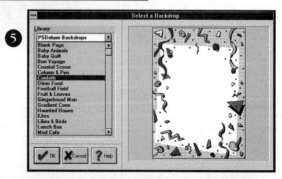

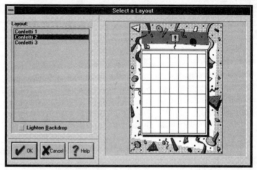

4. Select the calendar year. If you choose a monthly, weekly, or daily calendar project, more dialog boxes appear to help you narrow down the details about which month, week, or day, and times. Make the appropriate selections, and click OK.

5. Choose a backdrop graphic design, and click OK.

6. Choose a layout design, and click OK.

7. Use the Tool Palette and pull-down menus to fill in each layout element.

8. To add text or graphics to a calendar block, double-click the block to open the Edit Day dialog box. Based on the type of calendar project you select, the dialog box offers options for filling in both text and graphics. After filling in text or graphics, click OK to exit the dialog box.

9. Pull down the File menu, and select Save. In the File Save As dialog box, type in a file name, and click OK.

10. Pull down the File menu, and select Print. In the Print dialog box, choose any printing options, and click OK.

All of the instructions for individual calendar projects in this book are Windows steps. However, if you're using PSD-DOS or PSD-Mac, you can create the exact same projects. For the most part, your steps will be the same. There may be some slight differences in the instructions as noted.

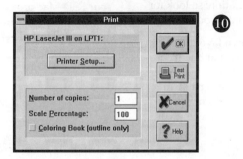

Calendars

PSD-DOS steps:

1. Select Calendar from the Project menu.

2. Select Create a new project.

3. Select the project orientation.

4. Select the calendar type.

5. Select the calendar year. Choose month, week, day, or times as appropriate to your project.

6. Choose Select a Backdrop from the menu list. Choose a backdrop design, and click Done.

7. Choose Select a Layout from the menu list. Choose a layout design.

8. Choose Fill In or Edit from the menu list. Fill in each layout element. Press Esc when done.

9. Choose Save from the menu list. Type in a file name, a description, and choose Save File.

10. Choose Print from the menu list, and select Print.

If you use PSD-DOS, your project steps will differ slightly. Instead of clicking OK when a task is complete as you do in Windows, you click Done (where applicable) when finished with each project step. Instead of using a Tool Palette or pull-down menus to fill in layout elements, you use a menu list and dialog boxes. Line Justify denotes horizontal justification, and Placement denotes vertical justification; so look for those commands to control positioning.

When creating your own layout, use the Add New Elements command to insert the various layout elements. If you ever become confused about using a menu or dialog box, look at the bottom of your screen for brief instructions telling you what to do.

PSD-Mac steps:

1. Select Calendar from the Project menu screen.

2. Select the calendar type.

3. Select the project orientation.

4. Select the calendar year. Choose month, week, day, or times as appropriate to your project and click OK.

5. Choose a backdrop graphic design, and click Save.

6. Choose a layout design, and click Print.

7. Use the Tool Palette and pull-down menus to fill in each layout element.

8. To add text or graphics to a calendar block, double-click the block to open the Edit Day dialog box. Based on the type of calendar project you select, the dialog box offers options for filling in both text and graphics. After filling in text or graphics, click OK to exit the dialog box.

9. Pull down the File menu, and select Save. In the Save dialog box, type in a file name, and click OK.

10. Pull down the File menu, and select Print. In the Print dialog box, choose any printing options, and click OK.

Your PSD-Mac project steps will vary ever so slightly. As in the Windows steps, you'll double-click a block to select it.

Yearly

Yearly calendars are always useful around the home, office, or school. This idea is a perfect project for advertising your company or business. Follow these steps to create a yearly calendar that you can give to customers, clients, associates, and others. By adding your company name, address, and phone number to a yearly calendar, you create instant advertising! Have the calendars printed on quality paper in large quantities at your local printing store.

1. Project: Choose Calendar. • Choose Yearly. • Choose Tall. • Choose 1995 (or year of your choice).
   • Click OK.

2. Backdrop: Choose Ocean & Jungle.
   • Click OK.

3. Layout: Choose Ocean & Jungle 2.
   • Click OK.

4. Edit Calendar block: Double-click block. • Font: NewZurica. • Style: Bold. • Under Month Blocks, choose Underlined. • Click OK.

5. Edit Headline: Double-click block.
   • Font: NewZurica. • Style: Bold.
   • Type your company name.
   • Click OK.

6. Click on New Object tool. • Choose Text. • Move and resize block to fit underneath headline. • Double-click Text block. • Font: Boulder.
   • Font Size: Medium. • Justification Horizontal: Center. • Justification Vertical: Center. • Type company phone number. • Press Enter to start a new line. • Change Font Size: Extra Small. • Type address.
   • Click OK.

7. Click on New Object tool.
   • Choose Text. • Move block to bottom of calendar page. • Resize to fill smaller space, as shown in example. • Double-click Text block. • Font: Boulder. • Font Size: Large. • Justification Horizontal: Center. • Justification Vertical: Center. • Type year.
   • Click OK. • Use the Color controls to set Behind Text color to pink.

Design Tip

Shaded square graphics make great backgrounds for calendars. Try using a large graphic layered behind your calendar block. Shade the graphic at 30% or 40%. This creates a nice screened background to your calendar design. Be sure to choose bold calendar fonts or thick lines so they are visible on top of the shaded art.

Monthly

If you're having trouble keeping up with family schedules, try this idea for a monthly calendar.

1. Project: Choose Calendar. • Choose Monthly. • Choose Wide. • Choose Calendar year and month. • Click OK.

2. Backdrop: Choose Blank Page. • Click OK.

3. Layout: Choose Calendar 5. • Click OK.

4. Edit Headline block: Double-click block. • Shape: Round Top. • Click OK.

5. Edit Column graphic: Double-click block. • Choose Bat & Gloves. • Click OK. • Pull down the Object menu and choose Shadow. • Select On.

6. Click on New Object tool. • Choose Row Graphic. • Move graphic to bottom of calendar page. • Resize to fill space as shown in example. • Double-click Row Graphic. • Choose Baseball & Bat. • Click OK.

7. Edit Calendar block with text: Double-click block. • From Edit Day dialog box, select day to fill in. • Click Edit Text button to open the Text dialog box. • Font: NewZurica. • Font Size: Medium. • Justification Horizontal: Center. • Justification Vertical: Center. • Type in text pertaining to day selected. • Click OK to return to Edit Day dialog box. • Repeat this sequence to fill in other days in your calendar. • When finished, click OK in the Edit Day dialog box.

8. Edit Calendar block with graphics: Double-click block. • From the Edit Day dialog box, select day to fill in. • Click Select Graphic button to open the Select a Square Graphic dialog box. • Choose an appropriate graphic. • Click OK to return to Edit Day dialog box. • Repeat this sequence to fill in other days in your calendar. • When finished, click OK in the Edit Day dialog box.

Design Tip

Remember, you can use regular square graphics in your calendar project as well as Calendar Icons.

Variation

Hang your calendar in a visible place, such as on a refrigerator door, for all to see. Print out extra graphics to cut and paste onto the calendar as needed.

Weekly

Weekly calendars are great for tracking daily events. This project shows a nifty weekly school calendar for the week of April 3, 1995.

1. Project: Choose Calendar. • Choose Weekly. • Choose Tall. • Choose April, 1995, and April 1st Starting Day (substitute dates as needed). • Click OK.

2. Backdrop: Choose Kites. • Click OK.

3. Layout: Choose Kites 2. • Click OK.

4. Edit Text block (at bottom of project): Double-click block. • Font: Chaucer. • Font Size: Large. • Click OK.

5. Edit Calendar block with text: Double-click block. • From Edit Day dialog box, select day to fill in. • Click Edit Text button to open the Edit Text dialog box. • Font: NewZurica. • Style: Bold. • Font Size: Medium. • Type in text pertaining to day selected. • Click OK to return to Edit Day dialog box. • Repeat this sequence to fill in other days in your calendar. • When finished, click OK in the Edit Day dialog box.

6. Edit Calendar block with graphics: Double-click block. • From the Edit Day dialog box, select day to fill in. • Click Select Graphic button to open the Select a Square Graphic dialog box. • Choose an appropriate graphic. • Click OK to return to Edit Day dialog box. • Repeat this sequence to fill in other days in your calendar. • When finished, click OK in the Edit Day dialog box.

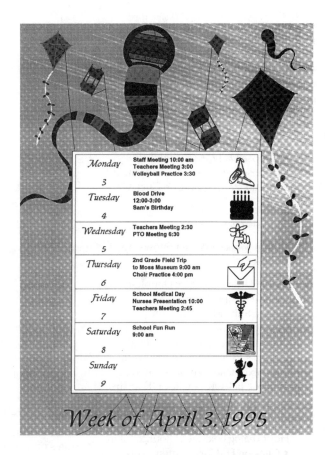

Week of April 3, 1995

Design Tip

If you're using PSD version 1.2, you can resize your calendar blocks to be bigger. To make maximum use of the project shown on this page, move the headline block to the top of the page, changing Behind Text color to white or blue. Resize the calendar block to fill the remaining space on the page. Now you have a bigger calendar!

Make a Monthly Office Calendar

Print out and copy a month's worth of blank weekly calendars to distribute to everyone in the office. They can fill in their own schedules and appointments!

Make a Pocket Calendar

Feeling really creative and experimental? Try designing a pocket-size version of your calendar project. Watch out for small point sizes and illegible fonts.

Daily

A daily calendar can help you organize each hour of your day. Follow these project steps for creating a daily calendar to use at work.

1. Project: Choose Calendar.
   • Choose Daily. • Choose Tall.
   • Choose Calendar year, month, day, and starting hour. • Click OK.

2. Backdrop: Choose Winter Snowscape. • Click OK.

3. Layout: Choose Winter Snowscape 1.
   • Click OK.

4. Edit Headline block. • Double-click block. • Shape: Round Top.
   • Font: Subway. • Click on Customize button. • Text Effect: Thick Outline. • Text Fill: Blend Down. • Colors: Set Text to white and Text Blend to blue, shaded at 10%. • Click OK. • Click OK again.

5. Edit Calendar block with text: Double-click block. • From Edit Hour dialog box, select hour to fill in.
   • Click on Edit Text button to open the Text dialog box. • Font: Subway.
   • Font Size: Medium.
   • Justification Horizontal: Center.
   • Justification Vertical: Center.
   • Type in text pertaining to hour selected. • Click OK to return to Edit Hour dialog box. • Repeat this sequence to fill in other hours in your calendar. • When finished, click OK in the Edit Hour dialog box.

6. Edit Calendar block with graphics: Double-click block. • From the Edit Hour dialog box, select hour to fill in.
   • Click Select Graphic button to open the Select a Square Graphic dialog box. • Choose an appropriate graphic. • Click OK to return to Edit Hour dialog box. • Repeat this sequence to fill in other hours in your calendar. • When finished, click OK in the Edit Hour dialog box.

Make a Picture Calendar

Calendars that you purchase in stores often have pictures and printed scenes attached to them. If you're using a continuous feed printer (one where the paper is one long sheet), you can design your own picture calendars. First, use the Sign project type (Tall orientation) to design a picture. Print it out, but don't tear the page from the rest of the paper in your printer. Instead, go on to make a monthly calendar design. Print it out. Now you have a picture calendar. You can continue this sequence to make designs for all twelve months of the year! You don't have to feel left out if you don't have a continuous feed printer. Simply tape your pages together to create the calendar.

Variation

Design a month's worth of daily schedules, punch holes along the left edge, and bind them in a 3-ring notebook. This makes a great day planner for yourself, or to give to someone else!

Event

If your school, office, or family likes to organize schedules around events, design your own event calendar that clearly marks a month's worth of activities. Use event calendars to help keep school or office staff informed of important monthly happenings. The project on this page shows how to make a seasonal event calendar for school.

1. Project: Choose Calendar. • Choose Monthly. • Choose Wide. • Choose 1995 and October (substitute as needed). • Click OK.

2. Backdrop: Choose Bats & Pumpkins patterned backdrop. • Click OK.

3. Layout: Choose Calendar 2. • Click OK.

4. Edit Column graphic: Click block. • Click Delete tool.

5. Edit Headline block: Double-click block. • Font: Boulder. • Type: OCTOBER (substitute month chosen in step 1). • Click OK. • Use the Color controls to change Behind Text to yellow. • Move block up to make room for square graphic block below.

6. Click on New Object tool. • Choose Square Graphic. • Double-click Square Graphic block. • Choose Pumpkin. • Click OK. • Click on Frame tool. • Choose Drop Shadow. • Resize block to fill space below headline. • Use the Color controls to change Behind Object to light blue.

7. Click on New Object tool. • Choose Text. • Double-click Text block. • Font: NewZurica. • Style: Bold. • Font Size: Small. • Type in calendar event text. • Click OK. • Move and resize block where needed on calendar, as shown in example.

8. Repeat step 7 to add as many Text blocks as needed.

Design Tip

Watch your fonts! For maximum legibility in your calendar text, be sure to use fonts that are legible at small point sizes. NewZurica is a reliable font, whether bold or regular. Avoid script fonts, such as Signature, when fitting text into a tiny area.

Other Ideas

Clubs, community organizations, churches, and other groups will find this project idea useful in many ways. Event calendars make great mailers, too!

Team

Keeping track of sports schedules can be a breeze with PSD. Here's a project idea for keeping monthly team games organized at school.

1. Project: Choose Calendar.
   • Choose Monthly. • Choose Tall. • Choose a year and month. • Click OK.

2. Backdrop: Choose Blank Page. • Click OK.

3. Layout: Choose Calendar 6. • Click OK.

4. Edit Text block: Resize block to fill space across top of project.
   • Double-click Text block. • Font: Boulder. • Font Size: Extra Large. • Type team name on first line. • Press Enter to start new line. • Change Font: Moderne. • Font Size: Medium. • Type title of game schedule on second line. • Click OK. • Resize block to fit text if necessary. • Use the Color controls to set Behind Text to green.

5. Edit Row graphic: Double-click block. • Choose Football Players. • Click OK. • Resize to fill space at bottom of project, as shown in example. • Click on Frame tool. • Choose None.

6. Add information about next month's schedule: click on New Object tool. • Choose Text. • Double-click Text block. • Font: NewZurica. • Font Size: Small. • Justification Horizontal: Center. • Justification Vertical: Center. • Type information about the next month's schedule. • Click OK. • Resize to fit at bottom of calendar block, across empty day boxes.

7. Edit Calendar block with text: Double-click block. • From Edit Day dialog box, select day to fill in. • Click Edit Text button to open the Edit Text dialog box. • Font: NewZurica. • Font Size: Medium. • Justification Horizontal: Center. • Justification Vertical: Center. • Type in text pertaining to day selected. • Click OK to return to Edit Day dialog box. • Repeat this sequence to fill in other days in your calendar. • When finished, click OK in the Edit Day dialog box.

8. Edit Calendar block with graphics: Double-click block. • From the Edit Day dialog box, select day to fill in. • Click Select Graphic button to open the Select a Square Graphic dialog box. • Choose an appropriate graphic. • Click OK to return to Edit Day dialog box. • Repeat this sequence to fill in other days in your calendar. • When finished, click OK in the Edit Day dialog box.

Design Tip

Remember, you can use regular square graphics in your calendar project as well as Calendar Icons.

Variation

Attach your team calendar to a banner for added interest. Posted in a visible place, you can easily see a banner with a calendar of upcoming team games.

Wedding Planner

Design a wedding planner for yourself or a friend to keep track of numerous wedding preparations. This is a wonderful idea for a bridal shower or engagement gift. Create as many months or weeks as needed, bind them, design an attractive cover, and you've made a clever planner to use for yourself or give to someone.

1. Project: Choose Calendar. • Choose Weekly. • Choose Tall. • Choose 1995, May, week starting May 8 (substitute year, month, and specific week for your project). • Click OK.

2. Backdrop: Choose Lilies & Birds. • Click OK.

3. Layout: Choose Lilies & Birds 2. • Click OK.

4. Edit Headline block: Double-click block. • Font: Paramount. • Style: Bold. • Type: WEDDING PLANNER. • Press Enter to start new line. • Type the week on the second line. • Click OK.

5. Edit Calendar block with text: Double-click block. • From Edit Day dialog box, select day to fill in. • Click Edit Text button to open the Edit Text dialog box. • Font: Calligrapher. • Font Size: Medium. • Justification Horizontal: Center. • Justification Vertical: Center. •Type in text pertaining to day selected. • Click OK to return to Edit Day dialog box. • Repeat this sequence to fill in other days in your calendar. • When finished, click OK in the Edit Day dialog box.

6. Edit Calendar block with graphics: Double-click block. • From the Edit Day dialog box, select day to fill in.

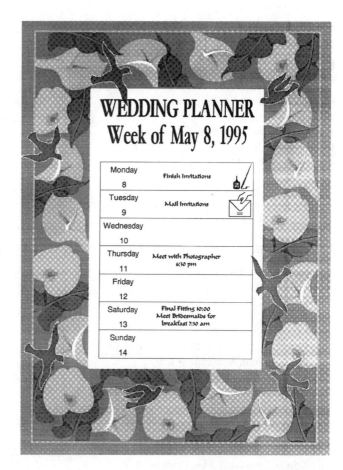

• Click Select Graphic button to open the Select a Square Graphic dialog box. • Choose an appropriate graphic. • Click OK to return to Edit Day dialog box. • Repeat this sequence to fill in other days in your calendar. • When finished, click OK in the Edit Day dialog box.

Design Tip

If you're using PSD version 1.2, you can enlarge your calendar block so it's bigger and easier to read. Enlarging the block will also give you more room to write in calendar information.

Variation

Modify the project shown on this page to become a shower planner for a baby or wedding shower. Use several weeks of dates to help you organize party details.

Calendars

Vacation Schedules

Here's a project idea to help you keep track of everyone's vacation schedules at the office. Use markers to block days and weeks off for each employee. This is also a good idea for school or home.

1. Project: Choose Calendar.
   • Choose Calendar type. • Choose Tall. • Choose 1995, or another appropriate Calendar year.
   • Click OK.

2. Backdrop: Choose Coastal Scene.
   • Click OK.

3. Layout: Choose Coastal Scene 2.
   • Click OK.

4. Edit Calendar block: Double-click block. • Font: Moderne. • Click OK. • Click on Frame tool.
   • Choose Thick Line.

5. Edit Headline block (year): Double-click block. • Font: Tubular. • Click OK.

6. Edit bottom text block: Double-click block. • Font: Steamer. • Font Size: Medium. • Justification Horizontal: Center. • Justification Vertical: Center. • Type: EMPLOYEE VACATION SCHEDULES. • Click OK.

7. Click on New Object tool.
   • Choose Text. • Double-click Text block. • Font: Steamer. • Font Size: Medium. • Justification Horizontal: Center. • Justification Vertical: Center. • Type your company department or heading.
   • Click OK. • Move block to upper left corner and adjust as necessary.

Variation

Create a calendar project with a screened art block. Follow this example:

1. After designing a calendar and editing the layout, choose a square graphic that you want to place in the background, such as World.

2. Resize the graphic and place on top of the calendar block, or wherever you want the art to appear.

3. Edit the color shading of the graphic to 30% or 40%.

4. Order the graphic to the back of the project (layer).

5. Edit calendar block, and make sure the color background is clear.

This should produce a calendar with a large picture shaded behind the months. Make sure you select bold, heavy lines and text for the calendar to show up on top of the shaded art.

Calendar Tip

Having trouble marking all the vacation schedules on an 8 1/2-by-11-inch sheet? Enlarge the calendar on a copying machine to make a big poster.

Advent

Advent calendars are special gifts for children counting down the days to Christmas. Each day of the calendar has a cut-out window, or flap, to reveal a picture underneath. The picture can be a part of a larger drawing, or individual graphics beneath each flap. You can see each day of the month revealed one at a time. Use your imagination to make a creative advent calendar for your family. These steps will start you off!

1. Project: Choose Calendar. • Choose Monthly. • Choose Tall. • Choose December, 1995 (substitute appropriate year).
   • Click OK.

2. Backdrop: Choose Blank Page.
   • Click OK.

3. Layout: Choose Calendar 10.
   • Click OK.

4. Edit Calendar block: Click block.
   • Click on Frame tool. • Choose None.

5. Edit Headline block (month): Double-click block. • Font: Calligrapher. • Click OK.

6. Click on New Object tool. • Choose Row Graphic. • Move block to bottom week of calendar and resize to fit across empty day boxes, as shown in example. • Double-click block. • Choose Nativity.
   • Click OK.

7. Using an Xacto knife or scissors, cut out the flaps, or windows, for each day box that will reveal a picture. Be careful not to cut out the entire day box; just cut portions of the paper to lift up and peek under.

8. Design and print out another calendar duplicating the one made in the steps above, except fill in the boxes for each day with a graphic. (You can also choose a large

graphic and design your calendar to reveal a piece of the picture each day.) • Double-click Calendar block. • From the Edit Day dialog box, select day to fill in. • Click Select Graphic button to open the Select a Square Graphic dialog box. • Choose an appropriate graphic. • Click OK to return to Edit Day dialog box.
• Repeat this sequence to fill in other days in your calendar.
• When finished, click OK in the Edit Day dialog box.

9. Using glue, carefully attach the graphic calendar to the back of the first calendar sheet created. Make sure the flaps you have cut will open to reveal a picture on the calendar underneath.

Another Idea

Another option is to paste small graphics printed out from other project pages onto a blank sheet of paper. Attach this paper behind the calendar made in steps 1–7 above. Make sure you line up the pictures under the flaps that you want to see each day. You may even try attaching holiday treats, sequins, glitter, and so on, under the flaps to be opened.

Parties, Holidays & Other Celebrations

Within this next group of projects, you'll find ideas for every kind of party or holiday get-together. These ideas use a variety of project types: greeting cards, signs, banners, and letterhead. If you're unclear about the menu sequences for a particular party project, refer to previous project sections that show the menus for creating a specific project type.

- Party Banner
- Decorations
- Games/Birthday Party
- Gift Tags
- Wrapping Paper
- Games/Baby Shower
- Place Cards
- Party Favors
- Place Mats
- Place Mat Puzzles
- Reunion Banner

Party Banner

Every party needs a banner. Anniversaries are no exception, whether it's a wedding anniversary or a company anniversary. Here's a simple wedding anniversary banner you can create.

1. Project: Choose Banner. • Choose Horizontal.

2. Backdrop: Choose Doves & Ribbon. • Click OK.

3. Layout: Choose Doves 3. • Click OK.

4. Fill in Headline block: Double-click block. • Font: Subway. • Font Size: Medium Over Medium. • Shape: Top Arch. • Type: Happy Anniversary. • Click OK.

5. Click New Object tool. • Choose Text. • Move block below headline, resizing to fill remaining space. • Double-click Text block. • Font: Sherwood. • Font Size: 120-point. • Justification Horizontal: Center. • Justification Vertical: Center. • Type: DAVE & PAT (substitute your anniversary couple's names). • Press Enter to begin a new line. • Change Font: Boulder. • Font Size: Extra Small. • Type: 50 YEARS! • Click OK. • Use the Color Palette to change text color to blue.

Design Tip

Try turning your banners into streamers. Choose a graphic or pattern to spread out all over your banner. Print it out, then cut the banner into two streamers. Tape the streamers to a doorway, ceiling, or even a fan! To put some bounce in your streamers, fold them accordion-style and hang.

Coordinate Your Party!

Design matching place mats, place cards, invitations, and other party decorations to coordinate with your anniversary banner design. Why spend all that money for stuff that gets thrown away; use your computer to make your own paper products!

Decorations

Add a festive touch to your home, office, store, or classroom window with decorative holiday signs and banners designed with the Print Shop programs. Follow these instructions to create a Christmas sign to place on a window or door.

1. Project: Choose Sign. • Choose Tall.

2. Backdrop: Blank Page. • Click OK.

3. Layout: No Layout. • Click OK.

4. Click New Object tool. • Choose Square Graphic. • Double-click square graphic. • Choose Candy Cane. • Click OK. Resize graphic as large as possible, almost filling page. • Move block to middle of page.

5. Click New Object tool. • Choose Headline. • Move block to top of page. • Resize to fill space as shown in example. • Double-click headline block. • Font: Chaucer. • Shape: Double Arch Up. • Type: Merry. • Click OK.

6. Click New Object tool. • Choose Headline. • Move block to bottom of page. • Resize to fill space as shown in example. • Double-click headline block. • Font: Chaucer. • Shape: Double Arch Up. • Type: Christmas. • Click OK.

Design Tip

Use several holiday sign designs to decorate a front door or window with holiday pictures and messages. This is a fun project for kids to do. Add color to the project with crayons, markers, or paint. Add extra features like glitter, bows, or sequins to make your holiday signs stand out.

Variation

Follow the same steps above, or vary them slightly. Use the following holiday square graphic art to make other decorations for your windows: Holiday Stamp, Holly, Biblical Angel, Ornament, or Menorah.

Games/ Birthday Party

You can use the Print Shop programs to make all sorts of party games for children and adults. Here's a project idea for a variation of the ever-popular birthday game, Pin-the-Tail-on-the-Donkey.

1. Project: Choose Banner. • Choose Horizontal.

2. Backdrop: Choose Stretch Dog. • Click OK.

3. Layout: Choose Stretch Dog 1. • Click OK.

4. Fill in Headline block: Double-click block. • Font: Tubular. • Shape: Rectangular. • Type: Pin the Tail on the Puppy. • Click OK.

Variation

For yet another spin on the old "pin the tail" game, why not try "put some ketchup on the hot dog?" (Good idea for older kids and teens.) This time, select the Hot Dog banner art. Follow the steps below to create the project. Hang your banner in a safe place that won't damage a wall. (You may even want to hang construction

paper or posterboard behind the banner in case an errant marker used in the game finds another target besides the Hot Dog art.) Give each game participant a different colored marker. Blindfold them, spin them around, then have them find the wall and draw a line of "ketchup" on the hot dog. The best looking line wins.

1. Project: Choose Banner. • Choose Horizontal.

2. Backdrop: Choose Hot Dog. • Click OK.

3. Layout: Choose Hot Dog 5. • Click OK.

4. Fill in Headline block: Double-click block. • Font: Boulder. • Shape: Arc Up. • Type: Put Some Ketchup on the Hot Dog! • Click OK.

5. Pull down the Project menu. • Choose Banner Length. • Set a Fixed Banner Length at 4 pages. • Click OK.

Design Tip

After printing out the banner, cut out the dog's shape, minus the tail. Attach to a wall or outdoor fence. Make separate tails out of construction paper for children to pin onto the banner.

Gift Tags

The greeting-card type of project also makes great gift tags for any occasion. To make a miniature card as a gift tag, just print out your project at 50 percent of its original size. Follow the steps below to make a Christmas gift tag.

1. Project: Choose Greeting Card.
   • Choose Side Fold.

2. Backdrop: Choose Blank Page.
   • Click OK.

3. Layout: Choose No Layout.
   • Click OK.

4. Click on New Object tool. • Choose Square Graphic. • Double-click square graphic block. • Choose Holly. • Click OK. • Resize block as large as possible. • Move to center of card.

5. Select Inside of Card.

6. Backdrop: Choose Blank Page.
   • Click OK.

7. Layout: Choose No Layout.
   • Click OK.

8. Click on New Object tool. • Choose Square Graphic. • Double-click square graphic block. • Choose Holly. • Click OK. • Move block to top of card, as shown in example.

9. Click on New Object tool. • Choose Headline. • Move block to center of card, resize as shown. • Double-click headline block. • Font: Signature. • Shape: Slanted Left. • Type: Merry Christmas. • Click OK.

10. When you're ready to print, select Print. • Choose Output Size from the Print menu. • Change Scale Percentage (output) to 50%. • Print your card, fold it, trim it, and you have completed your project!

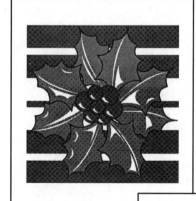

Design Tip

Make wrapping paper that matches your gift tag design by following the steps in the next project.

Font Tip

Here's a nifty headline tip. To "de-slant" italicized fonts, such as Signature, Standout, and Chaucer, use the Slanted Left shape!

Wrapping Paper

Believe it or not, you can even make your own wrapping paper using your computer! Simply design a pattern using various backdrops and graphic blocks. Print it out and color it with markers or paint. What a great way to create personalized wrapping paper for any occasion. The steps below show how to make wrapping paper.

1. Project: Choose Sign. • Choose Tall.

2. Backdrop: Choose Gifts.
   • Click OK.

3. Layout: Choose No Layout.
   • Click OK.

4. Click on New Object tool.
   • Choose Square Graphic. • Move block to upper left corner of page.
   • Double-click square graphic block. • Choose Birthday Hippo.
   • Click OK. • Resize block if necessary.

5. Repeat step 4 seven more times, each time moving the graphic to a different location creating a staggered look like the one shown in the example.

Variation

For another birthday-wrap project, follow these steps:

1. Project: Choose Sign. • Choose Wide.

2. Backdrop: Choose Red Balloons.
   • Click OK.

3. Layout: Choose No Layout.
   • Click OK.

4. Click on New Object tool.
   • Choose Square Graphic. • Move graphic to top left corner.
   • Double-click graphic block.
   • Choose Calendar Icons library.
   • Choose Balloon. • Click OK.
   • Use the Color Palette to set balloon graphic to blue.

5. Repeat step 4 to fill the whole page with balloons, changing the color each time.

Get Coordinated!

Make a gift tag that matches your wrapping paper design by following the project steps in the preceding project.

Design Tip

If one printed page isn't enough to wrap your gift, print out several copies and tape them together to form a larger sheet of wrap.

Games/ Baby Shower

Use the notepad orientation from the letterhead project type to make game forms for baby or bridal showers. The form will print two to a page. To have enough to pass out at the party, have the form copied on a copier. Follow these steps to create a shower game.

1. Project: Choose Letterhead.
   • Choose Notepad.

2. Backdrop: Choose Wet Duck.
   • Click OK.

3. Layout: Choose No Layout.
   • Click OK.

4. Click on New Object tool. • Choose Border. • Double-click Border.
   • Choose Thin Border. • Click OK.

5. Click on New Object tool. • Choose Headline. • Move block to top of page. • Resize block to fill width, as shown in example. • Double-click headline block. • Font: Scribble.
   • Shape: Arc Up. • Type: WELCOME TO MELISSA'S BABY SHOWER (substitute your guest of honor's name). • Click OK.

6. Click on New Object tool. • Choose Text. • Resize block to fill space below headline block, as shown in example. • Double-click Text.
   • Font: NewZurica. • Font Size: 14-point (choose Other, type 14, and click OK). • Justification Horizontal: Center. • Justification Vertical: Center. • Type: You're now an official contestant in our Perilous Purse Scavenger Hunt. Look through your purse for any of the items listed below. Tally up your points and wait to see if you won! Good luck! • Click OK.

7. Click on New Object tool. • Choose Text. • Resize block to fill left side of remaining space on page (in essence, creating a column), as

shown in example. • Double-click block. • Font: Jester. • Font Size: 20-point (choose Other, type 20, and click OK). • Justification Horizontal: Left. • Justification Vertical: Top. • Type a partial list of items that the guest may find in her purse. (Rest of list should continue in step 8.) • Click OK.

8. Click on New Object tool.
   • Choose Text block. • Resize block to fill right side of remaining space on page (in essence, creating a column), as shown in example.
   • Double-click block. • Font: Jester. • Font Size: 20-point (choose Other, type 20, and click OK). • Justification Horizontal: Left. • Justification Vertical: Top.
   • Type a partial list of items that the guest may find in her purse.
   • Click OK.

WELCOME TO MELISSA'S BABY SHOWER

You're now an official contestant in our Perilous Purse Scavenger Hunt. Look through your purse for any of the items listed below. Tally up your points and wait to see if you won! Good luck!

Driver's License (1)
Fifty-cent piece (5)
Lipstick (1)
Gum (1)
Tissue (1)
Package of Tissues (3)
Breath Mint (3)
Pencil (1)
Pen (1)
Safety Pin (3)
Button (3)
Pad of Paper (3)
Calendar (3)
Lint (1)
Mirror (1)
Comb (1)
Brush (1)
Spoon (5)
Straw (5)

Perfume (3)
Baby Bottle (5)
Baby Pictures (3)
Pet Pictures (5)
Jewelry (1)
Peanuts (5)
Pacifier (5)
Crayon (3)
Screwdriver (5)
Flashlight (5)
Sunglasses (1)
Coupons (3)
Book of Matches (3)
Toothpick (5)
Business Card (1)
Camera (5)
Fruit (5)
Calculator (3)
Something Unknown (5)

Design Tip

When placing text blocks over graphics or backdrop art, be sure to choose a bold font with a large enough point size to be legible over the design. Often the design of the art behind the text makes it difficult to read the type. Choosing a prominent font and size, or shading the background art, are solutions for this kind of problem.

Place Cards

You can design instant place cards for holiday dinners, or other seated occasions. Create your card using the greeting-card project type. Print out your project at 50 percent of its original size. The steps below show how to make a Thanksgiving dinner place card.

1. Project: Choose Greeting Card.
   • Choose Top Fold.

2. Backdrop: Choose Blank Page.
   • Click OK.

3. Layout: Choose No Layout.
   • Click OK.

4. Click on New Object tool.
   • Choose Square Graphic. • Move graphic to left side of project, resizing as shown in example.
   • Double-click Square Graphic block. • Choose Apple Basket.
   • Click OK.

5. Click on New Object tool.
   • Choose Text. • Move block to right side of project, resizing as shown in example. • Double-click Text block. • Font: Calligrapher.
   • Font Size: Large. • Justification Horizontal: Center. • Justification Vertical: Center. • Type family member's name. • Click OK.

6. Click on New Object tool.
   • Choose Horizontal Ruled Line.
   • Move line to top of project, resizing as shown in example.
   • Double-click block. • Choose Flower Vine. • Click OK.

7. Click on New Object tool.
   • Choose Horizontal Ruled Line.
   • Move line to top of project, resizing as shown in example.
   • Double-click block. • Choose Flower Vine. • Click OK.

8. Print and fold card, trimming if necessary. • Prop up to make into a place card for the table.

Variation

Here's an idea for a more formal, yet incredibly simple place card. Follow these steps:

1. Project: Choose Greeting Card.
   • Choose Top Fold.

2. Backdrop: Choose Blank Page.
   • Click OK.

3. Layout: Choose No Layout.
   • Click OK.

4. Click New Object tool. • Choose Border. • Double-click Border.
   • Choose Double Diamond
   • Select Wide Border. • Click OK.

5. Click New Object tool. • Choose Text block. • Resize block to fit inside border. • Double click text block. • Font: Signature. • Font Size: 30-point (choose Other: type 30, and click OK). • Justification Horizontal: Center. • Justification Vertical: Center. • Type the person's name. • Click OK.

3-D Place Cards

Be creative and add decorations to your place cards; glue on silk flowers, lace, candy corn, ribbons, dried flowers, candy canes, and more.

Design Tip

Place cards work best as top-fold greeting card projects. You can personalize each place card on your computer before you print them out.

Party Favors

Use the Print Shop programs to design simple party favors for any party; paper baskets, folded paper boxes, teepees, or origami sculptures. The following steps tell you how to create a Halloween party favor.

1. Project: Choose Sign. • Choose Wide.

2. Backdrop: Choose Bats & Pumpkins. • Click OK.

3. Layout: Choose No Layout. • Click OK.

4. Print out your design. • Add color to printed design with crayons, markers, or paint.

5. Place page, design side down, on table. • Place handful of candy in center of paper. • Pull up all four corners and edges of paper and gather them together. • Tie favor edges with curling ribbon.

Design Tip

For best results, print out your party-favor designs onto relatively thin or lightweight paper. The favors will then be much easier to wrap around candy or prizes.

Variation

Any craft projects that you make out of paper you can make with your Print Shop printouts. To see what other crafty paper projects you can create, explore craft books at your local library or bookstore.

Place Mats

You can easily design party place mats for any holiday or special gathering using your computer. Here's a simple children's birthday party place-mat idea.

1. Project: Choose Sign. • Choose Wide.

2. Backdrop: Choose Dino Birthday. Click OK.

3. Layout: Choose No Layout. • Click OK.

4. Click on New Object tool. • Choose Headline. • Move block to top of page, resizing to fill space as shown in example. • Double-click headline block. • Font: NewZurica. • Style: Bold. • Shape: Top Arch. • Type: Matt is 6 years old! (substitute your child's name and age). • Click OK.

Party Idea

Set out crayons as party favors and let kids color their place mats. Have a contest and give a prize for the best-looking place mat. If you're using PSD (DOS or Windows), you can even print out the place mats using the Coloring Book option!

Design Tip

Place mats aren't just for kids. You can design wonderful paper place mats for adult parties and get-togethers, too. Best of all, you can easily throw them away when dirty! Why spend lots of money on store-bought paper place mats when you can use your computer and design your own!

Place Mat Puzzles

Design a place mat with games and puzzles for children to do. Add fun column graphics on the sides and make a game or puzzle to fit the inside space. This makes a great idea for a party game with a prize going to the first one done! Follow these instructions for a fun puzzle place mat:

1. Project: Choose Sign. • Choose Wide.

2. Backdrop: Choose Blank Page. • Click OK.

3. Layout: Choose No Layout. • Click OK.

4. Click on New Object tool. • Choose Column Graphic. • Move to left side of page. • Resize to fill depth. • Double-click column graphic. • Choose Balloons. • Click OK.

5. Repeat step 4, this time moving graphic to right side of page.

6. Click on New Object tool. • Choose Headline. • Move block to top of page, resizing to fill space. • Double-click headline block. • Font: Bazooka. • Click OK.

7. Click on New Object tool. • Choose Text. • Move block to left side of page, below headline block. • Resize to fill space as shown. • Double-click text block. • Type in game instructions that you make up. • Click OK.

8. Repeat step 7, this time placing block on right side of page.

9. Click on New Object tool. • Choose Headline. • Move block to bottom of page. • Double-click headline block. • Font: Bazooka. • Type in birthday message. • Click OK. • Resize block to fit text.

10. Use the New Object tool and Color Palette to add shaded Square graphics of different colors that "float" behind place mat text.

Parties, Holidays & Other Celebrations

Reunion Banner

Big parties call for big signs. Use the Print Shop programs to make creative banners for your large gatherings. The following steps show how to make a directional banner for a family reunion.

1. Project: Choose Banner. • Choose Horizontal.

2. Backdrop: Choose Balloons. • Click OK.

3. Layout: Choose Balloons 2. • Click OK.

4. Fill in Headline block: Double-click block. • Font: Bazooka. • Font Size: Large Over Small. • Shape: Rectangular. • Type: SMITH REUNION UP AHEAD (substitute your family name). • Click OK.

Variation

Make banners for all your reunion activities; pie-eating contests, sack-race finish lines, and even pennants for the big softball game!

Design Tip

Avoid getting overzealous with your banner creations by trying to fit too much text onto a banner. The old saying "less is more" applies here. Also, if you want to be able to read the banner at quite some distance, use a bold, block font in a really large point size for maximum legibility.

Coordinate It!

Coordinate your reunion banner design with the reunion card design found in the Cards project part of this book.

Business Projects

This next group of projects features ideas for your business, whether it's an office, restaurant, or store. You'll find ideas for every kind of professional use. These ideas will use a variety of project types: letterhead, signs, greeting cards, and others. If you're at all unclear about the menu sequences for a particular business project, refer to the project sections that show the menus for creating that specific project type.

To: Sharon Parker
From: Vicki Crabtree
Re: Secretarial Pool
Date: 6-1-95

Now that summer hours have commenced, we are opening the executive secretarial pool to all departments. If you need summer help of any kind, call Joy Tull at extension 5400.

Please be aware that the upper management groups will still have priority over the secretarial pool.

Let me know if we can be of further assistance to you.

- Newsletter
- Memo
- Order Form
- Labels
- Menu
- Coupon
- Bulletin Board Notice
- Inspirational Message
- Fax Cover Sheet
- Employee of the Month Award
- Report Cover Sheet

- Résumé
- Mileage Report
- Transparencies
- Name Tag
- Time Sheet
- Packing List
- Brochure
- Sale Coupon

Newsletter

Newsletters can help you get the word out about office promotions and policies, upcoming sale events, volunteer activities, and more. The project idea on this page shows you how to create a simple, one-page newsletter promoting local events related to your business. This project is a great idea for mailing or handing out to customers.

1. Project: Choose Letterhead.
   • Choose Single Page.

2. Backdrop: Choose Blank Page.
   • Click OK.

3. Layout: Choose No Layout.
   • Click OK.

4. Click on New Object tool.
   • Choose Headline. • Move Headline block to very top of page.
   • Resize to fill space, as shown in example. • Double-click headline block. • Font: Heather. • Shape: Arc Up. • Type: The Music News (substitute your newsletter name).
   • Click OK.

5. Click on New Object tool.
   • Choose Square Graphic. • Move graphic below headline block and to the left, as shown in example.
   • Resize block slightly. • Double-click square graphic block.
   • Choose Music, or a graphic pertaining to your company.
   • Click OK.

6. Click on New Object tool.
   • Choose Text. • Move beneath Headline block, resizing to fill space as shown in example.
   • Double-click text block. • Font: NewZurica. • Style: Bold.
   • Justification Horizontal: Center.
   • Justification Vertical: Center.
   • Type your company name, address and phone number, as many lines as needed. • Click OK.
   • Click on Frame tool.
   • Choose Drop Shadow.

7. Click on New Object tool.
   • Choose Text. • Move block to left side of page, resizing to fill remainder of space. • Double-click text block. • Font: Paramount.
   • Font Size: 14-point.
   • Justification Horizontal: Left.
   • Justification Vertical: Top.
   • Type your newsletter article.
   • Click OK. • Click on Frame tool.
   • Choose Thin Line.

8. Click on New Object tool.
   • Choose Text. • Move block to right side of page, resizing to fill remainder of space (leave room for one more square graphic block).
   • Double-click text block. • Font: Paramount. • Font Size: 14-point.
   • Justification Horizontal: Left.
   • Justification Vertical: Top.
   • Type another newsletter article.
   • Click OK.

9. Click on New Object tool.
   • Choose Square Graphic.
   • Move block to bottom right corner of page. • Resize slightly to fill space, as shown in example.
   • Double-click square graphic.
   • Choose A TO Z, or a graphic pertaining to your article.
   • Click OK.

Memo

Memos are an essential part of any interoffice communication. Put your PSD program to use creating memos that communicate effectively and efficiently. Follow these project steps to make a stylish memo that communicates with flair.

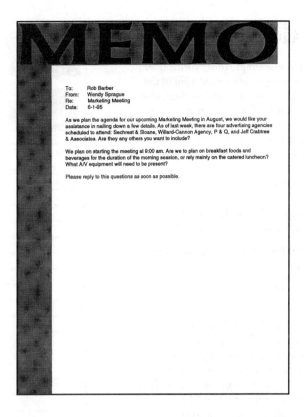

1. Project: Choose Letterhead.
    • Choose Single Page.

2. Backdrop: Choose Blank Page.
    • Click OK.

3. Layout: Choose No Layout.
    • Click OK.

4. Click on New Object tool. • Choose Headline. • Move block to very top of page. • Resize block to fill width of page, as shown in example. • Double-click headline block. • Font: Sherwood. • Shape: Rectangle. • Click the Customize button. • Under Shadow Effect, choose Silhouette. • Under Color, change Shadow to blue-gray, shaded at 50%. • Click OK. • Type: M E M O (space between each letter). • Click OK.

5. Click on New Object tool. • Choose Text. • Move block to left of page, resizing to fill page depth, as shown in example. • Double-click block. • Press the Spacebar once. • Click OK. • Use the Color Palette to change Behind Text color to blue-gray, shaded at 50%.

6. To add a Text block to memo for typing in text, click on New Object tool. • Choose Text. • Resize block to fill remaining space on page. • Double-click block. • Font: NewZurica. • Font Size: 12-point (choose Other, type 12, and click OK). • Justification Horizontal: Left. • Justification Vertical: Top. • Type in memo information. • Click OK.

Variation

For another spin on the same memo project, try following these steps:

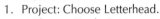

1. Project: Choose Letterhead.
    • Choose Single Page.

2. Backdrop: Choose Blank Page.
    • Click OK.

3. Layout: Choose No Layout.
    • Click OK.

4. Click on New Object tool. • Choose Headline. • Move block to top of page. • Resize to fill width. • Double-click headline block. • Font: Heather. • Shape: Top Arch. • Click Customize button. • Under Shadow Effect: Choose Silhouette. • Under Color, change Shadow color to blue-gray, shaded at 50%. • Click OK. • Type: M E M O. • Click OK.

5. Click on New Object tool. • Choose Column Graphic. • Double-click column graphic. • Choose Pen. • Click OK. • Click on Rotate tool. • Rotate graphic 90 degrees. • Move block to bottom of page. • Resize to fill width.

Order Form

You can make simple order forms using PSD. The single-page orientation of the letterhead project type makes them easy to create. Or you can also create order forms using the notepad orientation. (If you use the notepad orientation, you can print two forms to a page). Follow these instructions to make a full-size, single-page order form:

1. Project: Choose Letterhead.
   • Choose Single Page.

2. Backdrop: Choose Blank Page.
   • Click OK.

3. Layout: Choose No Layout.
   • Click OK.

4. Click on New Object tool.
   • Choose Row Graphic. • Move block to very top of page. • Resize block to fill width of page, as shown in example. • Double-click row graphic block. • Choose Orange Slices. • Click OK.

5. Click on New Object tool.
   • Choose Headline. • Move block to top of page, resizing to fit between oranges in row graphic.
   • Double-click headline block.
   • Font: NewZurica. • Style: Bold.
   • Shape: Top Arch. • Type your company name. • Click OK.

6. Click on New Object tool.
   • Choose Text. • Move block beneath row graphic block.
   • Resize to fill space as shown.
   • Double-click text block. • Font: NewZurica. • Style: Bold. • Font Size: Large. • Justification Horizontal: Center. • Justification Vertical: Center. • Type title of order form. • Click OK. • Click on Frame tool. • Choose Thin Line.
   • Use Color Palette to set Background color to blue.

7. Click on New Object tool.
   • Choose Text. • Move block below the text block containing the order form title (set in step 6).
   • Resize block to fill remaining space. • Double-click text block.
   • Font: NewZurica. • Font Size: Small. • Justification Horizontal: Left. • Justification Vertical: Center. • Type your order form information; use the Spacebar to space out words, if needed. Use the Shift key and the hyphen key (-) to make lines. • Click OK. • Click on Frame Tool. • Choose Thin Line.

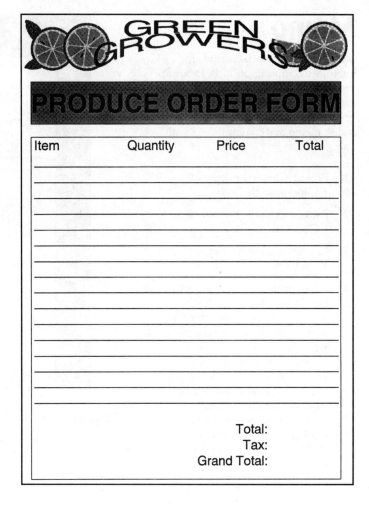

More Forms

Use your Print Shop program to design all sorts of office documentation: invoice form, packing slip, expense reports, purchase order form and so on. Adding crisp graphics can call attention to any form you use in your office or store.

Labels

Design your own labels for mailing packages, file folders, equipment, and more. Here's a project idea for a mailing label created with the notepad orientation of the letterhead project type.

1. Project: Choose Letterhead.
   • Choose Notepad.

2. Backdrop: Choose Blank Page.
   • Click OK.

3. Layout: Choose No Layout.
   • Click OK.

4. Click on New Object tool. • Choose Text. • Move block to upper left corner of page. • Double-click text block. • Font: Jester. • Style: Bold. • Font Size: Medium. • Justification Horizontal: Left. • Justification Vertical: Top. • Type your company name and address, upper- and lowercase letters. • Click OK. • Click on Frame tool. • Choose Thick Line. • Resize block to fit text and a square graphic, as shown in example.

5. Click on New Object tool. • Choose Square Graphic. • Double-click square graphic block. • Choose Apple Basket, or a graphic pertaining to your company. • Click OK. • Move block to fit inside lower right corner of text block. • Enlarge slightly, as shown in example.

Variation

Here's another label idea you can try. Use the first three steps above to start your project, then follow these steps:

1. Click on New Object tool. • Choose Mini-border. • Move mini-border to upper left corner of page. • Double-click mini-border. • Choose Triangle. • Click OK.

**Carol's Country Crafts
80748 East Jefferson Ave.
Kansas City, KS 00000**

2. Click on New Object tool.
   • Choose Square Graphic.
   • Double-click square graphic block. • Choose PSDeluxe Calendar Icons library. • Choose Exclamation. • Click OK. • Move block inside upper left corner of mini-border.

3. Click on New Object tool.
   • Choose Text. • Move block beside square graphic. • Resize smaller. • Double-click text block. • Font: NewZurica. • Font Size: Extra Small. • Type in return address. • Click OK.

4. Click on New Object tool.
   • Choose Text. • Move block to lower right corner of mini-border. • Double-click text block. • Font: NewZurica. • Font Size: 12-point (choose Other, type 12, and click OK). • Type in address. • Click OK. • Resize to fit text.

Menu

You can quickly design all kinds of menus for your restaurant, company dinner, or any special event requiring a menu. There are numerous food-related graphics you can choose. This project idea shows how to make a very simple menu.

1. Project: Choose Sign. • Choose Tall.

2. Backdrop: Choose Blank Page. • Click OK.

3. Layout: Choose No Layout. • Click OK.

4. Click on New Object tool. • Choose Column Graphic. • Double-click column graphic block. • Choose Mod Cafe Cups. • Click OK. • Click on Frame tool. • Choose Drop Shadow. • Use the Color controls to change Behind Object color to blue, 80% shaded. • Resize block to fill entire depth of left side of page.

5. Click on New Object tool. • Choose Headline. • Double-click Headline block. • Font: Sherwood. • Shape: Rectangular. • Type: THE COFFEE HUT (substitute your restaurant name). • Click OK. • Click on Frame tool. • Choose Drop Shadow. • Use the Color controls to set Behind Object to yellow, 80% shaded. • Resize block to fill top portion of project, as shown in example.

6. Click on New Object tool. • Choose Text. • Move block below headline block. • Resize to fill remaining space. • Double-click text block. • Font: Chaucer. • Font Size: Medium Large. • Justification Horizontal: Center. • Justification Vertical: Top. • Type in menu selections and prices. • Click OK.

Plasticize It!

Laminate your menus to use them over and over! Also use the sign projects to post daily specials, or insert "Daily Special" flyers within your existing menus.

Coupon

Make your own coupons to distribute to your customers. Use the notepad orientation from the letterhead project type to design coupons for your products or services. Follow the instructions below:

1. Project: Choose Letterhead.
   • Choose Notepad.

2. Backdrop: Choose Blank Page.
   • Click OK.

3. Layout: Choose No Layout.
   • Click OK.

4. Click on New Object tool. • Choose Mini-border. • Move border to upper left corner of page. • Double-click border. • Choose Joined Lines. • Choose Wide Border. • Click OK. • Resize block to leave room for headline and text block, and one square graphic block, as shown in example.

5. Click on New Object tool. • Choose Headline. • Move block inside mini-border. • Resize block to fill space as shown in example. • Double-click Headline block. • Font: Boulder. • Shape: Double Arch Up. • Type: 40% OFF! (substitute your coupon headline). • Click OK.

6. Click on New Object tool. • Choose Text. • Move block inside mini-border. • Resize to fit below headline block. • Double-click text block. • Font: NewZurica. • Font Size: 18-point (choose Other, type 18, and click OK). • Justification Horizontal: Center. • Justification Vertical: Center. • Type your coupon message, including coupon expiration date (set expiration date in a smaller size). • Press Enter to move to new lines. • Type company name on last line changing font and size. • Font: Subway. • Font Size: Medium. • Click OK.

40% OFF!

Bring this coupon in and save 40% off pet supplies!
Expires 12-95
THE PET SHOP

7. Click on New Object tool.
   • Choose Square Graphic. • Move block inside mini-border, to the right corner. • Resize to fit.
   • Double-click square graphic block. • Choose Pets, or a graphic pertaining to your company.
   • Click OK.

Bargain, Bargain, Bargain

Everyone's looking for a bargain, and you can give them one with your PSD coupons. Use your coupons with mailings, advertising flyers, or newsletters. They're a great way to advertise and bring in business. Don't forget to include an expiration date (or you'll live to regret it).

Bulletin Board Notice

Use the sign project type to make all kinds of bulletin board notices, or other signs to post, including memos. Here's a quick project idea for soliciting participants for a corporate softball team. Follow these steps:

1. Project: Choose Sign. • Choose Tall.

2. Backdrop: Choose Blank Page. • Click OK.

3. Layout: Choose Sign 2. • Click OK.

4. Fill in Square graphic: Double-click first square graphic block. • Choose Baseball. • Select Apply to All Squares. • Click OK.

5. Fill in Headline block: Double-click block. • Font: Boulder. • Shape: Rectangular. • Type PLAY BALL! • Click OK.

6. Fill in Text block: Double-click block. • Font: Tribune. • Font Size: Use different sizes for different parts of your message. • Justification Horizontal: Center. • Justification Vertical: Center. • Type in message details. • Click OK. • Click on Frame tool. • Choose Double Line.

PLAY BALL!

Sign up at the front desk for our company coed softball league.

Practice starts May 8 at 6:00
League starts June 1.
If you can't come play, come cheer us on for another league-winning year!
See Max Williams in Financing
for further details!

Design Tip

Use bulletin-board notices to promote company events, advertise open positions, recognize someone's hard work, provide sign-up sheets for special activities, solicit volunteer work, and more. Be sure to keep your designs simple and legible. Crowding the page with too much text or art will only defeat the purpose of the design—to communicate effectively!

Inspirational Message

Use Print Shop signs and banners to make inspirational messages for your staff, sales team, or customer service center. Here's an easy sign idea to make.

1. Project: Choose Sign. • Choose Wide.

2. Backdrop: Choose Blank Page. • Click OK.

3. Layout: Choose No Layout. • Click OK.

4. Click on New Object tool. • Choose Border. • Double-click border. • Choose Paperclips. • Select Wide Border. • Click OK.

5. Click on New Object tool. • Choose Headline. • Move block to top of project, as shown in example. • Double-click headline block. • Font: Subway. • Shape: Rectangular. • Type: TEAMWORK. • Click OK. • Resize block to fit text.

6. Click on New Object tool. • Choose Text. • Move block below Headline block, resizing to fill remaining space. • Double-click text block. • Font: Boulder. • Font Size: Medium. • Justification Horizontal: Center. • Justification Vertical: Center. • Type: YOU'RE THE PAPER CLIP THAT KEEPS US TOGETHER! • Click OK.

Post It!

Use sign and banner projects to post sales goals, company mottoes, motivational sayings, and other communication you want your staff or office to remember.

Design Tip

Borders with art, such as the one used in the project on this page, are perfect for adding pizzazz to an ordinary piece of paper. For your own company's messages, try using borders such as Medallion Center, Memo Planes, Quadline, and Triangle.

Add Color

For added emphasis on your inspirational message project, print your sign out on colored paper. Use bold, neon colors for fun and sporty messages. Use pastels for more subtle signs.

Fax Cover Sheet

When your company or office needs to send a fax, use a handy fax cover sheet made with the Print Shop programs. The project idea below shows how to make an eye-catching fax sheet.

1. Project: Choose Sign. • Choose Tall.

2. Backdrop: Choose Blank Page. • Click OK.

3. Layout: Choose Sign 4. • Click OK.

4. Fill in Headline block: Double-click block. • Font: Subway. • Type: FAX. • Click OK.

5. Fill in Text block: Double-click block. • Font: Subway. • Font Size: 68-point (choose Other, type 68, and click OK). • Justification Horizontal: Center. • Justification Vertical: Full. • Type: TO: FROM: DATE: # of PGS (use the Shift key and the hyphen key to make lines as shown in illustration). • Click OK. • Click on Frame tool. • Choose Thick Line.

FAX

TO: _____

FROM: _____

_____

DATE: _____

# of PGS _____

Fax Tip

Once you've found a fax cover design you like, have it printed in large quantities to keep near your fax machine.

Design Tip

Avoid using hard-to-read fonts in your fax project. Styles such as Signature or Standout are difficult to read, especially at small point sizes. Stick with legible, reliable fonts, like NewZurica, Paramount, Subway, and Moderne. Try to avoid tiny point sizes when making a fax cover sheet. Stick with 12-point or larger for best readability.

Employee of the Month Award

Here's a great idea for recognizing your employees. Design an Employee of the Month award using PSD. Follow these simple instructions:

1. Project: Choose Sign. • Choose Wide.

2. Backdrop: Choose Blank Page. • Click OK.

3. Layout: Choose No Layout. • Click OK.

4. Click on New Object tool. • Choose Border. • Double-click border. • Choose Celtic. • Select Wide Border. • Click OK.

5. Click on New Object tool. • Choose Headline. • Move block to top of page, resize as shown in example. • Double-click headline block. • Font: Sherwood • Shape: Arc Up. • Type: EMPLOYEE OF THE MONTH. • Click OK.

6. Click on New Object tool. • Choose Text. • Move block below headline block. • Resize to fill remaining space. • Double-click text block. • Font: Boulder. • Font Size: Large. • Justification Horizontal: Center. • Justification Vertical: Center. • Type your employee's name. • Press Enter to start new line. • Change Font Size: Medium. • Type accomplishment, and date. • Click OK. • Use the Color Palette to change Behind Text to 50% shaded green.

7. Click on New Object tool. • Choose Text. • Double-click text block. • Press Spacebar once. • Click OK. • Resize block to fill inner space of award. • Click on Frame tool. • Choose Thick Line. • Pull down Object menu. • Choose Order. • Choose Send to Back.

Design Tip

Have your finished award copied onto parchment or other quality paper. You can then have it framed to hang in an office.

Report Cover Sheet

Putting together an important presentation? Make an effective title cover that's sure to stand out. Follow these steps to make a report cover sheet.

1. Project: Choose Sign. • Choose Tall.

2. Backdrop: Choose Blank Page. • Click OK.

3. Layout: Choose No Layout. • Click OK.

4. Click on New Object tool. • Choose Text. • Move block to middle of page. • Double-click block. • Font: Paramount. • Style: Bold. • Justification Horizontal: Center. • Justification Vertical: Center. • Type report title. • Click OK. • Resize block to fit text, as shown in example.

5. Click on New Object tool. • Choose Square Graphic. • Double-click square graphic block. • Choose PSDeluxe Calendar Icons. • Choose Money. • Click OK. • Use the Color Palette to shade the Graphic Object at 40%. • Resize to fill space as shown in example. • Pull down Object menu. • Select Order. • Choose Send to Back.

6. Click on New Object tool. • Choose Mini-border. • Double-click border. • Choose Diamond Corners. • Click OK. • Resize block to encompass previous two blocks, as shown in example.

More Covers

You can find dozens of uses for report cover sheets designed with your Print Shop program: employee manuals, training materials, client presentations, quotes, equipment operation instructions, and more.

Résumé

You can even design a professional-looking résumé using your Print Shop program! Here's a simple one-page résumé design.

1. Project: Choose Letterhead.
   • Choose Single Page.

2. Backdrop: Choose Blank Page.
   • Click OK.

3. Layout: Choose Letterhead 20.
   • Click OK.

4. Fill in Horizontal Ruled Line: Double-click line. • Choose Scotch.
   • Click OK.

5. Fill in Text block 1 (top): Double-click block. • Font: NewZurica. • Style: Bold. • Font Size: 12-point (choose Other, type 12, and click OK). • Justification Horizontal: Full. • Justification Vertical: Center. • Type your name. • Press Enter to start new line. • Change Justification Horizontal: Center. • Type address. • Press Enter to start new line. • Type phone number. • Click OK.

6. Fill in Text block 2: Double-click block. • Font: NewZurica. • Font Size: 12 (choose Other, type 12, and click OK). • Justification Horizontal: Left. • Justification Vertical: Full. • Type your résumé information; career objective, education, work experience. Underline any headings. Leave extra lines between chunks of information. • Click OK.

HERB FELTNER
203 West Springmill Road, Carmel, IN 00000
(000) 000-0000

CAREER OBJECTIVE:
Head Chef of prestigious restaurant

EDUCATION:
B.A. degree in Restaurant Management from Pennsylvania University, Philadelphia, PA, 1975

B.F. degree in Cooking from Les School de Paris, France, 1980

M.B.A. degree in Computer Science from Yale University, Yale, CT, 1973

Associates degree in Computer Book Publishing from Alpha University, Carmel, IN 1970

WORK EXPERIENCE:
1991-1994
Head Chef: Alphado Restaurant, Indianapolis, IN
Responsibilities include preparing daily specials, supervising kitchen staff of 20, maintaining kitchen stock and supplies, overseeing cooking of nightly entrees, salads, and desserts. Also responsible for managing banquet menus, special events, and holiday events. Specialties include Baked Alaska, Rice Pudding Cakes, Chicken L'Orange with Marmalade Sauce.

1984-1991
Staff Chef: Questra Restaurant, Creal Springs, LA
Responsibilities included food preparation, assisting with menu selections, and delegating kitchen responsibilities. Attended annual Creole Cooking Seminar led by Jacques du Chance, New Orleans. Specialties included: Orange Jumbayla, Crawfish Gumbo, Gator Souffle, Blackened Blue Gill in Red Wine Sauce.

1979-1983
Staff Cook: Ed's Diner, Chicago, IL
Responsibilities included food preparation, kitchen clean up, and creating Saturday Night Special. Specialties included Turkey Pot Pie, Meat Loaf au Gratin, and Cream of Broccoli and Carrot Soup.

HOBBIES:
Horseback riding, golf, entering cooking contests, and programming computers.

Member of Chefs of America Club, since 1980

Design Tip

Use a better paper stock for printing your résumé. Remember to check for misspellings or typos before printing it out!

More Layouts

The best-looking résumés are simple in design. You'll find Letterhead 10, 14, 15, and 20 to be equally ideal for making résumés.

Business Projects

Mileage Report

If you do a lot of traveling for your company, why not custom-make your own mileage report? Follow these simple steps:

1. Project: Choose Letterhead
   • Choose Single Page.

2. Backdrop: Choose Blank Page
   • Click OK.

3. Layout: Choose Letterhead 38.
   • Click OK.

4. Fill in Square graphic (upper right): Double-click block.
   • Choose PSDeluxe Calendar Icons library. • Choose Car Trip
   • Click OK. • Click on Flip tool.
   • Choose Horizontal. • Use the Color Palette to set Behind Object to light gray.

5. Fill in Text block 1 (top): Double-click block. • Font: Boulder. • Font Size: Medium Large. • Type: Mileage Report. • Press Enter to start new line. • Change Font: NewZurica. • Font Size: Small.
   • Type your name and company information on the remaining lines, as shown in example. • Click OK. • Click on Frame tool
   • Choose Thin Line

6. Fill in Text block 2 (middle): Double-click block. • Font: NewZurica. • Font Size: 12 (choose Other, type 12, and click OK).
   • Style: Bold. • Justification Horizontal: Left. • Justification Vertical: Full. • Type in your report category headings on first line. Fill middle of block with blank lines by holding Shift key down and pressing Hyphen key (-). • On last lines of block, add totals and signature areas. • Click OK.

7. Fill in Ruled Line (bottom): Double-click line. • Choose Traditional. • Click OK.

MILEAGE REPORT

Bill Sprague
GTF Electronics Corporation
Account # 10092

Date:	Miles Travelled:	Destination:	Milage:	$Gas:

TOTALS:_____

Signature _____

Variation

Customize this same report to do double-duty as a family vacation mileage chart. You can also design a form for keeping track of basic car maintenance.

Design Tip

Many of the square graphics make great logos for businesses, especially when modified to your taste. Use logos you design with PSD on letterhead, forms, and envelopes.

Transparencies

Slide presentations and visuals are an important part of business communications. Use your PSD program to custom-make your visual materials for any type of presentation. The following example reveals some basic techniques for creating presentation visuals. Information is precise, graphics are clean, and the overall image is professional.

1. Project: Choose Sign. • Choose Wide.

2. Backdrop: Choose Blank Page. • Click OK.

3. Layout: Choose No Layout. • Click OK.

4. Click on New Object tool. • Choose Text. • Double-click Text block. • Font: NewZurica. • Style: Bold. • Font Size: Medium. • Justification Horizontal: Center. • Justification Vertical: Center. • Type: CUSTOMER SERVICE GROUP (substitute your own message). • Click OK. • Resize block to fit text. • Move block to upper left corner of page. • Click on Frame tool. • Choose Drop Shadow.

5. Click on New Object tool. • Choose Text. • Double-click text block. • Font: NewZurica. • Style: Bold. • Font Size: Small. • Justification Horizontal: Center. • Justification Vertical: Center. • Type your presentation message. • Click OK. • Resize block to fit text. • Move block to lower right corner of page. • Click on Frame tool. • Choose Thin Line.

6. Click on New Object tool. • Choose Text. • Double-click Text block. • Press Spacebar once. • Click OK. • Resize block into long, horizontal, rectangular shape, as shown in example. Block should connect to first text block (see example). • Use the Color Palette to change Behind Text color to light gray. • Pull down Object menu. • Choose Order. • Choose Send to Back to place block behind first text block.

7. Click on New Object tool. • Choose Text. • Double-click text block. • Press Spacebar once. • Click OK. • Resize block into long, vertical, rectangular shape, as shown in example. Block should connect with second text block and horizontal block set in step 6, overlapping as shown (see example). • Use the Color Palette to change Behind Text color to light gray. • Pull down Object menu. • Choose Order. • Choose Send to Back to place block behind second text block.

CUSTOMER SERVICE GROUP

One of the most overlooked aspects of customer service is "word-of-mouth"...An unhappy customer rarely tells the management about his/her dissatisfaction. Rather, he/she will tell friends and family about poor service received.

Design Tip

There are literally hundreds of presentation visuals you can create using your PSD program. Use them to make slides, transparencies for overhead projection, or illustrations for reports and other documents. Remember to use large, legible point sizes, and keep your visuals free from too much artwork.

Name Tag

Name tags are useful at meetings, seminars, and other group events. If you find that plain, old name tags from your local stationery store are boring, why not design your own? Here's a project idea to start you out.

1. Project: Choose Letterhead.
   • Choose Notepad.

2. Backdrop: Choose Blank Page.
   • Click OK.

3. Layout: Choose No Layout.
   • Click OK.

4. Click on New Object tool.
   • Choose Mini-border. • Set mini-border in upper left corner of page, sizing as shown in example.
   • Double-click mini-border.
   • Choose Blue Check. • Click OK.

5. Click on New Object tool.
   • Choose Text. • Double-click text block. • Font: Subway. • Font Size: Large. • Justification Horizontal: Center. • Justification Vertical: Top. • Type: HELLO. • Press Enter to start a new line. • Change Font Size: Medium. • Type: MY NAME IS. • Click OK. • Resize block to fit text. • Move block to fit inside of mini-border. • Click on Frame tool. • Choose Thin Line.

How Do I Attach Them?

Just trim the printed tags, and use tape to attach them to lapels and jackets. You can even take your printed tags to a printer and have them made into sticky tags. Better yet, many computer stores sell adhesive blank tags that you can put in your printer and print your name tag design right onto them!

Design Tip

Remember, the Notepad project prints out two to a page. It's a good idea to put as many name tags as you can fit onto your project page. Use the Copy and Paste commands (read about them in the Basic Print Shop Deluxe Skills section of this book).

Time Sheet

As most of the projects in this section show, PSD can really come in handy around your business or office. We've tried to show you different ideas for making forms with your computer. Here's another one. Create your own Time Sheet form for keeping track of hours and days worked.

1. Project: Choose Letterhead.
   • Choose Single Page.

2. Backdrop: Choose Blank Page.
   • Click OK.

3. Layout: Choose No Layout. • Click OK.

4. Click on New Object tool. • Choose Text. • Double-click text block.
   • Font: Heather. • Font Size: Medium Large. • Justification Horizontal: Left. • Justification Vertical: Top. • Type: TIME SHEET. • Press Enter to start new line. • Change Font: NewZurica.
   • Font Size: Small. • Type detailed information, such as Employee name and number. • Click OK.
   • Move and resize block to fit in upper left corner of page, as shown in example. • Click on Frame tool.
   • Choose Thin Line. • Use the Color Palette to set Behind Text color to light gray.

5. Click on New Object tool. • Choose Text. • Move block below first text block. • Resize to fill space, as shown in example. • Double-click text block. • Font: NewZurica.
   • Font Size: Small. • Justification Horizontal: Left. • Justification Vertical: Top. • Type time sheet categories. • Press Enter to start a new line. • Change Font Size: Large. • Hold down the Shift key, and press the Hyphen key to type in 7 lines. • Click OK.

6. Click on New Object tool.
   • Choose Text. • Move and resize block to fit in lower left corner of page, as shown in example.
   • Double-click text block. • Font: NewZurica. • Font Size: Medium.
   • Justification Horizontal: Left.
   • Justification Vertical: Full.
   • Type: Signature:. • Press Enter to start new line. • Hold down the Shift key and press the Hyphen key to make a line. • Press Enter to start a new line. • Type: Supervisor's Signature:. • Hold down the Shift key and press the Hyphen key to make a line. • Click OK. • Use the Color Palette to set Behind Text color to light gray shaded at 50%.

Design Tip

Remember to use the Colors option to change shading and backgrounds of your layout elements. You can create some distinctive looks for any of your projects by simply experimenting with the color commands. Just remember, certain colors print out darker than others. This effects legibility of text or visibility of art that are over such colors.

Packing List

This project teaches you how to create a packing list to include in boxes or packages your office ships. If you're using one of the square graphics as a company logo or illustration, set it in the background of this form as a piece of shaded art.

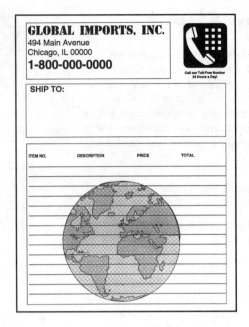

1. Project: Choose Letterhead.
   • Choose Single Page.

2. Backdrop: Choose Blank Page.
   • Click OK.

3. Layout: Choose No Layout.
   • Click OK.

4. Click on New Object tool.
   • Choose Text. • Double-click text block. • Font: Steamer. • Font Size: Medium Large. • Justification Horizontal: Left. • Justification Vertical: Top. • Type: GLOBAL IMPORTS, INC. • Press Enter to start new line. • Change Font: NewZurica. • Font Size: Medium. • Type address on two lines. • Press Enter to start new line. • Style: Bold. • Type in phone number. • Click OK. • Move and resize block to fit in upper left corner of page. • Click on Frame tool. • Choose Thin Line.

5. Click on New Object tool.
   • Choose Square Graphic. • Move block to upper right corner. • Double-click square graphic block. • Choose Phone. • Click OK.

6. Click on New Object tool.
   • Choose Text. • Move block to upper right corner, beneath square graphic block. • Resize as small as possible. • Double-click text block. • Font: NewZurica. • Font Size: Extra Small. • Justification Horizontal: Center. • Justification Vertical: Top. • Type: Call our Toll-Free Number 24 Hours a Day! • Click OK.

7. Click on New Object tool.
   • Choose Text. • Move block below first text block. • Resize to fill width of page. • Double-click text block. • Font: NewZurica. • Font Size: Medium. • Justification Horizontal: Left. • Justification Vertical: Top. • Type: SHIP TO:. • Click OK. • Click on Frame tool. • Choose Thin Line.

8. Click on New Object tool.
   • Choose Text. • Move and resize block to fit in bottom half of page. • Double-click text block. • Font: NewZurica. • Font Size: 12-point (choose Other, type 12, and click OK). • Type packing list information categories. • Press Enter to start new line. • Change Font Size: Medium. • Hold down the Shift key and press the Hyphen key to make lines that fill up the rest of the block. • Click OK. • Click on Frame tool. • Choose Thin Line.

9. Click on New Object tool.
   • Choose Square Graphic.
   • Double-click square graphic.

• Choose World, or an appropriate graphic
• Click OK.
• Use the Color Palette to change Object shading to 10%. • Resize graphic to fit in lower text block.
• Pull down the Object menu.
• Choose Order.
• Choose Send to Back.

Brochure

You probably didn't know you can use your basic PSD program to make a professional-looking brochure. It's not too hard. Here's an example of a tri-fold brochure, showing just one side: the outside page with front and back covers. The project page is divided into three portions that fold to make a brochure page.

1. Project: Choose Sign. • Choose Wide.

2. Backdrop: Choose Blank Page. • Click OK.

3. Layout: Choose No Layout. • Click OK.

4. To set front page of brochure, click on New Object tool. • Choose square graphic. • Move block to upper right corner of page; resize to fill space. • Double-click square graphic block. • Choose Running Computer. • Click OK.

5. Click on New Object tool. • Choose Text. • Double-click text block. • Font: NewZurica. • Font Size: Medium. • Style: Bold. • Justification Horizontal: Center. • Justification Vertical: Center. • Type: Is your computer on the go? And is it going faster than you? • Press Enter to start new line. • Change Font: Boulder. • Font Size: Extra Small. • Type company name. • Click OK. • Move and resize block to fit in bottom right corner.

6. To set back page of brochure, click on New Object tool. • Choose text block. • Double-click text block. • Font: Boulder. • Font Size: 12-point (choose Other, type 12, and click OK). • Justification Horizontal: Left. • Justification Vertical: Top. • Type your company name. • Press Enter to start new line. • Change Font: Moderne. • Type in address. • Click OK. • Resize block to fit text. • Click on Frame tool.

• Choose Thin Line. • Click on Rotate tool. • Rotate the block 90 degrees to the right. • Move block to upper right corner of middle brochure page.

7. Click on New Object tool. • Choose Square Graphic. • Double-click square graphic block. • Choose PSDeluxe Initial Caps library. • Choose Stamp. • Click OK. • Move and resize block to fit lower right corner of middle page.

8. To set inside flap page of brochure, click on New Object tool. • Choose Square Graphic. • Double-click square graphic block. • Choose PSDeluxe Squares library. • Choose Floppy Disk 3.5. • Click OK. • Move and resize block to fit in upper left corner of left brochure page. • Click on Rotate tool. • Tilt graphic slightly.

9. Click on New Object tool. • Choose Text. • Move block beside square graphic set in step 8. • Double-click text block. • Font: New-Zurica. • Style: Bold. • Font Size: Small. • Justification Horizontal: Center. • Justification Vertical: Top. • Type: Don't Let Technology Get the Best of You! • Click OK. • Resize block to fit text.

10. Click on New Object tool. • Choose Text. • Move and resize block to fit in bottom half of page. • Double-click text block. • Font:

New-Zurica. • Font Size: Extra Small. • Justification Horizontal: Left. • Justification Vertical: Top. • Type more brochure information, as shown in example. • Click OK.

11. Click on New Object tool. • Choose Square Graphic. • Double-click square graphic. • Choose Floppy Disk 5.25, or an appropriate graphic. • Click OK. • Move and resize block to fit in lower right corner of brochure page, as shown in example.

Sale Coupon

Here's an idea for a sale coupon you can make with PSD. Follow these instructions:

1. Project: Choose Letterhead.
    • Choose Notepad.

2. Backdrop: Choose Blank Page.
    • Click OK.

3. Layout: Choose No Layout.
    • Click OK.

4. Click on New Object tool. • Choose Mini-border. • Move mini-border to upper left corner of page. • Double-click mini-border. • Choose Triangle. • Click OK.

5. Click on New Object tool. • Choose Square Graphic. • Double-click square graphic block. • Choose Sale. • Click OK. • Move block inside upper left corner of mini-border. • Resize block to almost overflow border.

6. Click on New Object tool. • Choose Text. • Double-click text block. • Type in coupon message, expiration date, and company name. Use varying fonts and sizes for emphasis. • Click OK. • Click on Rotate tool. • Rotate block 90 degrees. • Move block and resize to fit inside remaining coupon space.

School Projects

In this next group of projects, you'll find many things to make for your school or classroom. These ideas will use a variety of project types: letterhead, signs, greeting cards, and others. If you're at all unclear about the menu sequences for a particular school project, refer to the project sections that show the menus for creating that specific project type.

- Newsletter
- Award Certificates
- Bulletin Board Notices
- Flash Cards
- Educational Worksheets
- Assignment Sheets
- Classroom Games
- Program for School Play
- Cue Cards
- Grade Book
- Attendance Sheet
- Permission Slips
- Buttons

Newsletter

Newsletters can help you get the word out about school events and happenings. The project idea on this page shows you how to create a simple, one-page newsletter. This project is a great idea for mailing or take-home handouts.

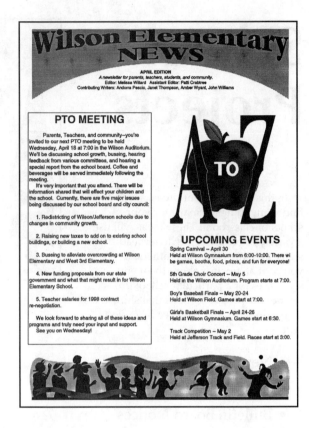

1. Project: Choose Letterhead.
    • Choose Single Page.

2. Backdrop: Choose Blank Page.
    • Click OK.

3. Layout: Choose No Layout.
    • Click OK.

4. Click on New Object tool.
    • Choose Headline. • Move block to top of page. • Resize to fill width. • Double-click headline block. • Font: Heather. • Shape: Top Arch. • Click Customize button. • Under Shadow Effect, choose Silhouette. • Under Color, change Shadow to blue, 20% shaded. • Click OK. • Type: Wilson Elementary NEWS. • Click OK.

5. Click on New Object tool.
    • Choose Text. • Move block below headline. • Resize to fill space. • Double-click text block. • Font: NewZurica. • Font Size: Extra Small. • Justification Horizontal: Center. • Justification Vertical: Center. • Type your edition information. • Click OK.

6. Click on New Object tool.
    • Choose Text. • Move block to middle of page and place on the left. • Resize to fill space. • Double-click text block. • Font: NewZurica. • Justification Horizontal: Center. • Font Size: Medium. • Type: PTO MEETING. • Press Enter to start new line. • Change Font Size: 12-point. • Justification Horizontal: Left. • Type your newsletter article.

7. • Click OK. • Click on Frame tool. • Choose Thin Line.

8. Click on New Object tool.
    • Choose Square Graphic. • Move and resize graphic to fit on right side of page. • Double-click square graphic block. • Choose A TO Z. • Click OK.

9. Click on New Object tool.
    • Choose Text. • Move block to middle, right side. • Resize to fill space. • Double-click text block. • Font: NewZurica. • Justification Horizontal: Center. • Justification Vertical: Top. • Font Size: Medium. • Type: UPCOMING EVENTS. • Press Enter to start new line. • Change Font Size: 12-point. • Justification Horizontal: Left. • Type your newsletter article. • Click OK.

10. Click on New Object tool.
    • Choose Row Graphic.
    • Move block to bottom of page. • Resize to fill page width, as shown in example. • Double-click row graphic block. • Choose Parade, or a graphic pertaining to your article. • Click OK.

Award Certificates

Certificates are a great idea for recognizing students, staff, or faculty. Design your own using your Print Shop Deluxe program. Follow these simple instructions:

1. Project: Choose Sign. • Choose Wide.

2. Backdrop: Choose Blank Page. • Click OK.

3. Layout: Choose No Layout. • Click OK.

4. Click on New Object tool. • Choose Square Graphic. • Stretch block to fill entire page. • Double-click square graphic block. • Choose PSDeluxe Initial Caps library. • Choose Border & Stars. • Click OK. • Use the Color controls to change Object shading to 50%.

5. Click on New Object tool. • Choose Headline. • Move block to top of page, resize to fit inside enlarged graphic block. • Double-click headline block. • Font: Sherwood. • Shape: Top Arch. • Type: MATH AWARD (or your award title). • Click OK. • Use the Color controls to change Behind Object color to clear.

6. Click on New Object tool. • Choose Text. • Move block to bottom of page, resizing to fill remaining space. • Double-click text block. • Font: Calligrapher. • Font Size: Medium. • Justification Horizontal: Center. • Justification Vertical: Center. • Type: For Outstanding Achievement in Math, we hereby award highest honors to (name of

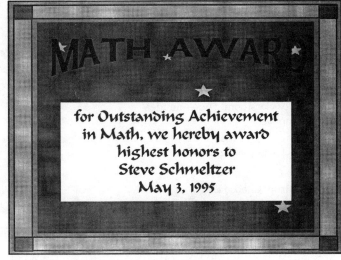

recipient). Substitute your own award message. • Click OK. • Use the Color controls to change Behind Text to white.

Design Tip

Have your finished award copied onto parchment or other quality paper. You can then have it framed to hang.

Stretching Tip

If you're using Windows, hold down the Ctrl key while resizing the block in step 4. This will give you "stretching" capabilities. If you're using a Mac, hold down the Option key while resizing. If you're using DOS, use the Stretch command.

Bulletin Board Notices

You can make all kinds of clever bulletin board notices to hang around the school or classroom. Here's an idea for a club notice.

1. Project: Choose Sign. • Choose Tall.

2. Backdrop: Choose UFO. • Click OK.

3. Layout: Choose UFO 1. • Click OK.

4. Fill in Headline block (upper left corner): Double-click block. • Font: Boulder. • Type: HEY. • Click OK.

5. Fill in second Headline block (inside UFO): Double-click block. • Font: Stylus. • Type: SCIENCE CLUB. • Click OK.

6. Fill in third Headline block (left beam): Double-click block. • Font: Tubular. • Type MEETING. • Click OK.

7. Fill in fourth Headline block (middle beam): Double-click block. • Font: Tubular. • Type date of meeting. • Click OK.

8. Fill in fifth Headline block (right beam): Double-click block. • Font: Tubular. • Type time of meeting. • Click OK.

Variation

Here's an idea for a Choir Rehearsal sign. Follow these steps:

1. Project: Choose Sign. • Choose Wide.

2. Backdrop: Choose Blank Page. • Click OK.

3. Layout: Choose No Layout. • Click OK.

4. Click on New Object tool. • Choose Headline. • Move and resize block to fill top of page. • Double-click headline block. • Font: Heather. • Shape: Top Arch. • Type: C H O I R (type spaces between each letter). • Click OK.

5. Click on New Object tool. • Choose Square Graphic. • Double-click square graphic. • Choose Music. • Click OK. • Move and stretch block to fill middle of page, as large as possible.

6. Click on New Object tool. • Choose Text. • Move and resize block to fill bottom of page. • Double-click text block. • Font: Heather. • Font Size: Large. • Type: P R A C T I C E Wednesday, Mar 6 at 3:00 p.m. • Click OK.

Design Tip

If you don't have a color printer, be sure to add color to your bulletin board signs. Use crayons, markers, or paint. Another good idea is to print your project on colored paper.

Flash Cards

You can design word flash cards, alphabet flash cards, addition and subtraction flash cards, and even multiplication cards. Follow these steps to create the flash cards shown:

1. Project: Choose Sign. • Choose Tall.

2. Backdrop: Choose Blank Page. • Click OK.

3. Layout: Choose No Layout. • Click OK.

4. Click on New Object tool. • Choose Mini-border. • Move border to upper left corner of page. • Double-click mini-border block. • Choose Balloons. • Click OK. • Resize if necessary, as shown in example.

5. Click on New Object tool. • Choose Square Graphic. • Move block inside mini-border. • Resize to fill space. • Double-click square graphic block. • Choose PSDeluxe Calendar Icons library. • Choose Balloon. • Click OK.

6. Click on New Object tool. • Choose Text. • Move block inside mini-border. • Resize to fill space. • Double-click block. • Font: Paramount. • Font Size: 96-point (choose Other, type 96, and click OK). • Style: Bold. • Justification Horizontal: Center. • Justification Vertical: Center. • Type: B b. • Click OK. • Resize to fit text if necessary.

7. Repeat step 4, this time moving the mini-border to the upper right corner of the page, and choosing Diamond Corners for the border art.

8. Repeat step 5, moving block inside mini-border created in step 7, selecting PSDeluxe Calendar Icons library and choosing Car Trip.

9. Repeat step 6, moving block inside mini-border created in step 7 and substituting new text, C c.

10. Repeat step 4 again, moving the mini-border to the lower left corner of the page, and choosing Celtic for border.

11. Repeat step 5 again, moving block inside mini-border created in step 10, selecting PSDeluxe Calendar Icons library, and choosing Heart.

12. Repeat step 6 again, moving block inside mini-border created in step 10 and substituting new text, H h.

13. Repeat step 4 one more time, moving the mini-border to the lower right corner of the page, and choosing Memo Planes for border.

14. Repeat step 5 one more time, moving block inside mini-border created in step 13, selecting PSDeluxe Calendar Icons library, and choosing Plane graphic.

15. Repeat step 6 one more time, moving block inside mini-border created in step 13 and substituting new text, P p.

Design Tip

For extra sturdiness, have your flash cards laminated, or glue them to heavier cardboard or posterboard.

Copy and Paste

If you're using Windows or Mac, you can use the Copy and Paste commands from the Edit menu to do steps 7–9, 10–12, 13–15. Once you've copied a block, double-click it to fill it in with new text or art.

Educational Worksheets

Creative worksheets are fun to make using your computer. Whether it's classroom games, activity pages, match-'em-ups, or even coloring pages, your Print Shop Deluxe program can help you design them all. Here's an idea for a weekly review worksheet.

1. Project: Choose Sign.
   • Choose Tall.

2. Backdrop: Choose Sheep in Field.
   • Click OK.

3. Layout: Choose Sheep in Field 1.
   • Click OK.

4. Fill in first Headline block (upper left corner): Double-click block.
   • Font: Tubular. • Type: WEEKLY REVIEW. • Click OK.

5. Edit second Headline block (cloud 2): Click block to select. • Click on Delete tool.

6. Click on New Object tool.
   • Choose Text. • Move block to cloud 2 and resize to fit inside of cloud. • Double-click text block.
   • Font: NewZurica. • Font Size: Extra Small. • Justification Horizontal: Center. • Justification Vertical: Center. • Type worksheet instructions. • Click OK.

7. Click on New Object tool.
   • Choose Text. • Move block to sheep 1 and resize to fit. • Double-click text block. • Font: NewZurica. • Font Size: 12-point (choose Other, type 12, and click OK). • Justification Horizontal: Center. • Justification Vertical: Center. • Type worksheet question. • Click OK.

8. Fill in Text block 3 (2nd sheep): Double-click block. • Font: NewZurica. • Font Size: 12-point (choose Other, type 12, and click OK). • Justification Horizontal: Center. • Justification Vertical: Center. • Type another worksheet activity, such as multiplication problems to solve. • Click OK.

9. Fill in Text block 4 (3rd sheep on left side): Double-click block.
   • Font: NewZurica. • Font Size: 12-point (choose Other, type 12, and click OK). • Justification Horizontal: Center. • Justification Vertical: Center. • Type another worksheet activity, such as scrambled words. • Click OK.

10. Fill in Text block 5 (sheep on right side): Double-click block. • Font: NewZurica. • Font Size: 12-point (choose Other, type 12, and click OK). • Justification Horizontal: Center. • Justification Vertical: Center. • Type another worksheet activity, such as history questions. • Click OK.

11. Fill in last Headline block (at bottom of page): Double-click block.
    • Font: Jester.
    • Type GOOD JOB! STUDY HARD! or another positive message.
    • Click OK.

Worksheet Tip

For another activity for students to do, have them color in the worksheet when they've finished all the questions. The Sheep background art is fun to color.

Assignment Sheets

Organize your students with take-home assignment sheets to help them keep track of homework. Here's a sample sheet.

1. Project: Choose Letterhead.
    • Choose Single Page.

2. Backdrop: Choose Notebook.
    • Click OK.

3. Layout: Choose Notebook 1.
    • Click OK.

4. Fill in Headline block: Double-click block. • Font: Scribble. • Type: ASSIGNMENT SHEET. • Click OK.

5. Fill in Text block: Double-click block. • Font: Jester. • Font Size: 30-point (choose Other, type 30, and click OK). • Justification Horizontal: Left. • Justification Vertical: Center. • Type individual assignments. • Click OK.

Variation

Here's yet another idea for an assignment sheet. Follow these instructions:

1. Project: Choose Letterhead.
    • Choose Single Page.

2. Backdrop: Choose Blank Page.
    • Click OK.

3. Layout: Choose No Layout.
    • Click OK.

4. Click on New Object tool.
    • Choose Column Graphic.
    • Double-click column graphic block. • Choose Pen. • Click OK.
    • Move and resize block to fill left side of page.

5. Click on New Object tool.
    • Choose Headline. • Double-click headline block. • Font: Scribble.
    • Type: ASSIGNMENT SHEET.
    • Click OK. • Move and resize block to fill top of page.
    • Click OK.

6. Click on New Object tool.
    • Choose Text. • Move and resize block to fill remaining page space.
    • Double-click text block. • Font: NewZurica. • Font Size: Medium Large. • Justification Horizontal: Center. • Justification Vertical: Center. • Type assignment text.
    • Click OK. • Click on Frame tool.
    • Choose Thin Line.

ASSIGNMENT SHEET

History - read Chapter 4, fill in exercise 11 in your workbook.

Spelling - memorize your spelling list for quiz next Tuesday.

Math - practice your multiplication tables for test November 3rd.

English - Read Chapter 5.

Turn in Field Trip permission slip for next week's trip to the Planetarium!

Design Tip

The PSD Notebook backdrop art also makes a wonderful page for kids to doodle on, for daily journals and diaries. Print out a copy and duplicate it to create your own personal notebook.

Classroom Games

Your Print Shop program can help you add to the fun and excitement of classroom games. You can print out graphics, banners, and more. Here's an idea for a scavenger hunt game using a text book. Have the students look on specific pages of a text book to find answers to questions, and letters from the answers spell out a secret word. Print all the game instructions on an attractive sign project. Follow these instructions to see an example.

1. Project: Choose Sign. • Choose Tall.

2. Backdrop: Choose Haunted House. • Click OK.

3. Layout: Choose Haunted House 5. • Click OK.

4. Fill Headline block: Double-click block. • Font: Palatia. • Style: Bold. • Shape: Arc Up. • Click Customize button. • Under Shadow Effect, choose Silhouette. • Under Color, change Shadow to 100% white. • Click OK. • Type: HAUNTED HOUSE HISTORY HINTS. • Click OK.

5. Fill in Text block 1: Double-click block. • Font: NewZurica. • Font Size: 12-point (choose Other, type 12, and click OK). • Justification Horizontal: Left. • Justification Vertical: Top. • Type game instructions and questions, for example: PAGE 42: Find the name of the first President of the United States. Write the first letter of his first name in the first blank below. • Click OK.

6. Fill in Text block 2: Double-click block. • Font: NewZurica. • Font Size: 12-point (choose Other, type 12, and click OK). • Justification Horizontal: Center. • Justification Vertical: Center. • Type answer area: Write the clue letters from above in order! _ _ _ _ _ Did you solve the mystery? • Click OK.

Design Tip

Watch out for really small type. Cramming too much into a small space can make your design very difficult to read. Always avoid using a script font in a very small point size.

Coloring Project

When students finish with the game, have them color in the worksheet with crayons or markers.

Variation

Design your own travel games, party games, or class games with your Print Shop program. There are many simple game sheets you can make: tic-tac-toe, hangman, scrambled words and pictures, memory games, and more. Browse through activity books to find ideas you can try!

Program for School Play

Design a program to hand out to audience members at your next school play, recital, or concert. Create a front and back that you fold as this idea shows. Follow these steps:

1. Project: Choose Sign. • Choose Wide.

2. Backdrop: Choose Egyptian. • Click OK.

3. Layout: Choose Egyptian 1. • Click OK.

4. Fill in Headline block: Double-click block. • Font: Stylus. • Type: Swim a Mile Up the Nile, or the name of your play. • Click OK. • You may have to enlarge your block slightly to fit text.

5. Fill in Text block: Double-click block. • Font: Paramount. • Font Size: Medium. • Justification Horizontal: Center. • Justification Vertical: Center. • Type names of cast members and production people. • Click OK.

Variation

Turn your program sheet into a two-fold program. The preceding steps design the inside. Follow these steps to design an outside. Run the programs through a copy machine, using front and back of paper.

1. Project: Choose Sign. • Choose Wide.

2. Backdrop: Choose Egyptian. • Click OK.

3. Layout: Choose No Layout. • Click OK.

4. Click on New Object tool. • Choose Text. • Double-click text block. • Font: Paramount. • Style: Bold. • Font Size: Medium. • Justification Horizontal: Center. • Justification Vertical: Center. • Type: W E L C O M E to the Willard Jr. High SPRING PLAY (or similar text). • Click OK. • You may have to enlarge your block slightly to fit text. • Click on Rotate tool. • Rotate block 90 degrees and place on right side of page in blank space.

5. Click on New Object tool. • Choose Text. • Double-click text block. • Font: NewZurica. • Font Size: Small. • Justification Horizontal: Center. • Justification Vertical: Center. • Type program information, such as who helped with scenery and costumes. • Click OK. • You may have to enlarge your block slightly to fit text. • Click on Rotate tool. • Rotate block 90 degrees to the right and place on left side of page in blank space.

Other Ideas

This is a project you can use for any special program where you want to list participants, topics, schedule of events, skits, and so on. Design your own programs for seminars, recitals, trade shows, community meetings, or clubs.

School Projects

Cue Cards

Use the sign project type to make cue cards for your school play. Follow these instructions to see how:

1. Project: Choose Sign. • Choose Wide.

2. Backdrop: Choose Blank Page. • Click OK.

3. Layout: Choose No Layout. • Click OK.

4. Click on New Object tool. • Choose Text. • Resize block to fill entire page. • Double-click text block. • Font: NewZurica. • Font Size: 42-point (choose Other, type 42, and click OK). • Justification Horizontal: Left. • Justification Vertical: Top. • Type in as many lines from the play as will fit on a page. • Click OK. • You may want to color-code the lines for each actor.

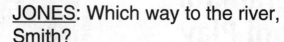

JONES: Which way to the river, Smith?
SMITH: I think we should head toward that pyramid on the right.
JONES: I thought we just came from there?
SMITH: Hmmmm. Perhaps you're right, Jones. Maybe we're lost.
JONES: I knew this would happen.

Cue Card Tip

Mount your cue cards on large posterboards; you can fit more to a board that way. If your printer uses continuous feed paper, you can print your cue cards out as one long strip.

When to Use Cue Cards

School plays aren't the only times cue cards can come in handy. They're also useful for presentation notes, class skits, band, and choir.

Grade Book

Design your own grade book with your Print Shop Deluxe program. The project steps shown here will help you create a sheet for grading ten students for ten assignments or tests.

1. Project: Choose Sign. • Choose Tall.

2. Backdrop: Choose Blank Page.
    • Click OK.

3. Layout: Choose No Layout.
    • Click OK.

4. Click on New Object tool. • Choose Headline. • Resize block to fill top of page. • Double-click headline block. • Font: Heather. • Shape: Squeeze. • Type: GRADE BOOK. • Click OK. • Use the Color controls to set Behind Object to light gray shaded at 30%.

5. Click on New Object tool. • Choose Text. • Resize block to fill upper middle, as shown in example. • Double-click text block. • Font: NewZurica. • Style: Bold. • Font Size: Small. • Type class name. • Press Enter to start new line. • Change Style and unselect Bold. • Type class information. • Click OK. • Click on Frame tool. • Choose Thin Line.

6. Click on New Object tool. • Choose Square Graphic. • Double-click square graphic block. • Choose PSDeluxe Initial Caps library. • Choose Grid. • Click OK. • Move and resize block, as shown in example.

7. Click on New Object tool. • Choose Text. • Resize block to fill left side of square graphic, as shown in example. • Double-click text block. • Font: NewZurica. • Style: Bold. • Font Size Small. • Justification Horizontal: Left. • Justification

GRADE BOOK

Mrs. Schoen's Creative Writing Class
Semester: _____
Class Attendance: _____
Finals Due: _____

James Kinkoph
Shawn Sechrest
Greg Loving
Kelly Hughes
Sherry Willard
Scott Farmer
Melissa Cannon
Steven Toliver
Anne Goodwin
Stacey Feder

Vertical: Full. • Type in ten student's names. (If you size the text block to be the same height as your grid and use full vertical justification, your names should line up. If not, experiment with different point sizes until the names line up as much as possible with the grid.)

More Sheets

Need more sheets for more student names? Print out several with new names typed onto each. Use the blank area at the top of the graphic block to fill in test dates and other grading information.

Attendance Sheet

Use Print Shop Deluxe to make your own class attendance sheet. Follow the instructions shown to create a sheet for keeping track of ten students for 20 days.

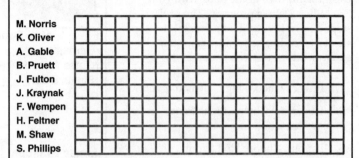

1. Project: Choose Sign. • Choose Wide.

2. Backdrop: Choose Blank Page. • Click OK.

3. Layout: Choose No Layout. • Click OK.

4. Click on New Object tool. • Choose Headline. • Resize block to fill top of page. • Double-click headline block. • Font: Boulder. • Type: ATTENDANCE SHEET. • Click OK. • Use the Color Palette to set Behind Object to light gray shaded at 20%.

5. Click on New Object tool. • Choose Square Graphic. • Double-click square graphic block. • Choose PSDeluxe Initial Caps library. • Choose Grid. • Click OK. • Move and resize block, as shown in example.

6. Repeat step 5, adding the same graphic onto the page. • Overlap the two blocks to make one large grid.

7. Click on New Object tool. • Choose Text. • Resize block to fill left side of square graphic, as shown in example. • Double-click text block. • Font: NewZurica. • Style: Bold. • Font Size: Small. • Justification Horizontal: Left. • Justification Vertical: Full. • Type in ten students' names. (If you size the text block to be the same height as your grid and use full vertical justification, your names should line up. If not, experiment with different point sizes until the names line up as much as possible with the grid.)

8. Click on New Object tool. • Choose Text. • Resize block to fill bottom, as shown in example. • Double-click text block. • Font: NewZurica. • Style: Bold. • Font Size: Medium. • Type class name and information. • Click OK. • Click on Frame tool. • Choose Thin Line.

More Sheets

Need more sheets for more student names? Print out several with new names typed onto each. Use the blank area at the top of the graphic blocks to fill in dates and other grading information.

Permission Slips

The Letterhead Notepad orientation is a handy size for school permission slips. Follow the instructions on this page to create a simple take-home permission slip for a class field trip.

1. Project: Choose Letterhead.
   • Choose Notepad.

2. Backdrop: Choose Blank Page.
   • Click OK.

3. Layout: Choose No Layout.
   • Click OK.

4. Click on New Object tool. • Choose Border. • Double-click Border.
   • Choose Thick Border. • Click OK.

5. Click on New Object tool. • Choose Headline. • Resize block to fill top of page. • Double-click headline block. • Font: Tribune. • Style: Bold. • Type: PERMISSION S L I P.
   • Click OK.

6. Click on New Object tool. • Choose Row Graphic. • Double-click row graphic block. • Choose ABC 123.
   • Click OK. • Move and resize block, as shown in example.

7. Click on New Object tool. • Choose Text. • Resize block to fill remainder of page, as shown in example. • Double-click text block.
   • Font: Tribune. • Style: Bold.
   • Font Size: Medium. • Justification Horizontal: Left. • Justification Vertical: Top. • Type permission slip details. • Click OK.

PERMISSION SLIP

Parent(s),

Mrs. Schoen's 8th grade class will be taking a field trip to the Metropolitan Art Museum on Friday, January 16. The bus will leave at 9:30 and return at 2:00. Students are to bring a lunch.

Please sign below to give your child permission to go and return the slip by January 14.

Thank you!

Signature _____

Two at a Time

Remember, the Letterhead Notepad project prints two to a page. Just trim into two pieces to distribute.

Buttons

How about a great project idea for school elections or team rallies? Make your own buttons to wear with your Print Shop Deluxe program. There are endless ideas to try. Just keep your design to about ¼ of a page. Once they're printed, trim them in a circular shape and attach them to clothes, hats, and jackets with tape or pins.

1. Project: Choose Letterhead.
   • Choose Notepad.

2. Backdrop: Choose Blank Page.
   • Click OK.

3. Layout: Choose No Layout.
   • Click OK.

4. Click on New Object tool.
   • Choose Square Graphic.
   • Double-click square graphic.
   • Choose PSDeluxe Calendar Icons library. • Choose Flag. • Click OK.
   • Resize block to fit in upper ¼ of page. • Use the Color controls to change Object color to blue.

5. Click on New Object tool.
   • Choose Headline. • Resize block to around top of square graphic block. • Double-click headline block. • Font: Boulder. • Shape: Arc Up • Type: VOTE. • Click OK.

6. Repeat step 5, this time resizing block to fit around bottom of Square graphic. • Change Headline Shape: Bottom Arc.
   • Type new message.

Variation

For an added effect, build your button over the International No square graphic. Just layer the same blocks created in the steps above over the inner section of the art. Shade the Square graphic itself to 50%.

Home Projects

With the capabilities of your Print Shop Deluxe program, you can make hundreds of creations for use around the house. The ideas in this next group of projects will certainly inspire you. These ideas use a variety of project types: letterhead, signs, greeting cards, and others. If you're at all unclear about the menu sequences for a particular home project, refer to the project sections that show the menus for creating that specific project type.

- Family Newsletter
- Signs for Around the House
- Chore Charts
- Allowance Charts
- Things To Do Lists
- Recipe Cards
- Phone Lists
- Address Books
- Videotape Labels
- Children's Growth Chart
- Travel Games
- Baby-Sitter Instructions

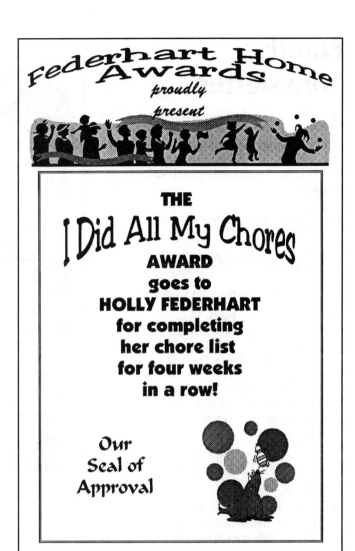

Family Newsletter

Newsletters are perfect for corresponding with family members, and they also make wonderful Christmas card inserts. The project idea on this page shows you how to create a simple one-page holiday newsletter.

1. Project: Choose Sign. • Choose Tall.

2. Backdrop: Choose Blank Page. • Click OK.

3. Layout: Choose Sign 6. • Click OK.

4. Fill in Headline block: Double-click block. • Font: Subway. • Shape: Arc Up. • Click Customize button. • Shadow: Silhouette• Colors: set Shadow to red.• Click OK. • Type: HOLIDAY NEWS FROM THE BAKER'S (substitute your family name) • Click OK.

5. Fill in Square graphic: Double-click block. • Choose Holiday Stamp. • Click OK.

6. Fill in Text block: Double-click block. • Font: Jester. • Font Size: 14-point (choose Other, type 14, and click OK). • Justification Horizontal: Left. • Justification Vertical: Center. • Type your family news article in letter form. • Click OK. • Click on Frame tool. • Choose Thick Line. • Use the Color Palette to set Behind Text to clear.

7. Fill in Row Graphic (bottom): Double-click graphic. • Choose Nativity. • Click OK.

8. Click on New Object tool. • Choose Square Graphic. • Stretch graphic to fit over text

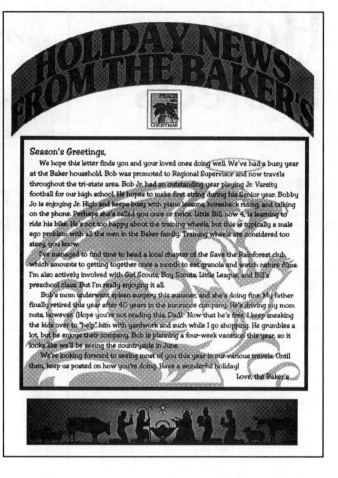

block, as shown in example. • Double-click square graphic block. • Choose Biblical Angel. Click OK. • Use the Color controls to change Object color to black, shaded at 10%. • Pull down the Object menu. • Select Order. • Choose Send to Back.

Stretching Tip

If you're using Windows, hold down the Ctrl key while resizing the block. This will give you "stretching" capabilities. If you're using Mac, hold down the Option key while resizing. If you're using DOS, use the Stretch command.

Extra! Extra!

If your newsletter needs more pages, just create a new sign project for each page needed. You can use a copier to print both sides of the newsletter paper.

Signs for Around the House

Use Print Shop signs to help family members remember chores and operate appliances, or simply leave them as notes. Sign projects are a breeze to design. Here's a great project idea for a sign to post by the microwave oven, with instructions telling how to operate it. Follow these simple steps:

1. Project: Choose Sign. • Choose Tall.

2. Backdrop: Choose Blank Page. • Click OK.

3. Layout: Choose Sign 19. • Click OK.

4. Fill in Border: Double-click Border. • Choose Southwest. • Click OK.

5. Fill in Headline: Double-click block. • Font: Librarian. • Shape: Perspective Bottom. • Type: HOW TO WORK THE MICROWAVE. • Click OK.

6. Fill in Text block: Double-click block. • Font: NewZurica. • Style: Bold. • Font Size: Medium. • Justification Horizontal: Left. • Justification Vertical: Center. • Type the instructions for operating your oven; use numbered steps. • Click OK.

Design Tip

Post your sign around the house in the area most appropriate. Use tape to hang on walls or appliances, but be careful that the tape won't damage anything. For sturdier signs, attach them to cardboard or posterboard.

HOW TO WORK THE MICROWAVE

1. Push power level 10.
2. Push in the amount of time.
    (60 = 1 minute)
3. Push start button.
4. Listen for beep.
5. Remove from oven. Careful--it's hot!

More Signs

Create similar instruction signs for the washer, dryer, dishwasher, and even for your computer! You can also create two signs that attach back to back to hang on the dishwasher: one saying the dishes are clean and the other saying they're dirty. You would then flip the sign to indicate whether the contents of the dishwasher are clean or dirty.

Chore Charts

Keep track of chores with a handy list. To make a simple chart using the notepad orientation from the letterhead project type, follow the steps included here.

1. Project: Choose Letterhead.
   • Choose Notepad.

2. Backdrop: Choose Blank Page.
   • Click OK.

3. Layout: Choose Notepad 12.
   • Click OK.

4. Fill in Square graphic (bottom left): Double-click block. • Choose Owl.
   • Select Apply to All Squares.
   • Click OK.

5. Fill in Square graphic (top left): Double-click block. • Choose Pushpin. • Click OK.

6. Fill in Text block (top): Double-click block. • Font: Bazooka.
   • Font Size: Large. • Type: CHORE CHART. • Click OK.
   • Resize to fit text. • Click on Frame tool. • Choose None.

7. Fill in Text block (middle): Double-click block. • Font: NewZurica.
   • Style: Bold. • Font Size: Medium Large. • Type in your list of chores as numbered steps. • Click OK.
   • Click on Frame tool.
   • Choose Thick Line.

CHORE CHART

1. Take out the trash.
2. Feed the dog.
3. Clean your room.
4. Put dirty clothes in hamper.
5. Wash the dishes.
6. Mow the lawn.
7. Walk the dog.

Design Tip

To make a chart with blank lines to fill in later instead of typing in text, hold down the Shift key and press the Hyphen key to draw lines across your text block.

Great Idea

Keep a master chore chart on a kitchen bulletin board or refrigerator to check off completed tasks.

Allowance Charts

Having trouble keeping track of everyone's allowance? Try this idea for making an allowance chart, using the weekly calendar project type. Follow these steps:

1. Project: Choose Calendar. • Choose Weekly. • Choose Tall. • Choose a year, month and specific week. • Click OK.

2. Backdrop: Choose Blank Page. • Click OK.

3. Layout: Choose Calendar 9. • Click OK.

4. Fill in Headline: Double-click block. • Font: NewZurica. • Style: Bold. • Shape: Rectangular. • Type: ALLOWANCE CHART and the name of the month. • Click OK.

5. Fill in Square graphic block: Double-click block. • Choose Lovable Pup, or other graphic. • Click OK. • You may want to enlarge the block slightly for a bigger graphic.

6. Fill in Calendar block: Double-click block. • To add text to the calendar, click Edit Text button. • Font: Tubular. • Font Size: Large. • Justification Horizontal: Center. • Justification Vertical: Center. • Type in text pertaining to calendar date. • Click OK. • Repeat sequence to add text to other dates. • To add graphics to the calendar, click Select Graphic button. • Choose a graphic. • Click OK. • Repeat this sequence to add more art. • When finished adding text and graphics, click OK to exit the Edit Day dialog box.

Allowance Chart/August		
Monday 7	TAKE OUT TRASH $1.00	
Tuesday 8	WASH THE DISHES $1.00	
Wednesday 9	WALK THE DOG $1.00	
Thursday 10	FOLD THE LAUNDRY $1.00	
Friday 11	CLEAN YOUR ROOM $1.00	
Saturday 12	PAYDAY	$
Sunday 13		

Design Tip

For a longer-lasting chart, select a monthly calendar. You can type each chore individually for each calendar date. Keep the point size large for easy reading. You may not have much room for graphics, but add them as appropriate to get the best visual appearance.

Home Projects

Things To Do Lists

Things To Do lists are helpful for tracking errands or keeping track of what you need to do. Follow these project instructions to create a nifty list you can carry with you.

1. Project: Choose Letterhead.
   • Choose Notepad.

2. Backdrop: Choose Blank Page.
   • Click OK.

3. Layout: Choose No Layout.
   • Click OK.

4. Click on New Object tool.
   • Choose Row Graphic. • Move graphic to bottom of page.
   • Resize to fill width, as shown in example. • Double-click row graphic. • Choose Ink Swash.
   • Click OK.

5. Click on New Object tool.
   • Choose Text. • Move block to left side of page. • Resize block to form left column. • Double-click text block. • Hold down the Shift key and press the Hyphen key to draw lines to fill entire block.
   • Click OK.

6. Repeat step 5, this time moving block to right side to form right column.

7. Click on New Object tool.
   • Choose Headline. • Double-click headline block. • Font: Boulder.
   • Shape: Double-Arch Up. • Click Customize button. • Under Colors, set Text to 30% shading. • Click OK. • Type: THINGS TO DO.
   • Click OK. • Click Rotate tool.
   • Rotate block slightly, as shown in example. • Resize block to fill space. • Pull down Object menu.
   • Choose Order. • Choose Send to Back.

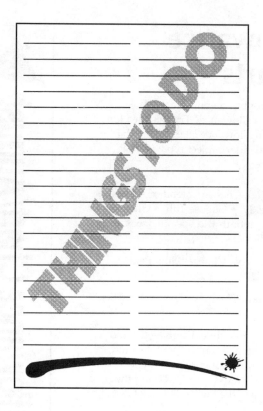

Variation

Here's another handy project idea for custom-making your own shopping list.

1. Project: Choose Letterhead.
   • Choose Notepad.

2. Backdrop: Choose Butterfly. • Click OK.

3. Layout: Choose Butterfly 4. • Click OK.

4. Fill in Border: Double-click Border.
   • Choose Double Line. • Click OK.

5. Fill in Headline: Double-click block.
   • Font: Heather. • Type: SHOPPING LIST. • Click OK.

6. Click on New Object tool. • Choose Text. • Move block to left, middle.
   • Resize to fill left column space.
   • Create lines: Hold down the Shift key and the hyphen key (-), and make lines from top to bottom of block.
   • Click OK.

7. Repeat step 6, this time placing the block on the right side and sizing to fill right column space.

Gift Idea

Design a special shopping list for a friend or family member. Take your design to a professional printer to make into an actual notepad.

Recipe Cards

You'll have plenty of fun whipping up your own recipe cards with your Print Shop Deluxe program. You can custom-design cards to fit any recipe book you have at home. You can make a special set of cards to give away as gifts. The following instructions show you how to design a card of your own.

1. Project: Choose Letterhead.
   • Choose Notepad.

2. Backdrop: Choose Blank Page.
   • Click OK.

3. Layout: Choose No Layout. • Click OK.

4. Click on New Object tool. • Choose Square Graphic. • Using just the top portion of the Notepad page, stretch the text block to fill upper half. • Double-click square graphic block. • Choose PSDeluxe Initial Caps library. • Choose Decor.
   • Click OK.

5. Click on New Object tool. • Choose Text. • Move block inside square graphic block. • Resize to fill space, as shown in example. • Double-click block. • Font: Chaucer.
   • Style: Bold, Underline. • Font Size: Medium. • Justification Horizontal: Center. • Justification Vertical: Center. • Type your recipe title. • Press Enter to start new line.
   • Change Font: Librarian. • Style: Bold. • Font Size: 12-point (choose Other, type 12, and click OK).
   • Type your recipe instructions.
   • Click OK. • Resize block to fit text, if necessary.

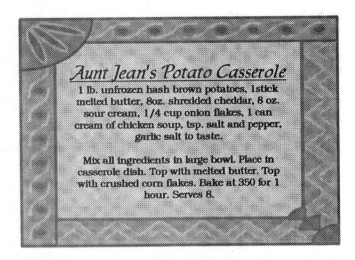

Stretching Tip

If you're using Windows, hold down the Ctrl key while resizing the block in step 4. This will give you "stretching" capabilities. If you're using Mac, hold down the Option key while resizing. If you're using DOS, use the Stretch command.

Design Tip

To protect your recipe cards, laminate them or place them in plastic covers. Also, try gluing them to index cards; punch holes at the top or side of the cards, and keep them in a ring-binder. This also makes a great gift!

Watch Out!

Be careful when layering text blocks over graphic drops or backdrops. To get maximum legibility of type, use a bold style, and shade the art to 10–20% shading.

Phone Lists

Design your own phone directory using Print Shop Deluxe. You can make a list of important numbers to keep by the phone. Use these instructions to help you.

1. Project: Choose Letterhead.
   • Choose Notepad.

2. Backdrop: Choose Blank Page.
   • Click OK.

3. Layout: Choose Notepad 18.
   • Click OK.

4. Fill in Column graphic: Double-click block. • Choose Herbs.
   • Click OK. • Resize block to fill vertical depth, making it as large as possible.

5. Switch the locations of the two text blocks. • Move the bottom block up to the top of the Notepad.
   • Move the other block to the bottom of the Notepad.

6. Fill in top Text block: Double-click block. • Font: StageCoach. • Style: Bold. • Font Size: Large.
   • Justification Horizontal: Center.
   • Justification Vertical: Center.
   • Type: PHONE LIST. • Click OK.
   • Click on Frame tool. • Choose Thick Line. • Use the Color controls to set Behind Text to yellow.

7. Fill in bottom Text block: Double-click block. • Font: Moderne.
   • Font Size: 16-point (choose Other, type 16, and click OK).
   • Justification Horizontal: Left.
   • Justification Vertical: Center.
   • Type in your own names and phone numbers. • Click OK.
   • Click on Frame tool. • Choose Thin Line.

PHONE LIST

Jean Jahnssen 000-0000
Kim Williams 000-0000
Aaron Williams 000-0000
Walt Winesburg 000-0000
Cathy Furlong 000-0000
Loretta Howell 000-0000
Rita Farmer 000-0000
Mildred Sechrest 000-0000
George Loving 000-0000
Lavern Williams 000-0000
Mima Willard 000-0000
Virginia Kinkoph 000-0000
Rachel Kinkoph 000-0000
Sally Sprague 000-0000
Pam Griswold 000-0000
Linda Yancy 000-0000
Mike Morris 000-0000
Jami Parent 000-0000
Mari Walker 000-0000
Fay Williams 000-0000
Jim Williams 000-0000

Variation

Another good idea is to design a special phone list to set by the phone in case of emergencies. On it, list just the emergency numbers your family needs to contact. Then make sure everyone knows where this list is. You might even want to miniaturize it and tape it to the phone itself.

Book Idea

Type up your entire phone list or minidirectory and enclose in a three-ring binder. Design an attractive cover sheet, too! If you save your phone list files, you can easily update them on your computer if anyone moves or changes numbers.

Address Books

Make your own address book to keep or give as a gift. You can even type in addresses before printing your book. Follow these steps for a good example:

1. Project: Choose Letterhead.
   • Choose Notepad.

2. Backdrop: Choose Blank Page.
   • Click OK.

3. Layout: Choose No Layout. • Click OK.

4. Click on New Object tool. • Choose Square Graphic. • Stretch block to fill entire Notepad page. • Double-click square graphic block.
   • Choose PSDeluxe Initial Caps library. • Choose French. • Click OK. • Use the Color controls to set Object at 50% shading.

5. Click on New Object tool. • Choose Text. • Resize block to fit inside graphic block, filling entire space as shown in example. • Double-click text block. • Font: NewZurica.
   • Style: Bold. • Font Size: Medium.
   • Justification Horizontal: Center.
   • Justification Vertical: Center.
   • Type in your addresses (if you're designing a book for a gift, type in blank lines). • Click OK.

Lisa & Bill Jamison
7899 KayBee Lane
Indianapolis, IN 00000

Jay & Ellen Moan
99403 Elm Street, Apt. A
Westville, GA 00000

Shawn Sechrest
905 Aspen Street
Breckenridge, CO 00000

Mima Willard
P.O. Box 2039, RR 9
Creal Springs, IL 00000

John & Andorra Pescio
843 Carmel Way
Orlando, FL 00000

Watch Out!

Be careful when layering text blocks over graphic drops or backdrops. To get maximum legibility of type, use a bold style and shade the art to 10–20% shading.

Stretching Tip

If you're using Windows, hold down the Ctrl key while resizing the block in step 4. This gives you "stretching" capabilities. If you're using Mac, hold down the Option key while resizing. If you're using DOS, use the Stretch command.

Videotape Labels

Tired of using those boring old stick-on labels on your videotapes? Design your own fun labels with your Print Shop Deluxe program. Follow these steps to see how:

1. Project: Choose Letterhead.
   • Choose Notepad.

2. Backdrop: Choose Blank Page.
   • Click OK.

3. Layout: Choose No Layout.
   • Click OK.

4. Click on New Object tool.
   • Choose Square Graphic.
   • Stretch block to fill top half of Notepad page. • Double-click square graphic block. • Choose PSDeluxe Calendar Icons.
   • Choose Television. • Click OK.

5. Click on New Object tool.
   • Choose Text. • Resize block to fit inside graphic block, as shown in example. • Double-click text block.
   • Font: NewZurica. • Style: Bold.
   • Font Size: Small. • Type your videotape label information.
   • Click OK. • Use Color controls to change Text to white.

Stretching Tip

If you're using Windows, hold down the Ctrl key while resizing the block in step 4. This gives you "stretching" capabilities. If you use a Mac, hold down the Option key while resizing. If you use DOS, use the Stretch command.

Variation

Here's a fast idea for another videotape label. Follow these instructions:

1. Project: Choose Letterhead.
   • Choose Notepad.

2. Backdrop: Choose Blank Page.
   • Click OK.

3. Layout: Choose No Layout.
   • Click OK.

4. Click on New Object tool. • Choose Mini-border. • Size mini-border to fill top left corner of page. • Double-click mini-border. • Choose Film Loop. • Click OK.

5. Click on New Object tool. • Choose Text. • Resize block to fit inside mini-border. • Font: NewZurica.
   • Style: Bold. • Font Size: Small.
   • Type your videotape label information.

Children's Growth Chart

Is your little monster growing like a weed? Use the banner project to create a fun chart to track your child's growth. Follow these instructions:

1. Project: Choose Banner. • Choose Vertical.

2. Backdrop: Choose Ogre. • Click OK.

3. Layout: Choose Ogre 5. • Click OK.

4. Fill in Headline block 1: Double-click block. • Font: Subway. • Type your child's name. • Click OK.

5. Fill in Headline block 2: Double-click block. • Font: NewZurica. • Style: Bold. • Type: GROWTH CHART. • Click OK.

Variation

For a girl's growth chart, select Kid Pyramid background art in step 2. Then choose Kid Pyramid 2 layout. Fill in blocks with information shown in example. For a more generic growth chart, select Ice Cream Cone background art in step 2. Then use Ice Cream Cone 4 layout.

How Does It Work?

Keep track of each month's growth by measuring your child's height against the chart. Mark each recording with a colorful marker.

Font Tip

If you're using a script font for your projects, avoid using all capital letters. Script fonts look best with both upper- and lowercase letters.

Home Projects

Travel Games

As you prepare for this year's family vacation, why not make your own travel games. The following steps show you how to make a simple License Plate Game form. To play the game, have travelers see how many state license plates they can mark off. The most X's wins!

1. Project: Choose Sign. • Choose Tall.

2. Backdrop: Choose Blank Page. • Click OK.

3. Layout: Choose No Layout. • Click OK.

4. Click on New Object tool.
   • Choose Square Graphic.
   • Stretch block to fill most of page.
   • Double-click square graphic block. • Choose PSDeluxe Initial Caps library. • Choose Grid.
   • Click OK.

5. Click on New Object tool.
   • Choose Headline block. • Resize block to fill top of page, as shown in example. • Double-click headline block. • Font: StageCoach. • Style: Bold. • Type: License Plate Game. • Click OK.

6. Click on New Object tool.
   • Choose Text. • Resize block to fit inside first grid column, from top to bottom, as shown in example. • Double-click text block. • Font: NewZurica. • Style: Bold. • Font Size: 30-point (choose Other, type 30, and click OK).
   • Justification Horizontal: Center.
   • Justification Vertical: Full.
   • Type 10 lines of state abbreviations. • Click OK. (If you size the text block to be the same height as your grid, and use full vertical justification, your states should line up in between grid lines. If not, experiment with different point sizes until the states line up as much as possible.)

7. Repeat step 6, moving the text block to the next grid column, and typing in 10 new abbreviations.
   • Repeat sequence to fill grid chart with abbreviations.

License Plate Game

AL	HI	NJ	UT	WA	AL	HI	NJ	UT	WA
AK	IA	NM	WY	MT	AK	IA	NM	WY	MT
AR	ID	NH	TN	VM	AR	ID	NH	TN	VT
AZ	IL	MD	VA	RI	AZ	IL	MD	VA	RI
CA	IN	NE	WV	TX	CA	IN	NE	WV	TX
CO	LA	KS	SC	SD	CO	LA	KS	SC	SD
CT	MN	MS	NC	ND	CT	MN	MS	NC	ND
DE	MO	MI	PA	KY	DE	MO	MI	PA	KY
FL	MA	ME	OH	NY	FL	MA	ME	OH	NY
GA	NV	OK	WI	MA	GA	NV	OK	WI	MS

Stretching Tip

If you use Windows, hold down the Ctrl key while resizing the block in step 4. This gives you "stretching" capabilities. If you use Mac, hold down the Option key while resizing. If you use DOS, use the Stretch command.

Baby-Sitter Instructions

For a practical list you can use at home, compose your own Baby-Sitter Instruction form. Include pertinent information, schedules, and emergency phone numbers. The example shown will help you get started.

1. Project: Choose Letterhead.
   • Choose Notepad.

2. Backdrop: Choose Cornflowers.
   • Click OK.

3. Layout: Choose No Layout. • Click OK.

4. Click on New Object tool. • Choose Headline. • Resize block to fit in top of white space. • Double-click headline block. • Font: Heather.
   • Type: BABY-SITTER INSTRUCTIONS. • Click OK.

5. Click on New Object tool. • Choose Text. • Resize block to fit inside remaining white space, as shown in example. • Font: NewZurica.
   • Style: Bold. • Font Size: Small.
   • Justification Horizontal: Center.
   • Justification Vertical: Center.
   • Type your instructions and information. • Click OK.

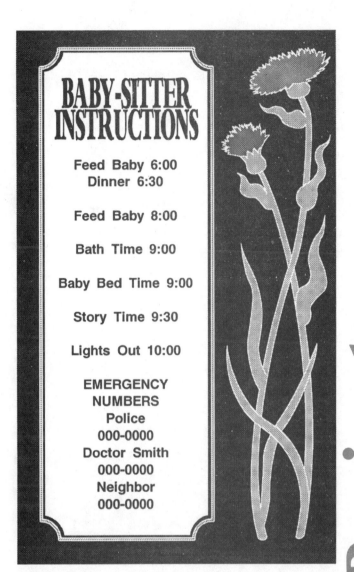

Club & Organi- zation Projects

This group of projects will give you even more ideas for using your Print Shop program. You'll find projects for your church, club, or community organizations. These ideas use a variety of project types: letterhead, signs, greeting cards, and others. If you are uncertain about the menu sequences for a particular project, refer to the project sections that show the menus for creating that specific project type.

- Church Newsletter
- Church Program
- Membership Forms
- Membership Cards
- Certificates and Awards
- Programs for Special Events
- Sign-Up Sheet
- Bumper Sticker

Church Newsletter

Use newsletters to communicate upcoming events, interesting articles, and special activities. The project idea on this page shows you how to create a simple, one-page newsletter for your church or synagogue. Use these same steps to make a newsletter for your club or organization.

1. Project: Choose Sign. • Choose Tall.

2. Backdrop: Choose Blank Page.
   • Click OK.

3. Layout: Choose Sign 16. • Click OK.

4. Switch the headline block and the ruled line block around. • Move the headline to the top of the page, and the ruled line below the headline.

5. Fill in Headline: Double-click block. • Font: Sherwood. • Shape: Top Arch. • Click Customize button. • Shadow Effect: Drop Shadow. • Position: Lower Right. • Colors: Shadow, light gray, shaded 50%. • Click OK. • Type the name of your church, synagogue, or club. • Click OK.

6. Fill in Horizontal Ruled Line: Double-click block. • Choose Scotch. • Click OK.

7. Click on New Object tool. • Choose Text. • Move and resize block to fit between Headline and Ruled Line, as shown in example. • Double-click text block. • Font: Moderne. • Font Size: Medium. • Justification Horizontal: Center. • Justification Vertical: Center. • Type the address of your church or synagogue. • Click OK.

8. Fill in text block on left side of page: Double-click block. • Font: Moderne. • Font Size: Small. • Justification Horizontal: Center. • Justification Vertical: Top. • Type the title of your article. • Press Enter to start new line. • Change Font Size: Extra Small. • Style: unselect Bold. • Type your newsletter article. • Click OK. • Click on Frame tool. • Choose Thin Line. • Leave room for square graphic, if desired.

9. Fill in text block on right side of page: (Reduce the size of the block, to allow room for square graphic to fit above it and text block to fit below it.) • Double-click text block. • Font: Moderne. • Style: Bold. • Font Size: Extra Small. • Justification Horizontal: Center. • Justification Vertical: Center. • Type the title of your article. • Press Enter to start new line. • Change Style: unselect Bold. • Justification Horizontal: Left. • Type your newsletter article. • Click OK. • Add a graphic to block if desired.

10. Click on New Object tool. • Choose Text. • Resize block to fit in remaining space on page, below right text block. • Double-click block. • Font: Moderne. • Style: Bold. • Font Size: Extra Small. • Justification Horizontal: Center. • Justification Vertical: Center. • Type in church or synagogue schedule. • Click OK. • Click on Frame tool. • Choose Thick Line.

11. Fill in bottom Horizontal Ruled Line: Double-click block. • Choose Scotch. • Click OK.

Church Program

You can design your own program publications for special musical presentations, plays, and other events using your Print Shop Deluxe program. The instructions on this page will help you create an interior design for a two-fold program.

1. Project: Choose Sign. • Choose Wide.

2. Backdrop: Choose Three Wise Men. • Click OK.

3. Layout: Choose No Layout. • Click OK.

4. Click on New Object tool. • Choose Headline. • Move block to top of page, resize to fill space as shown in example. • Double-click block. • Font: Chaucer. • Style: Bold. • Shape: Arc Up. • Click Customize button. • Choose Drop Shadow effect. • Under Colors, change Shadow to 50% light gray. • Click OK. • Type: A Christmas Cantata (or the name of your program). • Click OK.

5. Click on New Object tool. • Choose Text. • Move block to left side of project. • Resize block, as shown in example. • Double-click text block. • Font: Chaucer. • Style: Bold. • Font Size: 16-point (choose Other, type 16, and click OK). • Justification Horizontal: Center. • Justification Vertical: Center. • Type in the names of the cast or performers. • Click OK. • Use the Color controls to change Behind Text color to white.

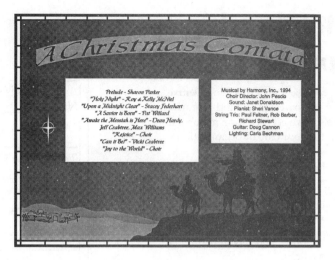

6. Click on New Object tool. • Choose Text. • Move block to right side of project. • Resize block, as shown in example. • Double-click text block. • Font: NewZurica. • Font Size: 14-point (choose Other, type 14, and click OK). • Justification Horizontal: Center. • Justification Vertical: Center. • Type in the names of the behind-the-scenes help. • Click OK. • Click on Frame tool. • Choose Thin Line. • Use Color controls to set Behind Text color to white.

7. Click on New Object tool. • Choose Border. • Double-click Border. • Choose Joined Lines. • Click OK.

Stretching Tip

If you are using Windows, hold down the Ctrl key while resizing the block. This gives you "stretching" capabilities. If you use Mac, hold down the Option key while resizing. If you use DOS, use the Stretch command.

Membership Forms

You can use your Print Shop Deluxe program to design all kinds of forms. Here's a project idea for a membership form for your club or organization.

1. Project: Choose Letterhead.
   • Choose Notepad.

2. Backdrop: Choose Blank Page.
   • Click OK.

3. Layout: Choose Notepad 12.
   • Click OK.

4. Fill in square graphic (top left): Double-click block. • Choose Hockey. • Click OK.

5. Fill in text block (top right): Double-click block. • Font: Boulder. • Font Size: 16-point (choose Other, type 16, and click OK). • Type: ALL AMERICAN-SPORTS CLUB. • Click OK. • Click on Frame tool. • Choose Thin Line. • Use Color Palette to change Behind Text color to yellow.

6. Fill in text block (middle): Double-click block. • Font: NewZurica. • Font Size: Small. • Justification Horizontal: Full. • Justification Vertical: Center. • Type your membership form with lines for name, address, phone number, and other information needed. Underline the top line, as shown in example. • Click OK.

7. Fill in square Graphic blocks (bottom): Double-click on first block. • Choose Baseball. • Click OK. • Repeat sequence to fill in each graphic with a different sport graphic: Basketball, Football, Soccer, Tennis.

ALL-AMERICAN SPORTS CLUB

MEMBERSHIP APPLICATION

Name _____

Address _____

_____

Telephone Number _____

Social Security Number _____

Birthdate _____

Sports Interests _____

_____

_____

_____

References _____

_____

Are you interested in participating in team sports or individual sports? _____

_____

Days or Nights available for team sports?

_____

Design Tip

Remember, the Notepad project type will print out two designs to a page; you'll have two of the same form to use.

Another Idea

Use similar project steps to create member record sheets that contain updated information about your club's members. Keep track of names, addresses, and phone numbers, as well as dues paid, titles, and interests.

Membership Cards

Make club membership cards with your Print Shop Deluxe program. The idea on this page is a club card given out by a dentist. Use these steps to make the card:

1. Project: Choose Letterhead.
   • Choose Notepad.

2. Backdrop: Choose Blank Page.
   • Click OK.

3. Layout: Choose No Layout. • Click OK.

4. Click on New Object tool. • Choose Mini-border. • Move block to top of Notepad page. • Resize to fill upper third of project page. • Double-click mini-border. • Choose Blue Check.
   • Click OK.

5. Click on New Object tool. • Choose Headline. • Move block inside mini-border, top. • Resize to fill space as shown in example.
   • Double-click headline block.
   • Font: Heather. • Shape: Arc Up.
   • Type: BRIGHT SMILES CLUB (or name of your club). • Click OK.

6. Click on New Object tool. • Choose Text. • Move block below headline block. • Resize to fill space, as shown in example. • Double-click text block. • Font: NewZurica.
   • Font Size: 16-point (choose Other, type 16, and click OK).
   • Justification Horizontal: Center.
   • Justification Vertical: Center.
   • Type: This card entitles that the bearer is in good standing with his/her dentist for taking good care of his/her teeth (or message of your choice). • Click OK.

7. Click on New Object tool.
   • Choose Square Graphic. • Move block beside text block. • Resize to fill space as shown in example.
   • Double-click square graphic block. • Choose Happy Tooth.
   • Click OK.

Business Cards

Use Print Shop Deluxe to design and print your business cards. There are endless possibilities. Although it may take a bit of experimenting to get the size just right, you can create some spiffy business cards for your organization, home, or office.

Design Tip

It may take some experimenting to get your business card size just right. Most cards measure 3 1/2"-by-2". For a more professional look, have a professional printer print your finished cards on stiffer paper, or you can laminate the cards.

Club & Organization

Certificates and Awards

Use the Sign project type to design certificates and awards to recognize outstanding individuals or achievements. The following instructions show you how to make an award for a club member.

1. Project: Choose Sign. • Choose Wide.

2. Backdrop: Choose American Flag. • Click OK.

3. Layout: Choose No Layout. • Select Lighten Backdrop. • Click OK.

4. Click on New Object tool. • Choose Border. • Double-click border. • Choose Diamond Corners. • Select Wide Border. • Click OK.

5. Click on New Object tool. • Choose Headline. • Move block to top of page, as shown in example. • Resize to fit. • Double-click headline block. • Font: Sherwood. • Shape: Arc Up. • Type: Citizen of the Year. • Click OK.

6. Click on New Object tool. • Choose Text. • Move block to middle of page. • Resize to fill remaining space. • Double-click text block. • Font: Calligrapher. • Font Size: 42-point (choose Other, type 42, and click OK). • Justification Horizontal: Center. • Justification Vertical: Center. • Type: Awarded to San Dee Phillips for outstanding community service above and beyond the call of duty. January, 1996 (substitute your recipient's name). • Click OK.

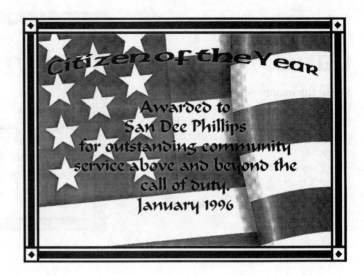

Design Tip

When placing text on top of a backdrop or graphic block, be sure to choose a font and point size that will be clearly visible. You can also shade the backdrop or art lighter so that text is more legible.

Frame It

Print your award on parchment paper, or another quality paper type. That way, you'll have a document suitable for framing. You can even take it to a frame shop to have it mounted and framed for giving.

Programs for Special Events

Is your club or community having a special event? Planning an upcoming seminar? Design a program to hand out to participants. With your Print Shop Deluxe program and the wide sign project type, you can design a cover and an interior to print on both sides of one sheet of paper. Fold the paper, and you have an instant program or brochure! Have the program printed up in large quantities. Here's a simple, elegant program cover idea.

1. Project: Choose Sign. • Choose Wide.

2. Backdrop: Choose Blank Page. • Click OK.

3. Layout: Choose No Layout. • Click OK.

4. Click on New Object tool. • Choose Row Graphic. • Move block to top of page. • Resize to fill entire width of page. • Double-click row graphic block. • Choose Bright Shapes. • Click OK.

5. Click on New Object tool. • Choose Row Graphic. • Move block to bottom of page. • Resize to fill entire width of page. • Double-click row graphic block. • Choose Bright Shapes. • Click OK. • Click on Flip tool. • Choose Horizontal and then Vertical.

6. Click on New Object tool. • Choose Headline. • Move block to right side of page. • Resize as shown in example. • Double-click headline block. • Font: Boulder. • Shape: Double Arc Up. • Type: COMMUNICATIONS SEMINAR (or title of your event). • Click OK.

7. Click on New Object tool. • Choose Text. • Move block below headline block. • Resize to fill space, as shown in example. • Double-click text block. • Font: NewZurica. • Font Size: Extra Small. • Justification Horizontal: Center. • Justification Vertical: Center. • Type: presented by. • Press Enter to start a new line. • Change Font Size: Small. • Type: TelePark Com. • Press Enter to start new line. • Change Font Size: Extra Small. • Type: Thursday, April 9 and Friday, April 10 • Click OK.

Design Tip

The project steps shown create a cover design. Follow similar steps to make an interior design, using the same two row graphics placed exactly as shown.

Sign-Up Sheet

Just about every club, organization, school, or office uses a sign-up sheet for various occasions. Follow the steps on this page to build a simple sign-up sheet for a team sport.

1. Project: Choose Sign. • Choose Tall.

2. Backdrop: Choose Blank Page. • Click OK.

3. Layout: Choose No Layout. • Click OK.

4. Click on New Object tool. • Choose Headline. • Move block to top of page. • Resize to fill entire width of page. • Double-click headline block. • Font: Boulder. • Type: SIGN UP. • Click OK.

5. Click on New Object tool. • Choose Row Graphic. • Move block beneath headline. • Resize to fill entire width of page. • Double-click row graphic block. • Choose Basketballs. • Click OK.

6. Click on New Object tool. • Choose Text. • Move block below row graphic. • Resize to fill space, as shown in example. • Double-click text block. • Font: NewZurica. • Style: Bold. • Font Size: 12-point (choose Other, type 12, and click OK). • Justification Horizontal: Center. • Justification Vertical: Full. • Type your sign up information. • Change Font Size: Medium. • Hold down the Shift key and press the Hyphen key to draw lines to fill the rest of the block. • Click OK.

7. Click on New Object tool. • Choose Square Graphic. • Double-click square graphic. • Choose Basketball. • Click OK. • Resize block to fill space, as shown in example. • Use the Color controls to change Object shading to 10%. • Pull down Object menu. • Choose Order. • Select Send to Back.

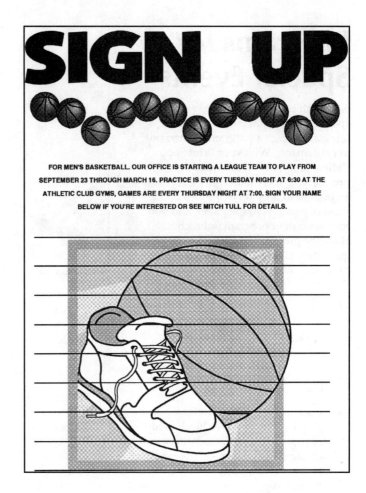

Design Tip

It's always a little tricky when you layer text over graphics, as in the project on this page. What will help you achieve maximum legibility is to shade your background art. Shading of 10–30% is rather light and will give you the best results.

Bumper Stickers

Ready for a fun project for your club or organization? Make your own club bumper stickers. You can take your finished design to a print shop to have them print copies onto adhesive paper. The following project shows you how to make a team-oriented bumper sticker.

1. Project: Choose Sign. • Choose Wide.

2. Backdrop: Choose Blank Page. • Click OK.

3. Layout: Choose No Layout. • Click OK.

4. Click on New Object tool. • Choose Row Graphic. • Move block to middle of page. • Double-click row graphic block. • Choose Football Players. • Click OK. • Stretch art as large as possible to fill space, as shown in example.

5. Click on New Object tool. • Choose Headline. • Move block above row graphic. • Resize as shown in example. • Double-click headline block. • Font: Boulder. • Type: GO GO GO GO (with spaces between each word, or type your own message). • Click OK.

6. Click on New Object tool. • Choose Headline. • Move block below row graphic. • Resize as shown in example. • Double-click headline block. • Font: Boulder. • Type: W I L D C A T S (with spaces between each letter, or type your own message). • Click OK.

Variation

For another bumper sticker design, follow these instructions:

1. Project: Choose Sign. • Choose Wide.

2. Backdrop: Choose Blank Page. • Click OK.

3. Layout: Choose No Layout. • Click OK.

4. Click on New Object tool. • Choose Row Graphic. • Move block to middle of page. • Double-click row graphic block. • Choose Music. • Click OK. • Stretch art as large as possible to fill space the size of a bumper sticker.

5. Click on New Object tool. • Choose Text. • Move and resize block to fit inside Music art, filling empty white space. • Double-click text block. • Font: Heather. • Font Size: 66-point (choose Other, type 66, and click OK). • Justification Horizontal: Center. • Justification Vertical: Center. • Type: SENIOR SONG-STERS CLUB (or your own message). • Click OK.

Design Tip

If you don't like how close together your headline words run, here's a tip for you. Use the Spacebar to add extra space between headline words. Three to five spaces is usually sufficient.

Craft Projects

The next project group shows you how to create crafty ideas using your computer. These ideas will use a variety of project types: letterhead, signs, greeting cards, and others. If you are uncertain about the menu sequences for a particular project, refer to the project sections that show the menus for creating that specific project type.

- Bookmarks
- Journal
- Garden Labels
- Luggage Labels
- Jar and Canning Labels
- Decorative Paper for Gift Boxes
- Postcards

Bookmarks

Bookmarks are easy projects to make for saving your place in a book, and they're perfect for gift-giving. There are two ways to design a bookmark: horizontally or vertically. The project steps on this page show you how to use the Letterhead project type to make a vertical bookmark.

1. Project: Choose Letterhead.
   • Choose Notepad.

2. Backdrop: Choose Blank Page.
   • Click OK.

3. Layout: Choose No Layout.
   • Click OK.

4. Click on New Object tool.
   • Choose Column Graphic.
   • Move graphic to middle of project page. • Resize to fill almost entire depth of page. • Double-click column graphic. • Choose Southwest Strip. • Click OK.

5. Click on New Object tool.
   • Choose Headline. • Click on Rotate tool. • Rotate graphic vertically, and resize to fit alongside left side of column graphic, as shown in example.
   • Double-click headline block.
   • Font: Sherwood. • Shape: Rectangular. • Type: DON'T LOSE MY PLACE! • Click OK.

6. Click on New Object tool.
   • Choose Mini-border. • Move and resize mini-border to fit around column graphic and headline block, as shown in example.
   • Double-click mini-border.
   • Choose Thin Border. • Click OK.

Variation

For a child's bookmark, follow these project steps:

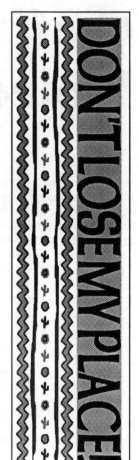

1. Project: Choose Letterhead.
   • Choose Notepad.

2. Backdrop: Choose Blank Page.
   • Click OK.

3. Layout: Choose No Layout. • Click OK.

4. Click on New Object tool.
   • Choose Row Graphic. • Double-click row graphic block. • Choose Bookworm. • Click OK. • Click on Rotate tool. • Rotate graphic to become a column graphic. • Resize to fill depth of page.

5. Click on New Object tool.
   • Choose Headline. • Double-click headline block. • Font: Boulder.
   • Shape: Double Arch Up. • Click on Customize button. • Change Text Effect to Thick Outline. • Change Shadow Effect to Silhouette. • Under Colors, set Text to white, Outline to black, and Shadow to Brown.
   • Click OK. • Type: JESSICA'S BOOK (substitute your child's name). • Click OK. • Click on Rotate tool. • Rotate block 90 degrees. • Move and resize block to fit on upper portion of bookmark design.

Journal

Create your own journal with a design from the Print Shop programs. You can even type in your entries right on screen. Here's a simple journal page design created with the notepad orientation from the letterhead project type. This prints out two designs to a page. Follow these instructions.

1. Project: Choose Letterhead.
   • Choose Notepad.

2. Backdrop: Choose Blank Page.
   • Click OK.

3. Layout: Choose No Layout. • Click OK.

4. Click on New Object tool. • Choose Column Graphic. • Move graphic to left side of project page. • Resize to fill entire depth of page.
   • Double-click column graphic.
   • Choose Pillar. • Click OK.

5. Click on New Object tool. • Choose Headline. • Move block to top of page. • Resize to fit, as shown in example. • Double-click headline block. • Font: Sherwood. • Shape: Rectangular. • Type: DAILY JOURNAL. • Click OK.

6. Click on New Object tool. • Choose Horizontal Ruled Line. • Move block directly below headline block.
   • Resize to fit, as shown in example. • Double-click Horizontal Ruled Line block. • Choose Flower Vine. • Click OK.

7. Click on New Object tool. • Choose Text. • Move block below Ruled Line. • Resize to fill remaining space. • Double-click text block.
   • Font: NewZurica. • Font Size: Medium. • Justification Horizontal: Left. • Justification Vertical: Bottom. • Type in lines by holding down the Shift key and hyphen (-) key. • Click OK when finished.

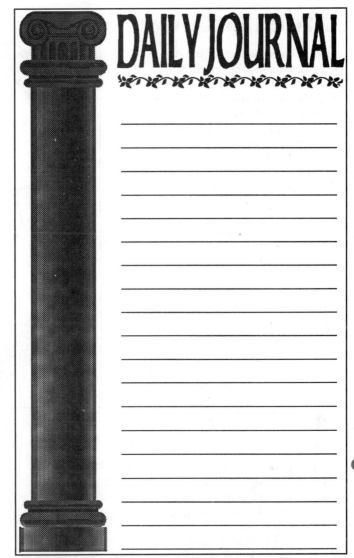

Variation

For another journal page idea, use the Pen Column graphic. Place the title at the bottom of the page. Use a Pennant Left headline shape to make the type look like it's coming from the pen point of the graphic.

Gift Idea

Print out a dozen copies of your journal page design and trim pages in two. Bind them together with a cover design to make a journal for gift-giving.

Garden Labels

Using the notepad letterhead project type, you can make designer garden labels for your green-thumb activities. Attach your printed and trimmed label to a sturdy piece of cardboard. Cover it with see-through plastic or laminate to protect it from the elements. You can staple these labels to sticks or wire posts, and place near each plant or garden row. Follow these steps to see how:

1. Project: Choose Letterhead.
   • Choose Notepad.

2. Backdrop: Choose Blank Page.
   • Click OK.

3. Layout: Choose No Layout.
   • Click OK.

4. Click on New Object tool.
   • Choose Square Graphic. • Move block to top of project page.
   • Resize to fill upper half of page.
   • Double-click square graphic block. • Choose PSDeluxe Initial Caps library. • Choose Victorian.
   • Click OK.

5. Click on New Object tool.
   • Choose Text. • Move block inside square graphic. • Resize to fill space, as shown in example.
   • Double-click text block. • Font: Chaucer. • Font Size: Large.
   • Justification Horizontal: Center.
   • Justification Vertical: Center.
   • Type: Violets, or the names of your particular garden plants.
   • Click OK.

Variation

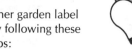

Need another garden label design? Try following these project steps:

1. Project: Choose Letterhead.
   • Choose Notepad.

2. Backdrop: Choose Blank Page.
   • Click OK.

3. Layout: Choose No Layout.
   • Click OK.

4. Click on New Object tool.
   • Choose Square Graphic.
   • Double-click square graphic block. • Choose PSDeluxe Initial Caps library. • Choose Scribble.
   • Click OK. • Resize block to fill half of page.

5. Click on New Object tool. • Choose Text. • Double-click text block.
   • Font: StageCoach. • Font Size: Large. • Justification Horizontal: Center. • Justification Vertical: Center. • Type in garden label.
   • Click OK. • Resize block to fit inside of square graphic. • Use the Color Palette to set Behind Text to white. • Click on Frame tool.
   • Choose Thin Line.

More Room

You can probably fit another label below the one you designed following the steps outlined. And remember, the Notepad orientation prints two projects to a page!

Labels for Luggage, Wallets, Purses

Here's a great idea for making sure your luggage, wallet, or purse has identification just in it case it gets lost. Make labels with your name and address, using your Print Shop program. Follow these easy steps:

1. Project: Choose Letterhead.
   • Choose Notepad.

2. Backdrop: Choose Blank Page.
   • Click OK.

3. Layout: Choose No Layout.
   • Click OK.

4. Click on New Object tool. • Choose Row Graphic. • Move block to top of project page. • Resize block to fill upper third of page, causing graphic to exceed page borders.
   • Double-click row graphic.
   • Choose Blue Blend. • Click OK.

5. Click on New Object tool. • Choose Text. • Move block on top of row graphic. • Resize to fill width, as shown in example. • Double-click text block. • Font: NewZurica.
   • Style: Bold. • Font Size: Medium.
   • Justification Horizontal: Left.
   • Justification Vertical: Top. • Type your name and address. • Click OK.

> **Marsha Washington**
> **908 Twelve Oaks Lane**
> **Sacramento, CA 00000**

Variation

For another luggage label design, follow these instructions:

1. Project: Choose Letterhead.
   • Choose Notepad.

2. Backdrop: Choose Blank Page.
   • Click OK.

3. Layout: Choose No Layout.
   • Click OK.

4. Click on New Object tool.
   • Choose Mini-border. •Move and resize mini-border. • Choose Quadline. • Click OK. • Use the Color Palette to set Behind Object to blue, 50% shaded.

5. Click on New Object tool.
   • Choose Text. • Move block inside mini-border. • Resize to fill width. • Double-click text block.
   • Font: Boulder. • Font Size: 18-point (choose Other, type 18, and click OK). • Justification Horizontal: Left. • Justification Vertical: Top. • Type your name and address. • Click OK.

Design Tip

Repeat these design steps to fill the Notepad page with lots of labels. You'll find many uses for them!

Craft Projects

Jar and Canning Labels

Personalize your handmade crafts, baked goods, or canned goods with creative labels designed on your computer. Use rubber cement or glue to attach your labels, or take them to a professional printer to have them made into stickers. Follow these easy steps:

1. Project: Choose Letterhead.
   • Choose Notepad.

2. Backdrop: Choose Blank Page.
   • Click OK.

3. Layout: Choose No Layout.
   • Click OK.

4. Click on New Object tool.
   • Choose Square Graphic. • Move block to upper portion of Notepad page. • Resize block to fill upper half. • Double-click square graphic block. • Choose PSDeluxe Initial Caps library. • Choose Inca.
   • Click OK.

5. Click on New Object tool.
   • Choose Text. • Move block inside of square graphic block.
   • Resize to fill space, as shown in example. • Double-click text block.
   • Font: Jester. • Style: Bold. • Font Size: Medium. • Justification Horizontal: Center. • Justification Vertical: Center. • Type: Aunt Nancy's Pickled Pears 9-7-95 (or the label for your project).
   • Click OK.

Variation

For another kind of canning label, try these project steps:

1. Project: Choose Letterhead.
   • Choose Notepad.

2. Backdrop: Choose Blank Page.
   • Click OK.

3. Layout: Choose No Layout.
   • Click OK.

4. Click on New Object tool.
   • Choose Mini-border. • Move and resize mini-border to fill upper half of page. • Double-click mini-border. • Choose Egyptian. • Click OK.

5. Click on New Object tool.
   • Choose Text. • Move block inside of mini-border. • Resize to fill space, as shown in example. • Double-click text block. • Font: StageCoach.
   • Style: Bold. • Font Size: Medium Large. • Justification Horizontal: Center. • Justification Vertical: Center. • Type the label for your project. • Click OK.

More Labels

You'll find many uses for labels designed on your PSD program. Try identification labels, file labels, garage tool labels, frozen food labels, lawn chair labels, book labels and so on.

Decorative Paper for Gift Boxes

Paper-covered boxes of various sizes make wonderful gifts. Plain ones are available at craft stores, or you can use small boxes you have at home (such as a shoe box). They're fun to decorate and store keepsakes in. Here's an idea for using your computer to make decorative paper to cover a special gift box, whether it's round or square. Simply print out a design you've created using your Print Shop program. Color it or paint it; then glue it to your box and box lid. Add a ribbon or bouquet of dried or silk flowers, and you will create a crafty gift to give or keep for yourself.

1. Project: Choose Sign. • Choose Wide.

2. Backdrop: Choose Blank Page. • Click OK.

3. Layout: Choose No Layout. • Click OK.

4. Click on New Object tool. • Choose Square Graphic. • Resize graphic block to fill entire page. • Double-click square graphic block. • Choose PSDeluxe Initial Caps library. • Choose French. • Click OK.

What Do I Do with It?

You'll find many uses for the fancy designs from your Print Shop program: pretty shelf paper, sheets of stationery, place mats, and more. Browse through a paper craft book to find other uses for around the house or for gift-giving.

Craft Projects

Postcards

Make your own personalized postcards to send. Follow the steps below to make the illustration shown.

Janet Donaldson
9403A East Main
Des Moines, IA 00000

1. Project: Choose Greeting Card.
   • Choose Top Fold.

2. Backdrop: Choose Crab on Beach.
   • Click OK.

3. Layout: Choose Crab on Beach 1.
   • Click OK.

4. Fill in Headline block: Double-click block. • Font: Subway.
   • Type: GREETINGS FROM FLORIDA! • Click OK.

5. Fill in Text block: Double-click block. • Font: Jester. • Font Size: 28-point (choose Other, type 28, and click OK). • Justification Horizontal: Center. • Justification Vertical: Center. • Type: From just another crab on the beach (or use your own postcard message).
   • Click OK.

6. Edit border: Leave border blank.

7. Select Inside of Card.

8. Backdrop: Choose Blank Page.
   • Click OK.

9. Layout: Choose No Layout.
   • Click OK.

10. Click on New Object tool.
    • Choose Vertical Ruled Line.
    • Double-click Vertical line.
    • Choose Traditional. • Click OK.
    • Move and resize block to fit in middle of page.

11. Click on New Object tool.
    • Choose Border. • Double-click border. • Choose Thin Border.
    • Click OK.

12. Click on New Object tool.
    • Choose Square Graphic. • Move block to upper right corner of page. • Double-click square graphic block. • Choose PSDeluxe Initial Caps library. • Choose Stamp. • Click OK.

13. Click on New Object tool.
    • Choose Text. • Double-click text block. • Font: NewZurica. • Font Size: Extra Small. • Justification Horizontal: Center. • Justification Vertical: Center. • Type: STAMP.
    • Click OK. • Move block to fit inside stamp art, resizing to fit as necessary.

14. Click on New Object tool.
    • Choose Square Graphic. • Move block to lower left corner of page.
    • Double-click square graphic block. • Choose PSDeluxe Square Graphics library. • Choose Starfish. • Click OK.

15. Click on New Object tool.
    • Choose Text. • Move block to lower right portion of page, resizing to fit. • Double-click text block. • Font: NewZurica. • Font Size: Small. • Type name and address of recipient. • Click OK.

Kids Cards

Children love receiving mail. Design some special child-oriented postcards for children in your local hospital, school, church, or for your own nieces, nephews, and cousins.

Design Tip

Print out your design, trim, and mount to heavy paper or cardboard. Don't forget to design the back of your card with a place to write a message.

Kid Stuff

Hey, kids (and parents)! The projects in this group are just for you. You can make all kinds of great things with the Print Shop Deluxe programs, such as Keep Out signs, coloring books, holiday ornaments, and more. Make sure you have a parent or teacher around to help you follow the steps for each project and to get you started. These ideas use a variety of project types: letterhead, signs, greeting cards, and others. If you're not sure how to build any of these projects, refer to the project sections that show the menus and dialog boxes for creating that specific project type.

Don't forget to color in your projects after you've printed them. Use crayons, markers, colored pencils, or paint. You can also use scissors and glue to add on to your creations. Be creative!

- Keep Out Sign
- Diary
- Christmas Ornaments
- Coloring Book
- Puzzles
- Storybook
- Memory Match-Up Game
- Flash Cards
- Play Money
- Play Menus
- Play Order Forms
- Lemonade Stand Banner
- Lawn-Mowing Sign
- Baby-Sitting Sign
- Notebook Cover
- School Report Covers
- Collection Chart
- Tickets to a Magic Show

Keep Out Sign

Make a Keep Out sign that really works. Use your Print Shop Deluxe program to design a sign for your door. Follow these steps to see how:

1. Project: Choose Sign. • Choose Tall.

2. Backdrop: Choose Woodpecker. • Click OK.

3. Layout: Choose No Layout. • Click OK.

4. Click on New Object tool. • Choose Headline. • Move block to top of backdrop white space, as shown in example. • Double-click headline block. • Font: Subway. • Type: KEEP OUT! • Click OK.

5. Click on New Object tool. • Choose Text. • Move block below headline block. • Resize to fill remaining space. • Double-click text block. • Font: Boulder. • Font Size: 58-point (choose Other, type 58, and click OK). • Justification Horizontal: Center. • Justification Vertical: Center. • Type: This means you! • Click OK. • Resize block to fit text, if necessary.

Add Some Color

After you print a sign, use crayons, markers, or paint to color it in. To make your sign sturdier, glue or tape it onto posterboard or cardboard.

Other Ideas

There are a couple of backdrops that make good Keep Out signs. Try using UFO, or Dragon (wide sign project). Once you've designed and colored a Keep Out sign for your door, why not make some for your brothers, sisters, or friends. This is also a good project idea for your secret clubhouse!

Diary

You can make your own designer pages to put into a diary or journal. First, design your page with lots of blank lines to write on. (If you use the notepad project from the letterhead type, you can print two diary designs on one page!) Print out several pages and trim them. You can punch holes in the sides and put them into a three-ring binder to make your own diary book. You can also staple a bunch together. Follow these steps to make your design:

1. Project: Choose Letterhead.
   • Choose Notepad.

2. Backdrop: Choose Blank Page.
   • Click OK.

3. Layout: Choose No Layout.
   • Click OK.

4. Click on New Object tool. • Choose Column Graphic. • Move block to left side of page. • Resize to fill depth of page, as shown in example. • Double-click column graphic block. • Choose Hearts.
   • Click OK.

5. Click on New Object tool. • Choose Headline. • Move block to top of page. • Resize to fill width, as shown in example. • Double-click headline block. • Font: Heather.
   • Shape: Pennant Right. • Type: MY DIARY. • Click OK.

6. Click on New Object tool. • Choose Text. • Move block below headline block. • Resize to fill remaining space as shown in example.
   • Double-click text block.
   • Justification Vertical: Full. • Hold down the Shift key and the hyphen key (-) to make lines throughout your block until it fills up.
   • Click OK.

7. Click on New Object tool.
   • Choose Square graphic. • Move block to very bottom right corner of page. • Double-click square graphic block. • Choose Teddy.
   • Click OK. • Use the Color Palette to change Behind Object color to white.

Design Tip

Want an idea for a boy's diary page? Use the same steps shown on this page. But when you come to step 4, choose Space Ships or Bat & Glove instead of Hearts.

Diary Tip

Use your diary to write about things such as: what happens to you each day, ideas you might have, poems, or stories. You can even sketch things! Read through your diary from time to time to see what you've been up to.

Kid Stuff

Christmas Ornaments

You can make paper Christmas ornaments to hang on your tree. Design them on your computer, color them, and cut them out. Add ribbon or string to hang them. It's easy! The project idea on this page shows how to make three different kinds of ornaments.

1. Project: Choose Sign. • Choose Tall.

2. Backdrop: Choose Blank Page. • Click OK.

3. Layout: Choose No Layout. • Click OK.

4. To make teddy bear ornament, click on New Object tool. • Choose Square Graphic. • Move block to upper left corner of project page. • Double-click square graphic block. • Choose PSDeluxe Initial Caps Library. • Choose Victorian. • Click OK. • Resize to hold another square graphic block.

5. Click on New Object tool. • Choose Square Graphic. • Move block inside first square graphic. • Resize block to fill inside of circle. • Double-click square graphic block. • Choose PSDeluxe Square Graphics library. • Choose Teddy. • Click OK.

6. To make candy cane ornament, click on New Object tool. • Choose Square Graphic. • Resize block, as shown in example. • Double-click square graphic block. • Choose Candy Cane. • Click OK. • Click on Flip tool. • Choose Horizontal.

7. To make angel ornament, click on New Object tool. • Choose Square Graphic. • Move block to bottom of project page. • Resize to fit, as shown in example. • Double-click square graphic block. • Choose Biblical Angel. • Click OK.

8. Click on New Object tool. • Choose Mini-border. • Move border around angel graphic. • Double-click mini-border. • Choose Music. • Select Wide Border. • Click OK.

Design Tip

Glue on glitter, bows, and other holiday stuff to make your ornaments really special. It's also a good idea to glue your ornaments to cardboard or posterboard, and then cut them out. This will make them very sturdy when hanging on the tree.

Coloring Book

You can make your own coloring book or coloring pages using your Print Shop Deluxe program. Find a graphic you like, enlarge it, print it out, and color! You can make several coloring pages and put them into a book. You can even print out coloring book outlines for all your art. Follow these steps to make the coloring page shown in the illustration.

1. Project: Choose Sign. • Choose Tall.

2. Backdrop: Choose Easter Basket.
   • Click OK.

3. Layout: Choose No Layout.
   • Click OK.

4. Pull down File menu. • Select Print.
   • Choose Coloring Book from the Print dialog box. • Click OK.

Use Square Graphics

You can also use square graphics as coloring pages. Start your project on an empty page with no layout. Add a square graphic. Stretch it to fill the entire page. Then print it out following the steps above. That was easy!

Make a Book

Make a coloring book to give to a friend. Pick out your favorite backdrop graphics and turn them into full page pictures following the steps above. When you've made a bunch, staple them together to make a book. Don't forget to design a cover for it!

Kid Stuff

Puzzles

Print out your favorite picture and turn it into a puzzle. Use scissors to cut your picture into smaller shapes. Put the pieces into a decorated envelope, and give them to a friend to put together. Follow these instructions to make a giant picture.

1. Project: Choose Sign. • Choose Tall.

2. Backdrop: Choose Blank Page. • Click OK.

3. Layout: Choose No Layout. • Click OK.

4. Click on New Object tool. • Choose Square Graphic. • Move block to top left corner of page. • Stretch to fill entire page, as shown in example. • Double-click square graphic block. • Choose Pumpkin. • Click OK.

5. Click on New Object tool. • Choose Border. • Double-click Border. • Choose Thick Border. • Click OK.

6. Print out your picture. • Color it using crayons or markers. • Cut the picture into shapes like puzzle pieces.

Stretching Tip

If you use Windows, hold down the Ctrl key while resizing the block in step 4. This will give you "stretching" capabilities. If you use Mac, hold down the Option key while resizing. If you use DOS, use the Stretch command.

More Puzzle Ideas

You can make all kinds of great puzzle projects with your Print Shop Deluxe program. Try making puzzle postcards. Send them to friends who have to put them together to read the message. Make puzzle party invitations. Friends have to put the puzzle together to find out where the party is. Think of your own great puzzle ideas!

Storybook

Have you ever wanted to write your own storybook? Now you can, using your computer! First, you must think of a story. Next, use your Print Shop Deluxe program to make each page of your storybook. Look at the steps below to see how we made a page from a storybook. You can create different pages for your book. You'll find lots of art to use to illustrate your story. If you can't find any art to go with your story, just print out the words, and draw your own picture on the page.

1. Project: Choose Sign. • Choose Tall.

2. Backdrop: Choose Sand Castle.
   • Click OK.

3. Layout: Choose No Layout.
   • Click OK.

4. Click on New Object tool. • Choose Square Graphic. • Move the block to the left side of the page. • Resize block as shown in example.
   • Double-click block. • Choose PSDeluxe Initial Caps library.
   • Choose Decor. • Click OK.

5. Click on New Object tool. • Choose Text. • Resize block and move it so it fits inside the square graphic block. • Double-click text block.
   • Font: Heather. • Font Size: Large.
   • Type: O. • Click OK.

6. Click on New Object tool. • Choose Text. • Move block beside square graphic. • Resize text block to fill space, as shown in example.
   • Double-click text block. • Font: Heather. • Font Size: 42-point (choose Other, type 42, and click OK). • Justification Horizontal: Left. • Justification Vertical: Top.
   • Type a paragraph from your story here. (Indent the first line 10 spaces by pressing the Spacebar 10 times.)
   • Click OK.

Make a Book

Once you've finished your story, color in the pages. You can punch holes along the sides and put your storybook into a three-ring binder. Now you have a book to share with a friend or family member.

Kid Stuff

Memory Match-Up Game

You can make really neat memory match game flash cards using the art on your Print Shop Deluxe program. Make a set of cards, like the ones in the illustration. Print out two copies, so you have two of the same card. Cut them out and mix them up. Place them face down on a table or floor. Turn over one card, and then turn over another to find the matching card. An instant game! Follow these instructions to see how to make your cards:

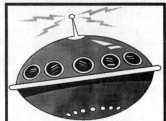

1. Project: Choose Sign. • Choose Wide.

2. Backdrop: Choose Blank Page. • Click OK

3. Layout: Choose No Layout. • Click OK.

4. Click on New Object tool. • Choose Square Graphic. • Move block to top left corner of page. • Stretch to fill top left corner, as shown in example. • Double-click square graphic block. • Choose Birthday Hippo. • Click OK. • Click on Frame tool. • Choose Thick Line.

5. Click on New Object tool. • Choose Square Graphic. • Move block to top right corner of page. • Stretch to fill top right corner, as shown in example. • Double-click square graphic block. • Choose Burger. • Click OK. • Click on Frame tool. • Choose Thick Line.

6. Click on New Object tool. • Choose Square Graphic. • Move block to bottom left corner of page. • Stretch to fill bottom left corner, as shown in example. • Double-click square graphic block. • Choose Leprechaun. • Click OK. • Click on Frame tool. • Choose Thick Line.

7. Click on New Object tool. • Choose Square Graphic. • Move block to bottom right corner of page. • Stretch to fill bottom right corner, as shown in example. • Double-click square graphic block. • Choose Spaceship. • Click OK. • Click on Frame tool. • Choose Thick Line.

8. Print out two copies of your page. • Cut apart the squares. • Follow the instructions in the tip on this page to play the game.

How to Play Memory Match-Up

Mix up the squares and spread them out on the floor or table, face down. Now turn over one card. Remember what it looks like. Turn over another card to see if you can find a match to the first card. If it's a match, you can pick up the two cards. If it's not a match, turn them back over and let someone else have a turn. The winner is the player with the most matched squares. You and your friends can take turns playing this memory match-up game!

Another Idea

Try making a Puzzle Match-Up game using the cards you made. Cut each card into two pieces. Mix them up and turn them over on a table or floor. Turn over one piece. Now turn over another piece and see if they go together. If they do, you have a match and can pick up the cards. If they don't match, turn them back over and let someone else try.

Flash Cards

You can make flash cards to help you with math or language. You can also make a set to help your little brother or sister. Follow these steps to create some number flash cards.

1. Project: Choose Sign. • Choose Wide.

2. Backdrop: Choose Blank Page. • Click OK.

3. Layout: Choose No Layout. • Click OK.

4. To make the first flash card, click on the New Object tool. Choose Text. • Move the block to the upper left corner. • Stretch to fill upper left corner, as shown in example. • Double-click text block. • Font: Boulder. • Font Size: Extra Large. • Justification Horizontal: Left. • Justification Vertical: Center. • Type: 3. • Click OK.

5. Click on New Object tool. • Choose Square Graphic. • Move block inside the text block. • Resize graphic block to fit a small picture. • Double-click square graphic block. • Choose Bunny. • Click OK.

6. Pull down Edit menu. • Choose Copy. • Pull down Edit menu again. • Choose Paste. • Now you should have two bunnies, but one is on top of the other. • Click on the top bunny, and move the block beside the first bunny. • To make another bunny, pull down the Edit menu again. • Choose Paste. • Click the top bunny and move the block to fit under the other bunny graphics.

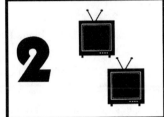

7. Repeat steps 4–7 to design different kinds of flash cards. Four flash cards will fit onto one project page.

Design Tip

You can resize your art squares, make some large or small, or flip them horizontally. You can even rotate your rabbits!

Play Money

Have you ever wanted to design your own play money? Now you can with the Print Shop Deluxe program. Look at the instructions below to see how to make your own play money.

1. Project: Choose Letterhead.
   • Choose Notepad.

2. Backdrop: Choose Blank Page.
   • Click OK.

3. Layout: Choose No Layout.
   • Click OK.

4. Click on New Object tool.
   • Choose Square Graphic. • Move block to upper left corner of page.
   • Resize to fit across page.
   • Double-click square graphic block. • Choose PSDeluxe Initial Caps library. • Choose Stamp.
   • Click OK. • Use the Color Palette to set Behind Object to green.

5. Click on New Object tool.
   • Choose Square Graphic. • Move block to middle inside of first graphic block. • Enlarge block slightly. • Double-click square graphic block. • Choose PSDeluxe Squares library. • Choose New Year's Baby. • Click OK.

6. Click on New Object tool.
   • Choose Headline. • Move block to top inside of first graphic block.
   • Resize to fill space across top, as shown in example. • Double-click headline block. • Font: Steamer.
   • Shape: Arc Up. • Type: PLAY MONEY. • Click OK.

7. Click on New Object tool.
   • Choose Text. • Resize block and move it so it fits inside the graphic block on the left side of the New Year's Baby. • Double-click text block. • Font: Boulder. • Font Size: 68-point (choose Other, type 68, and click OK). • Justification Horizontal: Center. • Justification Vertical: Center. • Type: $5. • Click OK.

8. Click on New Object tool.
   • Choose Text. • Resize block and move it so it fits inside the graphic block on the right side of the New Year's Baby. • Double-click text block. • Font: Boulder. • Font Size: 68-point (choose Other, type 68, and click OK). • Justification Horizontal: Center. • Justification Vertical: Center. • Type: $5.
   • Click OK.

Design Tip

You have room to make more money on your Notepad page. Repeat the steps in this project, but move your blocks into the empty parts of your page. Remember, the Notepad project prints out two to a page, so you'll have lots of "money" to cut out and play with.

Play Menus

Are you opening up a play restaurant? You'll need play menus to use. Here's an easy idea for making a play menu. (Follow the instructions under the Play Money project to make pretend money to use in your restaurant!)

1. Project: Choose Sign. • Choose Tall.

2. Backdrop: Choose Mod Cafe. • Click OK.

3. Layout: Choose Mod Cafe 1. • Click OK.

4. Fill in Headline block: Double-click block. • Font: Jester. • Type: Sally's Restaurant (or use your own name). • Click OK.

5. Fill in Text block 1: Double-click block. • Font: Jester. • Style: Bold. • Font Size: 40-point (choose Other, type 40, and click OK). • Type: Ham & Cheese Sandwiches .75 Chips .50 (add your own menu items). • Click OK.

6. Fill in Text block 2: Double-click block. • Font: Jester. • Style: Bold, Drop Shadow. • Font Size: 40-point (choose Other, type 40, and click OK). • Justification Horizontal: Center. • Justification Vertical: Center. • Type: Ice Cream Sundaes, 1.50 (type in your own desserts). • Click OK. • Move block down slightly.

7. Click on New Object tool. • Choose Square Graphic. Double-click square graphic block. • Choose Burger. • Click OK. • Move block between text blocks, resizing to fit. • Click on Rotate tool. • Tilt graphic, as shown in example.

Design Tip

You don't have to use the layout on this page. Make your own. Design your menu with goofy food and outrageous prices! Don't forget to color in your menu after you've printed it out.

Kid Stuff

Play Order Forms

You can make all sorts of fun order forms to play with. Here's a project idea for making an order form notepad for your play restaurant. Follow these steps:

1. Project: Choose Letterhead.
   • Choose Notepad.

2. Backdrop: Choose Cupcakes & Candy. • Click OK.

3. Layout: Choose No Layout.
   • Click OK.

4. Click on New Object tool.
   • Choose Headline. • Move block to top right corner of page.
   • Resize to fit, as shown in example. • Double-click headline block. • Font: Bazooka. • Font Size: Large. • Justification Horizontal: Center. • Justification Vertical: Center. • Type: MAY I TAKE YOUR ORDER PLEASE?
   • Click OK.

5. Click on New Object tool.
   • Choose Text. • Move block below headline block. • Resize to fill open space, as shown in example. • Double-click text block.
   • Hold down the Shift key and the hyphen key (-), and make lines throughout the block until you run out of room. • Click OK.

Design Tip

This project will print two to a page when you print it out on your printer. Print out five of these pages, trim each form, and staple them together to make an order pad.

Lemonade Stand Banner

Make a giant banner for your next lemonade stand. You can design a banner that's sure to make everyone notice. Follow these instructions to make a cool lemonade stand banner:

1. Project: Choose Banner. • Choose Horizontal.

2. Backdrop: Choose Art Deco. • Click OK.

3. Layout: Choose Art Deco 3. • Click OK.

4. Fill in Headline block: Double-click block. • Font: Boulder. • Font Size: Small/Large. • Type: FRESH SQUEEZED LEMONADE .50. • Click OK.

More Lemonade Stuff

Remember to make signs or flyers for your lemonade stand. Use the Sign project type to help you.

Make a Coupon

Follow the instructions under the Coupon project in this book to make nifty lemonade coupons for your friends!

Kid Stuff

Lawn-Mowing Sign

You'll drum up business all over the neighborhood with lawn-mowing signs made with the Print Shop Deluxe program. Here's an easy sign you can make.

1. Project: Choose Sign. • Choose Tall.

2. Backdrop: Choose Blank Page. • Click OK.

3. Layout: Choose Sign 15. • Click OK.

4. Fill in Headline block: Double-click block. • Font: Sherwood. • Shape: Arc Up. • Type: LAWN-MOWING. • Click OK. • Resize block to make it bigger, as shown in example.

5. Fill in Text block: Double-click block. • Font: Boulder. • Font Size: 86-point (choose Other, type 86, and click OK). • Justification Horizontal: Center. • Justification Vertical: Center. • Type: CALL BILLY SPRAGUE 000-0000 (but use your own name and phone number). • Click OK.

6. Fill in Mini-border: Double-click border. • Choose Geo. • Click OK.

Design Tip

If you're hanging your sign outside, you might want to cover it with clear plastic to protect it from the weather.

It's a Flyer

Use your sign design as a flyer to hand out to neighbors and friends or put in mail boxes. Print the design on colored paper to make it really stand out!

Baby-Sitting Sign

Let everyone in your neighborhood know you're available to baby-sit. Post your signs on poles, or hand them out as flyers. Here's a simple sign you can make.

1. Project: Choose Sign. • Choose Tall.

2. Backdrop: Choose Gingerbread Man. • Click OK.

3. Layout: Choose Gingerbread Man 5. • Click OK.

4. Fill in Headline block: Double-click block. • Font: Subway. • Shape: Arc Up. • Type: BABY-SITTING. • Click OK.

5. Fill in Text block (middle): Double-click block. • Font: Subway. • Font Size: Medium Large. • Justification Horizontal: Center. • Justification Vertical: Center. • Type: CALL JENNIFER JAHNSSEN 000-0000 (but use your name and phone number). • Click OK. • Use the Color controls to set Behind Text to clear.

6. Fill in Text block (bottom): Double-click block. • Font: Subway. • Font Size: Medium. • Justification Horizontal: Center. • Justification Vertical: Center. • Type: References Available. • Click OK. • You may have to move the block left or right to fit in space. • Use the Color controls to set Behind Text to clear.

Pass 'Em Out!

Advertise your business by placing signs in doorways and mailboxes around your neighborhood. Print them on colored paper so they will stand out.

Notebook Cover

Here's a nifty notebook cover idea. You can make different covers for all your school books!

1. Project: Choose Sign. • Choose Tall.

2. Backdrop: Choose Ocean & Jungle. • Click OK.

3. Layout: Choose Ocean & Jungle 5. • Click OK.

4. Fill in Headline block: Double-click block. • Font: Boulder. • Type: ENGLISH CLASS (or the name of your class). • Click OK.

5. Fill in Text block: Double-click block. • Font: NewZurica. • Style: Bold. • Font Size: Medium. • Justification Horizontal: Center. • Justification Vertical: Center. • Type your name, and the name of the class teacher. • Click OK.

Design Tip

Remember to add color to your notebook cover. Crayons, markers, and paint can make your notebook cover a work of art. You might also try printing your project on colored paper. Make colorful covers for all of your class notebooks!

Variation

There is some other cool backdrop art you can use to make notebook covers. Try using Confetti, Football Field, Notebook, UFO, Valentine Hearts, Volcano, and Woodpecker.

School Report Covers

Show your teacher how creative you can be with a cool report cover designed on your Print Shop Deluxe program. Follow these instructions to create the project shown:

1. Project: Choose Sign. • Choose Tall.

2. Backdrop: Choose Egyptian Party. • Click OK.

3. Layout: Choose Egyptian Party 1. • Click OK.

4. Fill in Headline block (top): Double-click block. • Font: Tribune. • Type: HISTORY. • Click OK.

5. Fill in Text block (middle): Double-click block. • Font: Stylus. • Font Size: 40-point (choose Other, type 40, and click OK). • Justification Horizontal: Center. • Justification Vertical: Center. • Type the title of your report. • Click OK.

6. Fill in Headline block (bottom): Double-click block. • Font: Boulder. • Type your name, as shown in example. • Click OK.

Variation

For a more serious report cover design, try building your project from scratch. Follow these steps:

1. Project: Choose Sign. • Choose Tall.

2. Backdrop: Choose Blank Page. • Click OK.

3. Layout: Choose No Layout. • Click OK.

4. Click on New Object tool. • Choose Border. • Double-click Border. • Choose a neat border design that you like. • Click OK.

5. Click on New Object tool. • Choose Text. • Move block to the middle of the page. • Double-click text block. • Font: NewZurica (or another font you like). • Justification Horizontal: Center. • Justification Vertical: Center. • Type in your report title and other information. • Click OK. • Click on Frame tool. • Choose Thin Line.

Collection Chart

Here's a project idea to help you keep track of your collection, whether it's sports cards, stamps, rocks, or shells. Follow these steps to make a chart for your football card collection:

1. Project: Choose Sign. • Choose Tall.

2. Backdrop: Choose Football Field. • Click OK.

3. Layout: Choose Football Field 1. • Click OK.

4. Fill in text block (top): Double-click block. • Font: Bazooka. • Font Size: Small. • Type: FOOTBALL CARD COLLECTION. • Click OK. • Click on Frame tool. • Choose Thin Line.

5. Fill in text block middle, left: Double-click block. • Font: NewZurica. • Font Size: Small. • Justification Horizontal: Left. • Justification Vertical: Center. • Type the name of your card, team, date, and maker. • Repeat sequence to fill text block with collection data. • Click OK when finished.

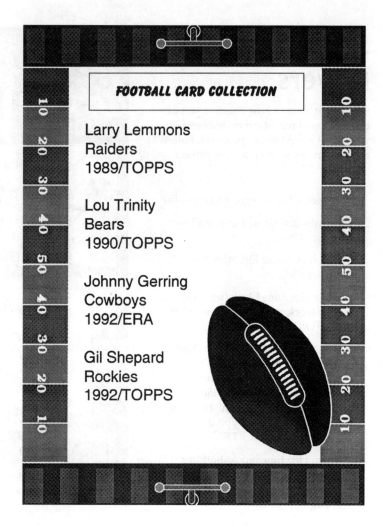

FOOTBALL CARD COLLECTION

Larry Lemmons
Raiders
1989/TOPPS

Lou Trinity
Bears
1990/TOPPS

Johnny Gerring
Cowboys
1992/ERA

Gil Shepard
Rockies
1992/TOPPS

Make a Book

If your collection uses several pages, punch holes in the sides and put them into a three-ring binder. This will keep you really organized!

Tickets to a Magic Show

Are you a budding magician? Use your computer to make tickets to a magic show that you put on. You can also use this design to create admission tickets to plays and puppet shows you and friends put on. Follow these instructions:

1. Project: Choose Letterhead.
   • Choose Notepad.

2. Backdrop: Choose Blank Page.
   • Click OK.

3. Layout: Choose No Layout.
   • Click OK.

4. Click on New Object tool. • Choose Square Graphic. • Double-click square graphic. • Choose PSDeluxe Calendar Icons library. • Choose Ticket. • Click OK. • Move the block to top of page. • Stretch to fill upper 1/3.

5. Click on New Object tool. • Choose Headline. • Double-click headline block. • Font: Boulder. • Shape: Arc Up. • Click on Customize button. • Shadow Effect: Silhouette. • Color: set Text white, and Shadow black. • Click OK. • Type: ADMIT ONE. • Click OK. • Use the Color Palette to change Behind Object to black. • Move block to fit inside ticket, covering some of the art.

6. Click on New Object tool. • Choose Text. • Double-click text block. • Font: Jester. • Style: Bold. • Font Size: Medium. • Justification Horizontal: Center. • Justification Vertical: Center. • Type: The Amazing Loudini's MAGIC SHOW (or the name of your show). • Change Text Color to white. • Click OK. • Use the Color Palette to change Behind Text to black. • Move block to fit inside ticket, beneath headline, covering some of the art.

Stretching Tip

If you use Windows, hold down the Ctrl key while resizing the block in step 4. This gives you "stretching" capabilities. If you use Mac, hold down the Option key while resizing. If you use DOS, use the Stretch command.

Design Tip

You may have to try a few times to overlap the text and headline block so that they cover the art underneath. You can also use the Order command to help you layer the blocks.

Basic Print Shop Deluxe Skills

What Are the Basics?

If you've never worked with The Print Shop Deluxe (PSD, for short) before, this section will give you some important information for getting around in the program, whether you're working in the Windows, DOS, or Mac version of the software. You'll find tips for using the mouse and keyboard, instructions for printing and saving your files, and everything you need to know about working with the various program elements.

 Start Your Engines!   Before we begin looking at the program, you need to have it up and running on your computer. To start the program, follow the instructions found in Section One under the heading "Starting the Program" (if you've not installed the program, follow the installation instructions located in Appendix A in the back of this book).

What's on Your Screen?

The *Project* or *Main menu* screen is the first screen you see after starting your program. This is where all of your projects start. This is also where you can exit the program. The Project menu displays the name of the program, project selections you can make, and a few extra buttons, such as Exit or Cancel. Figure 2.1 shows the Project menu from PSD-Windows version.

What's a Menu Anyway?   A menu is a list of commands that appear in a box or drop-down box.

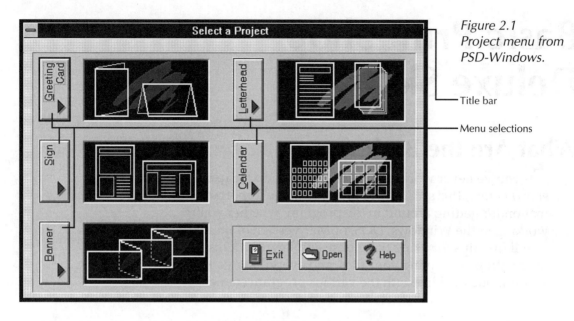

Figure 2.1
*Project menu from
PSD-Windows.*

Title bar

Menu selections

If you're using DOS or Mac versions of the software, your Project menu screens will look slightly different, *but only slightly*. The only differences are that the PSD-DOS menu shows a printer Setup button, and the PSD-Mac menu calls its Exit button Cancel.

MAC ***What Else Is Different?*** Both Windows and Mac programs let you open a saved file from the Project menu. In DOS, you save the files according to project type, and you can only open a saved file after selecting a project type.

In all three versions of the program, there are five distinct project types you can make: Greeting Cards, Letterheads, Signs, Calendars, or Banners. Before I show you how the program works, it's a good idea to go over the basics of using the mouse and the keyboard.

Windows Screen Tip If you're using PSD-Windows, you can make full use of your screen area by clicking on the Maximize button once you've opened a project to work on. Just click the upward arrow button located in the far upper right corner of the screen.

> *Help!*   Another wonderful feature of PSD is the Help
> function. If you're using Windows or DOS, just press
> the **F1** key on your keyboard, and the program will
> provide information or instructions pertaining to the
> screen you "called for help" from. If you're using Mac, click on
> the Help button, or select Help from the Apple menu. (On
> System 7, click on the Balloon Help icon.) Depending on your
> software, your Help system will "help" you read what you need
> to know. When you're finished, you can exit.

Navigating the Program

If you're a new computer user, you'll want to know some
basic information about working with the mouse and the
keyboard.

Using the Mouse

If you're a first-time mouse user, you'll soon find that using a
mouse to move around the screen is incredibly simple and
intuitive. First of all, place your right hand over the mouse, and
your index finger over the left mouse button. (Mac users don't
have a left or right button to worry about.) To move the mouse,
gently push it around on your desktop or mouse pad. As you
do, you'll notice something happening on your screen. A *mouse
pointer* (Windows and Mac) or *highlight bar* or *box* (DOS) moves
around on the screen as you move your mouse around on the
desk. Look at the following list of basic mouse actions:

- **Click**   A *click* is a quick tap or press of the mouse button.
  When you want to make a selection using the mouse,
  simply point the on-screen arrow at the item, and then click
  the left mouse button. (If you're using a Mac, you won't
  have a left or right mouse button; just click the one button!)

- **Double-click**   Some selections require a *double-click*: two
  quick taps of the mouse button.

- **Drag**   To move an object on your screen to a new position,
  you must drag it with the mouse. *Dragging* is pointing to
  the object, holding down the mouse button, and moving
  the mouse. When you reach the new position, let go of the
  mouse button.

> **DOS** **DOS Mouse Note** If you're using the PSD-DOS version, you will find uses for both the left and right mouse buttons in the program. Pressed simultaneously, they act like the Tab key; they take you to different sections of a menu. Clicking the right mouse button is the same as pressing Esc, which takes you back a step in your project.

Using the Keyboard

Broderbund designed PSD for mouse users, so it's a little tougher moving around PSD with your keyboard. If you happen to be using PSD-DOS, you can move around your screen using the arrow keys on the keyboard. *Highlight* your on-screen selection (surround it by a box), and press the Enter key. Aside from the arrow keys, you'll also find yourself using the Esc key to go backward a step in your project.

For both PSD-DOS and PSD-Windows programs, you have the option of using selection keys. *Selection keys* are shortcuts on the keyboard that correspond to menus or dialog box options. They open menus and choose commands, often when used in conjunction with the Alt key. Selection keys are usually bold or underlined when they appear in a menu or dialog box. For example, the word Exit on the Exit button has an underlined E (see Figure 2.1). If you press the letter E on the keyboard, you can exit the program from this screen. Look for these keyboard selection letter keys throughout PSD.

If you're using the Mac version of PSD, you can still use the keyboard, although not as fluidly as described above. The command key, the key with the strange-looking symbol on it (also has an apple on it), is used to activate keyboard shortcuts. Just press the key and the letter of the menu command you want to execute. (You'll have to memorize what all of those letters are!)

Of course, the most basic purpose for using the keyboard in PSD is to type in text. There are steps within the projects that require you to enter text from the keyboard. When you reach such a place, the arrow or highlight bar becomes a blinking line or vertical bar called a *cursor*. A cursor always indicates where to type the next letter. When typing is complete, you're back to moving around with the mouse or arrow keys.

How to Assemble a Project

Although the screens differ slightly from one program version to the next, the basic procedures are the same. You pick a project type, design it, and print it out. All of this happens through a variety of menus and dialog boxes (which you'll learn more about shortly).

You can assemble each project by using a series of menus and dialog boxes to choose borders and artwork, and type in text. Along the way, you can customize, experiment, and preview your work. At any point, you can stop and *edit* (or change) your project. You can save each project again and again. Unlike other intimidating software programs available, PSD is really quite foolproof.

For example, here's a sequence of menus and dialog boxes used to create a simple sign using PSD-Windows. Follow along with the numbers to see how each step progresses. It is surprisingly easy to create a project.

1.   First, select a project type from the Project menu screen. For this example, choose Sign. Simply click on the Sign button.

2.   Then select sign orientation. For this example, choose a Tall orientation by clicking on the Tall button.

3.   A backdrop dialog box (a box with different option selections) appears from which you can choose a particular backdrop graphic design for your project. You can view each design on the list before you make a selection. Choose a backdrop and click **OK**.

List of backdrops   Use these arrows to see more backdrops.   Preview of backdrop

4.   After choosing a backdrop, you pick out a layout for the sign.
     Choose a specific layout that meets your needs, and click on the
     OK button. (You'll learn more about layouts in the pages ahead.)

Select a layout from this list.   A preview of the layout

5. Once you select a layout, you're ready to fill it in. Choose the particular layout element you want to fill in by double-clicking on it; a dialog box will appear. In a Text or Headline dialog box, default options are already selected, and the cursor waits ready for you to type in text. If you want to choose a different font or size, or any other option, make your selection before typing in the text. In a Graphic dialog box, you'll see a list of available art to choose from; just make a selection. You can view what each looks like before choosing. To exit either kind of dialog box, click **OK**.

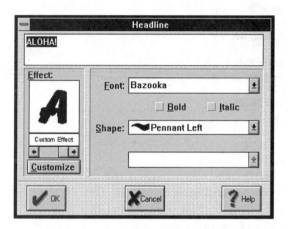

6. After you finish the sign, you're ready to save and print the project. You will learn how to do this later in this section.

7. Figure 2.2 shows what the finished sign looks like.

Figure 2.2
A finished project,
created with PSD-
Windows.

All versions of the Print Shop programs follow similar menu sequences. The menus and dialog boxes will look different, depending on what software type you have, but the idea is the same: to piece together a project, step by step. Mind you, you won't always follow the same sequence. In some projects, you'll skip steps to create a special design, and you don't have to fill in every layout element.

As you work on your project, you'll always see a picture on your screen of what the project currently looks like. At any time during the course of the project, you can exit the program, print, save, or select options. You'll find details about these functions in the pages ahead.

Menus and Dialog Boxes

Menus and dialog boxes are the keys to getting around in PSD. The menus and dialog boxes used in the program are very straightforward and easy to use. Familiarize yourself with the following information so you can easily jump around from project to project.

Using Menus

Menus are special lists that allow you to make choices regarding steps, designs, layouts, and more. In Windows and Mac, a menu bar appears at the top of the screen listing the names of menus that pull down to reveal various commands. Take a look at the menu list from PSD-Windows shown in Figure 2.3.

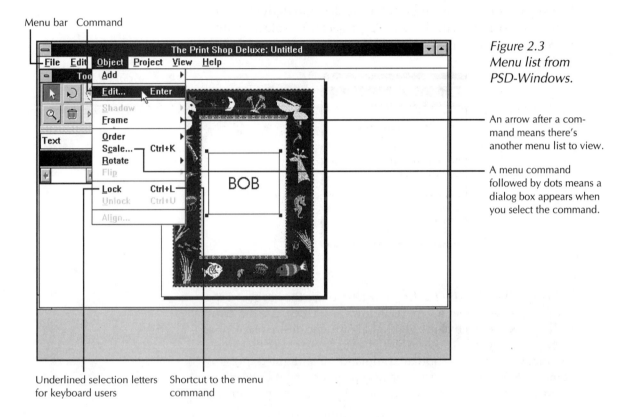

Menu bar   Command

Underlined selection letters   Shortcut to the menu
for keyboard users   command

Figure 2.3
Menu list from
PSD-Windows.

An arrow after a command means there's another menu list to view.

A menu command followed by dots means a dialog box appears when you select the command.

Why Is the Command Gray? Sometimes, an item on a menu list appears shaded in gray. This means you cannot select it for that particular task.

To use a Windows menu:

1. Click on the menu name in the menu bar using the mouse.

2. To choose a menu item, simply click on your selection.

To use a Mac menu:

1. Click on the menu name, and hold the mouse button down to keep the menu displayed.

2. Drag the mouse to highlight the item, and then let go of the mouse button to select.

PSD-DOS menus appear automatically based on what step of the project you're working on. Figure 2.4 shows the primary menu for working with PSD-DOS projects. To select an item from such a menu, just click on it with the mouse.

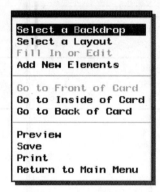

Figure 2.4
*A menu from
PSD-DOS.*

Want to Use the Keyboard? To use the keyboard to select a menu item (Windows and DOS), use the arrow keys to move the highlight bar to the desired selection; *highlighting* causes a black bar to appear over the command. When the appropriate command is highlighted, press Enter. PSD-Windows users can also press and hold the Alt key and press the underlined (selection) letter in the menu name.

Using Dialog Boxes

Sometimes PSD needs more information from you, such as what art options you want to apply, before it can perform a command you select. When it needs more information or has a group of options for you to choose from, it displays a dialog box. *Dialog boxes* are special boxes that give you more information about a particular command or ask you for more information. Figure 2.5 shows an example of a dialog box from the PSD-Windows version.

Buttons to turn
options on or off

Arrows indicate drop-down lists
that offer more selections.

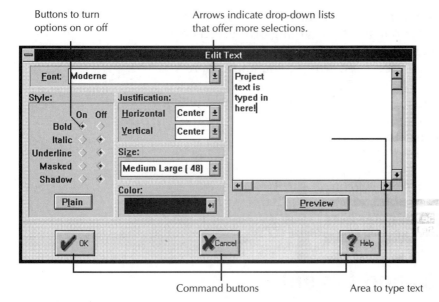

Figure 2.5
Dialog box from
PSD-Windows.

Command buttons

Area to type text

Dialog boxes feature many elements: a space for typing in text; drop-down menus from which to choose fonts and alignment; and option buttons you can use to turn on bold, italic, and other special treatments for your text and art. You can use your mouse to point at parts of the box and then click to make selections. You can also use the Tab key and the arrow keys on the keyboard to move from option to option.

To use a dialog box:

1. Click on the items you want to turn on, or type in text where applicable.

2. To exit the dialog box, click **OK** or **Done**. To exit without executing your selections, select **Cancel** or press **Esc**.

DOS

Two-Part Boxes   In DOS, you'll encounter dialog boxes containing two sections. In between the two sections is a Tab button. The top section contains a menu list. After choosing an item from the menu list, you can tab to the bottom section to continue your selections.

Press both mouse buttons at the same time to tab between the two menu sections, or click on the Tab button on the menu.

There are lists of art or fonts inside dialog boxes. Many of these menu lists are too long to fit everything on one screen. In these cases, you'll notice a *scroll bar* on the menu, with arrows on either end. When you see these arrows, you know there's more of the menu list to look at. To scroll through a list, move your mouse pointer to the top or bottom (depending on which direction you want to scroll). Click on the arrows or use the arrows on your keyboard to move up and down.

MAC *Mac U-Turns* If you're using PSD-Mac, some dialog boxes have a Return to Project menu button that looks like a U-turn. Clicking on it will take you to the Project menu screen.

Building Blocks and Layouts

Once you select a project, backdrop, and layout for your project, PSD displays several elements that resemble boxes on your screen. They will remain blocks until you fill them in. The blocks represent borders, graphic blocks, ruled line blocks, text blocks, and headline blocks. You can combine these elements in hundreds of different ways. Used together, these elements make up your layout.

A *layout* provides designated areas for each element of your project. It's kind of like having a map of where each part goes. All you have to do is plug in text, graphics, headlines, and borders in the places the layout designates they should go. Each element has an icon that represents what kind of block it is. Figure 2.6 shows a sample layout using every possible element.

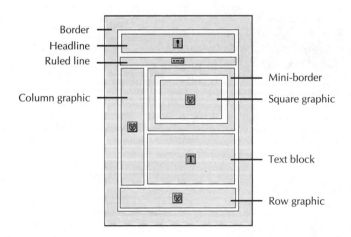

Border
Headline
Ruled line
Column graphic
Mini-border
Square graphic
Text block
Row graphic

Figure 2.6
Each layout element has an icon indicating what kind of block it is.

PSD comes with many layouts for each project type. You also have the option of designing your own layout. Each element block can be resized and moved around on the project page. At any point in your project, you can modify or completely change the layout you have chosen. When you finish with a project, you can always go back and edit the various elements.

To choose an element to fill in or edit:

1. First, move the mouse pointer over the layout element.

2. Double-click (Windows and Mac) or click (DOS) on the element to open a dialog box.

Inside the dialog box will be options or lists that you can choose from that will fill in the element with art or text. Windows and Mac users will find additional tools and menus to help edit layout elements (you'll learn about the Tool Palette in the pages to come).

> **MAC** **Mac Text Blocks** If you're using PSD-Mac, double-clicking on a text block element won't open a dialog box. Instead, it will let you type text into the block. To control fonts, sizes, and other options (items found in other PSD dialog boxes), use the Text menu on the menu bar.

Working with Text Elements

Text elements are an important part of your PSD projects. Not only can you select from a variety of typestyles to make your words look good, but you can also work with different sizes, colors, placement, and more. When it comes to text, you'll find many different possibilities with PSD.

There are two types of text elements: *Text blocks*, and *Headline blocks*. Text blocks are just regular text that you type into your project. Headline blocks are one or two lines of text that you can shape and style to catch the reader's eye. The following information will tell you all about the various text features and options. You can find these options in PSD dialog boxes that appear when you select a text element (see Figure 2.7). If you're using PSD-Windows or PSD-Mac, you also find the options in the pull-down menus or the Tool Palette (you'll learn more about the Tool Palette when we cover graphics).

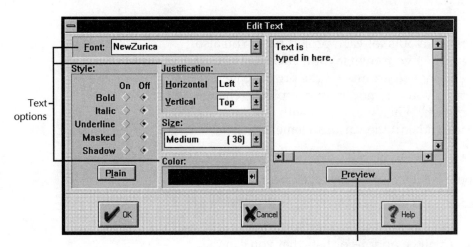

Figure 2.7
The Text dialog box
showing the various
text options from
PSD-Windows.

Click the Preview button to
see what text will look like.

Fonts

Fonts are the various styles of letters you can choose for your text. There are various fonts available, ranging in looks from chunky and fat to handwritten and soft. Professional printers classify fonts into two categories: *serif* and *sans serif*. These Latin-based words basically mean feet (serif) and without feet (sans serif). A typestyle like Paramount has little feet or appendages that extend from the bottom of the character. (See Figure 2.8 for an example.) You probably see this font style in newspapers and books. A typestyle like NewZurica does not have these appendages; instead each character is more block-like (see Figure 2.9). Block typestyles are more common in advertising (on billboards, for example).

C
is for
CAT — Serif characters have feet.

Figure 2.8
An example of a
serif font.

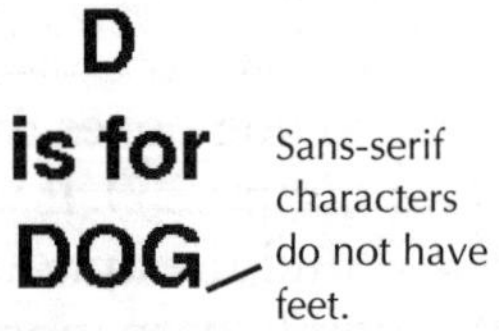

D
is for
DOG — Sans-serif characters do not have feet.

Figure 2.9
An example of a
sans-serif font.

You choose fonts when you fill in or edit a text block or a headline block. They appear in lists in which you can scroll through and select the font you want (see Figure 2.10). Appendix C of this book shows all of the basic PSD fonts.

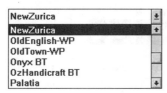

Figure 2.10
A font menu list from
PSD-Windows.

Styles and Effects

In addition to the different fonts, there are different styles, or looks, available for each font. You can italicize a font, make it bold, underline it, and more. See Figure 2.11 for some examples. These design options for changing the look of the text give you great flexibility in creating the perfect look for your project.

Figure 2.11
Examples of font
design options.

In addition to changing the way a font looks, you can also create special effects for your text. You can add shadows or frames, rotate text, and even change the text color. You'll find all of these options available in the various menus and dialog boxes.

Sizes

Not only are fonts available in different styles, but they are also available in different sizes. The sizes range from very large to very small. In the professional printing world, *point size* is the height of a font's characters, measured in points (one point equals 1/72 inch). Figure 2.12 shows some different point sizes.

10Point Size

18Point Size

24 Point Size

36 Point Size

You choose size from a list that ranges from extra large to extra small (see Figure 2.13). The list also offers you a chance to enter a specific point size not covered by the size ranges. If you're having trouble getting your text block to fit in medium size, and small is too small, select **Other** at the bottom of the size list. Then type a point size that is less than the medium size of 36-point. (Try 34, 32, and so on.)

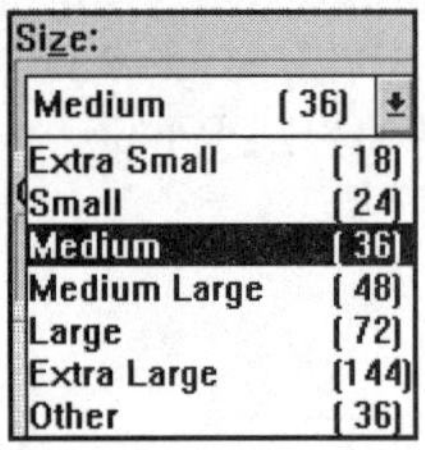

Figure 2.12
Examples of point sizes.

Size:	
Medium	[36]
Extra Small	[18]
Small	[24]
Medium	[36]
Medium Large	[48]
Large	[72]
Extra Large	[144]
Other	[36]

Figure 2.13
The Font Size list from PSD-Windows.

Positioning

Now that you know a little more about fonts, you need to know the different ways of displaying your text. There are numerous ways of placing your text within your text block. Vertical positioning (*placement)* in the PSD programs controls whether text is positioned at the top, center, or bottom of the block. Horizontal positioning (*justification* or *alignment)* controls whether all lines of text are lined up on the left or right of the block or are centered or justified in the block. Figure 2.14 shows examples of each.

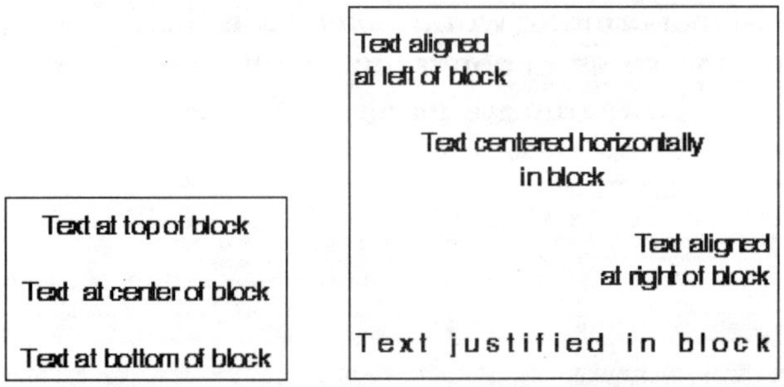

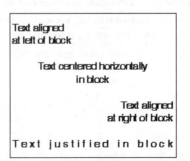

Figure 2.14
Examples of text positioning.

Justified text stretches out across the text block forming a left-aligned and right-aligned margin. Justified text can create some interesting text blocks, and is especially useful if you're doing a newsletter. Justified text appears frequently in newspapers and magazines.

Basic Corrections

You'll find many occasions for editing, or changing, your text block after you've typed in the words. For example, suppose you've misspelled a word. To make a correction, simply place the cursor where you need to edit, and use the keyboard keys to delete the wrong character or add the correct letter. If you notice your mistake after exiting the dialog box, just double-click the block, and open the dialog box again.

You can edit your text the way you do with a word processing program. This involves highlighting the word or words that you want to change. For example, if there's a word in the middle of your text block that you want to make stand out by choosing another typestyle, use the mouse or arrow keys to highlight the word. Here's how:

- Using the mouse, move the cursor to the word, and double-click to highlight.

- Using the keyboard, use the arrow keys to move the cursor to the word. Hold down the Shift key, and press the arrow keys until the entire word is highlighted.

Once you highlight a word, you can choose a new typestyle. Use these same techniques for entire blocks of text, changing sizes and styles and controlling the position of the text. Remember, you can only change what you highlight.

Editing Options

There are additional editing options you can use in the course of building your projects, such as changing a font to Bold or adding a frame or shadow to the text. Along with fonts, sizes, and positioning, these other options are available on the Tool Palette and from pull-down menus (Windows, Mac), or in your edit dialog box (DOS). You can select options anytime you're working on your project elements. Use the options to add special effects to text, control where things are placed, or change how your project looks. The following descriptions will briefly tell what each option does and where you can find it.

Option	Location	Function
Done	Dialog box (DOS)	Closes the dialog boxes and puts your changes into effect. Select this when finished editing (DOS only).
Colors	Color Palette (Windows, Mac), Dialog box (DOS)	Enables you to choose colors to use in your project. This is only useful if you have a color printer, or just want to see how different colors might look in your design. Using different colors on a monochrome printer will give you different intensities of black.
Frame	Tool Palette or Object Menu (Windows, Mac), Dialog box (DOS)	Places a box around the text block. The menu gives you several frame styles to choose from.
Move	Dialog box (DOS)	Moves a block and places it somewhere else on your project. In PSD-Windows and PSD-Mac, you can use the Pointer tool from the Tool Palette to drag and move blocks.
Resize	Dialog box (DOS)	Makes your block smaller or larger using the mouse or keyboard arrows. In PSD-Windows and PSD-Mac, you can use the pointer to click on a block corner, and drag the mouse to resize.

Rotate	Tool Palette or Object Menu (Windows, Mac), Dialog box (DOS)	Tilts your text; it works the same way as rotating a graphic. Just determine how many degrees to tilt your block.
Preview	Dialog box (Windows, Mac, DOS)	Shows you immediately how the text looks: font and size, and any special effects.
Order	Object Menu (Windows, Mac), Dialog box (DOS)	Positions, or layers, a block in the foreground or background of your project (useful for placing text over a square graphic, for example). The back drop is always the back layer, and the border is always the front layer.
Undo	Edit Menu (Windows, Mac), Dialog box (DOS)	Undoes your last action.
Delete	Tool Palette or Edit Menu (Windows, Mac), Dialog box (DOS)	Makes an entire block disappear.
Clear Text	Dialog box (DOS)	Empties your block of all text currently in it (DOS only).
Select All	Edit Menu (Windows, Mac), Dialog box (DOS)	Selects everything in the text block, making it easy to change all fonts or sizes.

To use an option with PSD-Windows or PSD-Mac:

1. If you're in a Text dialog box, just click on the option you want to select to turn it on. Select the option before typing text; or highlight the text to be changed, and choose the option.

2. If you're not in a Text dialog box, click your text block, and pull down a menu (such as the Edit or Object menu). Or click on the Tool Palette tools (you'll learn more about these under the topic of Graphics) to turn an option on.

To use an option with PSD-DOS, select the option from the Edit dialog box (see Figure 2.15). Select the option before typing text, or highlight the text to be changed, and then choose the option. You'll have to press Tab to move back and forth between the two parts of the dialog box.

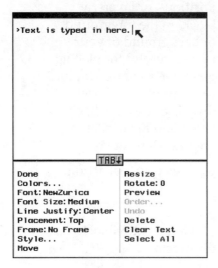

Figure 2.15
The Edit text dialog box from PSD-DOS.

Headlines Are Text, Too!

Because they have text in them, headline blocks work similarly to text blocks (see Figure 2.16). However, they can only be up to two lines long, and can be styled, shaped, and colored to create exciting messages or points of interest in your projects. One of the best features of PSD is the capability to shape your headline text. The Shape option, found in the Headline dialog box (Windows, Mac, and DOS), has 21 different shapes ranging from a plain old rectangle to a fancy double arch. These shapes can really add pizzazz to your layout.

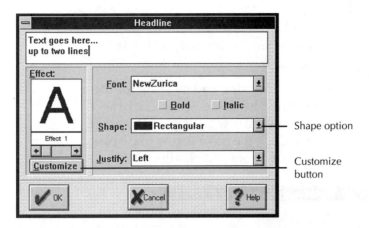

Figure 2.16
The PSD-Windows
Headline dialog
box.

To change a headline shape, just click the drop-down arrow in the dialog box (Windows and Mac), or click on the word Shape (DOS). A list of headline shapes will appear from which you can make a selection.

You can edit a headline in a variety of ways, just like a text block. The same options for controlling how text blocks look also apply to headline blocks. Refer to the previous table for descriptions of the various options.

Headline blocks have some special effects options not available in ordinary Text blocks. These effects can help you create a variety of eye-catching headlines for your projects. If you're using PSD-Windows or PSD-Mac, you'll find these special effects by clicking on the Customize button inside the Headline dialog box. If you're using PSD-DOS, these effects are found in your Headline dialog box under the options Shadow and Colors.

When PSD-Windows and PSD-Mac users click on the Customize button, a Custom Effect dialog box opens (see Figure 2.17). The following list describes the various options for customizing headline text. (PSD-DOS users can create these same effects by using the Shadow and Colors commands.) To exit this dialog box and return to the Headline dialog box, click OK.

Option	Effect
Text Effect	Changes outlining style of text.
Text Fill	Changes how text is filled in with color.
Shadow Effect	Changes type of shadow behind text.

Shadow Position	Changes positioning of shadow effect.
Shadow Fill	Changes how a silhouette effect is filled in.
Color	Controls coloring and shading for the designated headline items. Click the drop-down arrow to display the list of items. Click the color arrow to display the list of colors and shading.

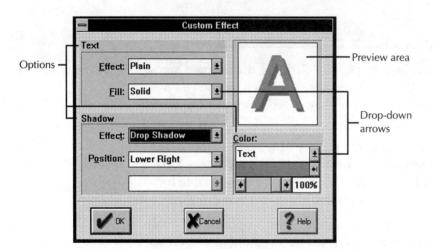

*Figure 2.17
The Custom Effect
dialog box from
PSD-Windows.*

Working with Graphic Elements

One of the most remarkable features of the Print Shop programs is the interchangeability of graphics. You can create hundreds of different looks for each project. Without graphics, you wouldn't be able to complete most of the projects in this book. Graphics are what make PSD so appealing.

What's a Graphic?

A *graphic* is any piece of artwork you include in your project: illustrations, backdrops, borders, and even ruled lines. There are three types of picture graphics in PSD: square, row, and column. Many of the PSD layouts have designated graphic elements. All you have to do is pick out a piece of art, and the computer immediately places it in your project. Figure 2.18 shows a sample square graphic.

Figure 2.18
A PSD square
graphic.

In addition, you can also select from dozens of backdrop graphics that vary in height and width, such as banner backdrops, calendar graphics, initial cap graphics, borders, miniborders, and horizontal and vertical lines. Even if these graphics aren't enough, you can always modify or change the look of your art by using the editing commands. Editing commands are available from dialog boxes, pull-down menus, or the Tool Palette. You can also purchase additional graphics libraries made specifically for The Print Shop Deluxe.

Graphic Options

Within the PSD-Windows and PSD-Mac pull-down menus and Tool Palette, or the PSD-DOS dialog box, you can choose a variety of graphic options for controlling how your art looks. Your options include colors, shadows, rotate, flip, stretch, and more. The following table details what each command does when you modify or edit a graphic. Compare the examples shown in the table to the regular square graphic in Figure 2.18.

Example	Option	Description
	Colors	Changes color, shading, and background (Behind Text) of your graphic.
	Shadow	Places a shadow behind a graphic, giving the graphic depth.

Frame

Puts a box around the graphic. There are several styles to choose from: thin, thick, double line, or drop shadow.

Rotate

Tilts the graphic block in varying degrees. PSD-Windows and Mac users can manually rotate the block with the Rotate tool from the Tool Palette, or specify exact degrees. PSD-DOS users can specify the exact angle of rotation in the dialog box.

Flip

Flips a graphic horizontally or vertically for a new perspective on your art.

Scale

Changes the size of the graphic block, larger or smaller.

Stretch

Distorts the shape of the block, squishing in or stretching out. To use the stretch option with PSD-Windows, hold down the Ctrl key while resizing the art. If you're using PSD-Mac, hold down the Option key while resizing.

Order

Positions, or layers, a block in the foreground or background of your project. This is useful for placing graphics underneath text and creating different layers of blocks. However, the backdrop art is always the back layer of your project, and the border is always the front layer.

Additionally, here are some other editing commands:

Option	Location	Function
Apply to All	Graphic dialog box	Applies your graphic edits to all graphic blocks of the same kind. For example, if your project has four square graphic blocks, you can apply the edits you make on the first block to all of the blocks, without having to select and modify each one separately. To use this command, click the check box (Windows, Mac) or select **Yes** (DOS), and any changes you make to the graphic from that point on are made to other like graphics blocks as well. (Move, Scale, Stretch, Copy, Order, and Undo commands do not work with the Apply to All command.)
Move	Dialog box (DOS only)	Repositions the graphic block in the project.
Copy	Edit Menu (Windows, Mac), Dialog box(DOS)	Duplicates the graphic block and lets you place the copy wherever you want. Windows and Mac users must use the Paste command to paste the copy into the project.
Undo	Edit Menu (Windows, Mac), Dialog box (DOS)	Undoes your last command.
Delete	Edit Menu (Windows, Mac), Dialog box (DOS)	Wipes out your block completely.

Release 1.2 If you're using PSD-DOS release 1.2, you'll find a new option for backdrops in your Edit menu—Page Blend. This new feature lets you blend the page color from one color to another. This is a special effect you can use with any of your backdrops. It gives you six effects: solid, blend across, blend down, double blend, radiant blend, and diagonal blend. Try them all out to see what color effects you can achieve.

If you're using the Windows or Mac version of PSD, you'll find a few extra editing commands at your fingertips. On the Object menu, there is a command for locking or unlocking your blocks. That's to keep them from being accidentally moved. When selected, this command locks your block into place so that it cannot be moved, rotated, flipped, scaled, stretched, resized, ordered, or deleted.

Also on the Object menu is a command for aligning blocks. This editing technique is good to use when "eyeballing" a block into place is too difficult. Select Align, and choose the alignment you want from the dialog box. There are 11 alignment options to choose from.

The View menu offers you a chance to see different perspectives of your project. You can zoom in for a closer look, zoom out, see the project at actual size or at various percentages of the actual size. Also on the View menu are options for hiding the backdrop or the Tool Palette. These options also expand on your viewing perspectives.

The Tool Palette

If you're using PSD for Windows or Mac, you'll find a slightly different approach for editing graphics. Instead of an editing dialog box, there is a handy-dandy *Tool Palette* that has icons for quick editing with a click of the mouse button. (Sorry DOS users, no Tool Palette for you. You can find all of your editing controls in the dialog boxes.)

The PSD-Windows Tool Palette has eight tools and a Color Control Panel. Take a look at Figure 2.19.

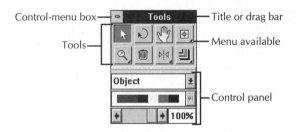

Figure 2.19
The Windows Tool Palette can help you modify graphic elements in a project.

The PSD-Mac Tool Palette has nine tools and a Color Control Panel. The extra tool found on the Mac palette is a Text tool used for working with text and text blocks. Take a look at Figure 2.20.

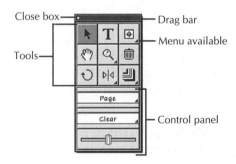

Figure 2.20
The Mac Tool Palette has nine tools and a control panel.

You can select a tool from the Tool Palette by simply clicking on the tool. Some tools have a tiny triangle in the lower right corner. This indicates there's a menu to see. To reveal the menu, move the pointer to the tool and hold down the mouse button. The menu will appear. (These menus are also available from the menu bar at the top of the window.)

You can drag your Tool Palette to another area of the screen by pointing at the Title bar (also called Drag bar), holding down the mouse button, and moving the mouse. You can close the Tool Palette by double-clicking on the Control-menu box (also called a Close box) or by selecting Hide Tools from the View menu on the menu bar. To return the palette to your screen, select Show Tools from the View menu.

Here's a list of the palette tools (except for the Mac Text tool) and what they do:

Tool	Name	Description
	Pointer tool	Mouse pointer arrow that selects the different elements in your layout; helps with resizing and moving elements around.
	Rotate tool	Tilts and turns an element in your layout.
	Hand tool	Moves your project around inside the window.
	New Object tool	Adds new elements to your layout, such as text blocks, square graphics, or borders.
	Zoom tool	Changes the display of your project. To get a close up, zoom in. To get a wide view, zoom out. There are also specific zoom sizes to select.
	Delete tool	Does exactly that; it deletes whatever you highlight on your layout.
	Flip tool	Flips an element horizontally, vertically, or both.
	Frame tool	Places borders around elements in your layout.
	Color Control Panel	Chooses specific colors and shading for parts of your layout.

More Graphics

In addition to the graphics you already know about, there are two more to learn: *initial caps* and *calendar graphics*. These square graphic types are available when you choose Other Libraries at the top of your Square graphic menu list (see Figure 2.21). You can find initial caps in the PSDeluxe Initial Caps file (Windows and Mac) or INITCAPS.PSG (DOS). Calendar graphics are in a file called PSDeluxe Calendar Icons (Windows and Mac) or CALENDAR.PSG (DOS).

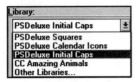

Figure 2.21
Choose Initial Caps
and Calendar Icons
from the Graphics
list.

Initial Caps

Initial caps are decorative boxes that you can use as backgrounds for single capital letters. See Figure 2.22 for an example. You can use initial caps graphics for creating projects, such as a certificate, that require a more formal look. You can also use them for the first letter of the first sentence at the beginning of a fairy tale, or in other documents that rely on a lot of text. Scaled large, they make nice backgrounds for blocks of text or a square graphic.

To use an initial cap, select the one you want from the list of graphics found in the Square graphic dialog box (choose **Other Libraries** and the initial caps file) and follow these steps:

1. Scale the graphic to the size you want.

2. Add a text or headline block on top of the initial cap background.

3. Type one letter in the block (see Figure 2.22).

To continue a sentence, just add another text block beside the initial cap graphic.

Figure 2.22
An example of an
initial cap graphic.

Calendar Graphics

Calendar graphics are great for fitting in small spaces, like in a calendar. They're monochrome (black-and-white) graphics, but you can change them to colors. You'll find uses for them in many PSD projects besides calendars.

To use, simply select the graphic you want from the calendar graphics file and scale it to fit, if necessary. Figure 2.23 shows how calendar graphics look in a calendar project.

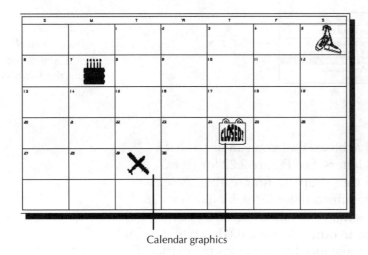

Calendar graphics

Figure 2.23 Examples of calendar graphics in a calendar.

Borders, Mini-borders, and Ruled Lines

The decorative borders and ruled lines can further your graphic potential when you're creating projects. A border or ruled line can give your project a distinct look, and a mini-border can draw attention to an important text or graphic block. Ruled lines can add some punch between text blocks. There's only one thing to remember about borders, mini-borders, and ruled lines: you cannot move, scale, or stretch regular borders, but you can modify mini-borders and ruled lines with editing commands. Knowing that, you can experiment with mini-borders and ruled lines to fashion a variety of graphic effects.

Using the Graphics Exporter

You can use the Graphics Exporter to export (send) your PSD graphics (except for banner backdrops, borders, mini-borders, and ruled lines) into other programs. When you installed PSD, the Graphics Exporter was automatically installed. You must close your PSD program to use the Graphics Exporter. (The first time you use your Exporter utility, you may have to "unpack" the program onto your hard disk drive. Just follow the prompts to do so.)

If you're using PSD-Windows:

1. Double-click on the **Graphics Exporter** icon in the The Print Shop Deluxe program group window.

2. Choose **Select a Graphics Library** from the main menu, and press **Enter**.

3. Choose your desired library, the exact graphic, and the file format you want to use. Also, select a destination for your exported graphic; where is it going?

4. When finished with selections, press **Enter** to export.

5. Select another graphic, or press Esc.

6. Select **Exit To DOS** to return to Windows.

For more information about the utility, consult your PSD-Windows manual. Now you can go into the program into which you exported your graphic.

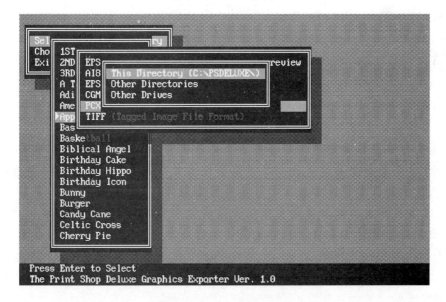

Figure 2.24
The Graphics
Exporter screen from
PSD-Windows and
PSD-DOS.

If you're using PSD-DOS:

1. Type **Export** at the DOS prompt, and press **Enter** to start.

2. Choose **Select a Graphics Library** from the main menu, and press **Enter**.

3. Choose your desired library, the exact graphic, and the file format you want to use. Also, select a destination for your exported graphic; where is it going?

4. When finished with selections, press **Enter** to export.

5. Select another graphic, or press Esc.

6. Select **Exit To DOS** to return to the DOS prompt.

   If you're using PSD-Mac:

1. Double-click on the **Exporter** icon to open the utility; click **OK**.

2. Select a library, and click **Open**.

3. Choose a graphic, and click **Export**.

4. Choose a file format (EPSF or PICT), and save the graphic to a particular destination.

5. Click **Save** and then **Quit** to exit the Exporter.

Importing Graphics from Other Programs

Good news for PSD-Windows and PSD-Mac users: you can import (bring in) graphics from other programs! If you're using PSD-Windows, you can import two kinds of other graphics: those created in an older version of NPS (The New Print Shop), or those made using Windows bit maps (BMP format), such as the Windows Paintbrush program or any other program that makes BMP files.

The easiest way to place a graphic that has been created in another program is to use the Windows Clipboard, which acts as a temporary storage space. Within the program the art originates from, copy the art to the Clipboard by using the **Copy** command from the **Edit** menu. Move to the PSD-Windows program, and open the project file into which you want to import the art. Next, select **Paste** from the **Edit** menu, and place your imported art into your project.

> *PSD-Windows Tip*   Graphics from New Print Shop or Windows' BMP files are *bit-mapped*, made from square dots. When you stretch or scale these graphics, the results will not be as smooth-looking as when you use your *scalable* graphics in PSD for Windows. Also, you cannot use New Print Shop full-panel graphics, borders, or fonts in your PSD program.

If you're working with PSD-Mac, you can import PICT files from other programs through the Scrapbook (a temporary storage place). Open the application that has the PICT file you want to use. Copy it to the Scrapbook with the **Edit Copy** command. Return to your PSD project, pull down the **Edit** menu, and choose the **Paste** command.

If you're a PSD-DOS user, you cannot import other graphics unless you have PSD release 1.2. This latest release does allow you to bring in new art (EPS, PCX, TIFF files) from other drawing programs. To import a graphic, just select **Add New Elements**, **Imported Graphics**, the desired file format, and the exact graphic location and art piece. Once the art is imported, you can move, scale, frame, and more.

Previewing Your Project

It's especially nice to be able to preview your project as a final check before you print it out, or just to see how it's progressing. The Preview function, available on PSD-Windows and PSD-DOS, is a valuable feature to use during any step of the project. Although you can certainly see a picture of your work on the project screen as you're putting it together, there are some projects in which you might want a bigger, overall view. Or perhaps you would like to see what it looks like in color. With PSD (Windows and DOS), you have expanded preview options.

There are three preview options to choose from: Color, Black and White, or Coloring Book. If you're using PSD-Windows, you must first pull down the **View** menu, and then select **Preview**. If you're using PSD-DOS, you can select **Preview** from the menu list.

When you select Color Preview from the Preview list, the screen will display a larger image of your project in color. You'll need a color monitor to see it in color, of course. If your project is too big to view in its entirety on one screen (a banner, for example), use the plus (+) key to go forward or minus (−) key to go backward and scroll along and view.

When you select Black & White Preview, the screen will display a monochrome image of your project. If you choose Coloring Book Preview, the screen will display your project in outline form, similar to a child's coloring book. You can later print out your project in Coloring Book style. Figure 2.25 shows an example of the Coloring Book preview option from PSD-DOS. Click **Done** or select **Esc** to stop the preview at any time.

Figure 2.25
The Coloring Book preview option from PSD-DOS.

Working with Files?

After you've finished a project, you're ready to save it and turn it into a file, assuming you plan to use it again. *Files* are created whenever you save a project you've made. Give each file you create a unique name to distinguish it from other files. Within a file is information pertaining to your project, whether it be a small greeting card or a large banner.

PSD offers several different ways to save a file, depending on which program version you have. You can save a file on your hard disk drive or a floppy disk.

There are two saving options you can use: a *Full Save* and a *Quick* or *Fast Save*. What's the difference? A Full Save includes all graphics you added to the project. A Quick Save just *references* the graphics. In other words, it codes the file with information on where to pick up those graphics, kind of like an ID number. A Full Save is handy when you want to give your file to another PSD user who doesn't have all the graphics you used in your project. A Full Save stores the complete project intact. However, a Full Save takes up a lot more room on your disk. Most of the time, Quick Save is the best way to save a file. However, keep in mind how your project will be used in the future and how much room you have on your disk when you make these choices.

Saving a File

To save a file when you have completed a project:

1. Select **Save** from the menu list. If you're using PSD-Windows or PSD-Mac, you'll have to pull down the **File** menu to choose **Save**.

2. Type in the name you want to give your project (eight-character maximum for PSD-Windows and PSD-DOS). Additionally, if you're using PSD-Windows or PSD-DOS, you may add a description of your project where indicated. A description may help you identify the project later on.

3. When finished, click **OK** (Windows), **Save File** (DOS), or **Save** (Mac).

To see how a file name is entered, look at Figure 2.26.

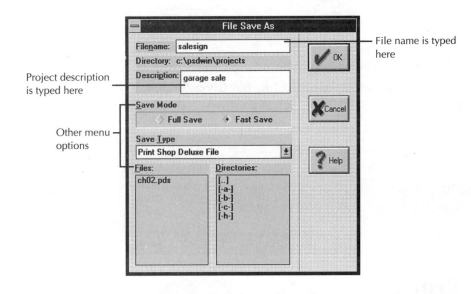

Project description is typed here

Other menu options

File name is typed here

Figure 2.26
The File Save As dialog box, PSD-Windows.

The Save As Command   Use Save As from the File menu to save a previously saved project under a new file name. For example, you could save a greeting card with the same graphic but different text.

If you'd like to start another project after saving your existing project, just open another project type. If you're using PSD-Windows or PSD-Mac, pull down the **File** menu, and choose **New**. If you're using PSD-DOS, select **Return to Main Menu**.

Using an Existing File

To work on a file you've created and saved before, you'll need to retrieve it first. If you're using PSD-Windows or PSD-Mac:

1.   Select the **Open** button on the Project menu screen. A dialog box will appear with a list of previously saved files.

2.   Highlight the project you want, and click on **OK** or **Open**.

The Open command is also available for PSD-Windows and PSD-DOS users; simply pull down the **File** menu and choose **Open**.

If you're using PSD-DOS:

1.   Select the project type from the first menu screen.

2.   The next menu gives you a chance to open an existing file. Choose **Load a saved project**.

3.   A list of previously saved files will appear, from which you can select your project.

Can't Find It in DOS?   If you don't see the file you're looking for, make sure the correct project type is selected.

Printing Your Project

The last thing to do when you've completed a project is print it out. Before you begin the steps for printing out a project, you need to set up your printer.

Setting Up Your Printer

PSD-Windows:

1. Select **Printer Setup** from the **File** menu.

2. A Printer Setup dialog box appears (see Figure 2.27), showing the current list of printer drivers available (the list is based on what you specified when you installed your Windows program).

*Figure 2.27
The Printer Setup
dialog box, PSD-
Windows.*

3. To choose further Windows printing options, select **Setup** from the Printer Setup dialog box.

4. Another dialog box appears. All the options in this dialog box are controlled by the Windows program, and not by PSD. If you need help with the other options, consult your Windows manual.

PSD-DOS:

1. Select **Setup** from the Project menu screen.

2. Depending on your printer make and model, and how you have it hooked up to your computer, enter the correct information where needed.

   The Select Printer option requires you to identify the printer model you are using. Select Printer Port is where you identify which port your printer is hooked up to. Usually, this is LPT1. Test Printer, when selected, will run a test of whether your printer and port settings are correct. If everything is correct, a message will print out: **Welcome to The Print Shop** or **Welcome to The Print Shop Deluxe**. If no message prints out during your Test Printer test, check each setting again, and consult your printer manual.

PSD-Mac:

1. Select **Page Setup** from the **File** menu.

2. Depending on your printer make and model, choose the settings you want.

Printing

To print your project:

1. Pull down the **File** menu, and choose **Print** (Windows and Mac), or select **Print** from the menu list (DOS).

2. Another menu or dialog box (see Figure 2.28) will appear offering you printing options, such as Number of Copies. After making any other appropriate selections, choose **OK** or **Print**, and the printer will be off and running.

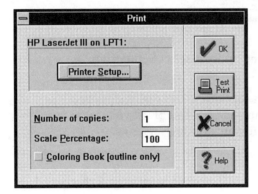

Figure 2.28
The Print dialog
box, PSD-Windows.

Because of the different size and scope of the projects you create with the Print Shop programs, there are several options to printing. For example, you can control the size of the printed project, whether it be a tiny gift enclosure card or an extra-large sign. Here are brief explanations about these other printing options. If you're using PSD-Windows or PSD-Mac, you'll find some of these options either in the Printer Setup dialog box (Windows) or by clicking the More Options button (Mac).

Option	Description
Test Paper Position	Positions the paper in the printer so that it prints out at the correct place (not available on PSD-Windows or PSD-Mac).
Number of Copies	Prints up to 99 copies of your project.
Output Size	Controls the size of your printout, based on percentages.
Paper Feed	Available option if you have a printer that can handle both single sheets of paper and continuous feed.
Print Quality	Changes your printout to different levels of DPI (dots per inch).
Print Backwards	Allows you to print your project backwards. (This isn't available for Mac and Windows users, and PSD-DOS users can use this only on sign projects.)
Coloring Book Option	Gives you a printout in outline form, very much like a child's coloring book.
Print Color Samples	Useful for those of you who have color printers.
Check SetUp	Printer setup options.
Poster Sized	Option available to PSD-Windows users that lets you print sign and calendar projects in extra-large sizes.
Scale Percentage	Allows you to scale how large your printed image prints out.

Exiting the Program

Once you've finished a project:

1. Pull down the **File** menu, and choose **Exit** (Windows and Mac). Or select **Return to Main Menu** on the menu list (DOS).

2. If your program takes you back to the Project menu or main entry screen, click on the **Exit** button.

 Faster Exits for All Using PSD-DOS? You can exit from within a project by pressing **Esc** until you reach a menu allowing you an exit to the Project menu.

Using PSD-Windows? Double-click on the **Control-menu box** in the upper left corner of your screen to exit the entire program.

Using PSD-Mac? Click on the **Close** button in the upper left corner of your window's title bar. Then pull down the **File** menu, and choose **Quit** to exit the application.

If you exit without saving your file, PSD will ask you if you want to save it. Make the appropriate response in the dialog box.

Wrap It Up

Now that you know your way around the Print Shop programs, you're probably ready to try a project. There are hundreds to choose from in the beginning of this book. Be inspired—get creative!

Installation Instructions

 If you need to install your Print Shop Deluxe (PSD) program version, follow these handy instructions:

Installing PSD for Windows:

1. Starting from the Program Manager screen in Windows, insert Print Shop Deluxe Disk 1 into drive A. (If you're using a different drive, insert the disk into that drive, and substitute that drive letter for A in the following instructions.)

2. Pull down the **File** menu from the menu bar, and select **Run**.

3. Type **a:setup** in the Command Line box. Click **OK**.

4. Enter the name of the disk drive and directory on which you want to install Print Shop Deluxe. If you do not specify a drive or directory, the program will install the copy on the C drive, in a directory named PSDWIN. Press **Enter** to continue.

5. Now the program will install itself. Follow the on-screen instructions to insert each disk.

6. When the installation procedure is complete, you'll be returned to the Program Manager window.

Installing PSD for DOS:

1. Insert PSD Disk 1 into drive A. (If you're using a different drive, insert the disk into that drive, and substitute that drive letter for A in the following instructions.) Type **A:** and press **Enter**. (If you have Windows on your computer, you must exit Windows to install PSD.)

2. At the DOS prompt, type **Install** and press **Enter**. An introduction screen will appear, detailing how the installation program works. Press **Enter**, and the installation screen will appear.

3. Select Install The Print Shop Deluxe by pressing **Enter**. (Or click the left mouse button.) A screen appears, asking you to enter a name. Type your name and press **Enter**. You can type in a second name, company, or school name on the second line, and press Enter afterward. Press **Enter** again to confirm. (If you make a

mistake, select **Edit**, and use the arrow keys to edit. Press **Enter** to continue.)

4. The next instruction will ask you to enter the source drive letter, disk drive, and the directory on which you want to install Print Shop Deluxe. If you do not specify a drive or directory, PSD will install the copy on the C drive, in a directory named PSDELUXE. Press **Enter** to continue. Press **Enter** again to confirm.

5. Now PSD will install itself. Follow the on-screen instructions to insert each disk.

6. Another screen will appear, asking if you want to install more fonts. If so, insert the fonts disk and press **Enter** (or click the left mouse button).

7. When you have installed Print Shop Deluxe, press **Enter** and you will return to the installation screen. Select **Exit Install** and press **Enter** to leave the installation program.

> **Installing Release 1.2**   If you're installing PSD release 1.2, the installation screen in Step 3 will give you four choices. Choose "Install The Print Shop Deluxe" by pressing **Enter** to install the program. If you have an earlier version of PSD on your computer, the program will ask if you would like to install over that version. If you say yes, PSD saves your earlier project files. The program automatically installs all fonts in the release 1.2 installation.

Installing PSD for Macintosh:

1. Insert Print Shop Deluxe Disk 1 into the floppy drive. (Make sure you turn off all virus detection applications.)

2. Double-click the **Disk 1** icon.

3. Double-click the **Installer** icon, and click **OK** on the Installer title screen.

4. Click **Install** to create a Print Shop Deluxe folder with the Print Shop Deluxe program in it. (If you want to choose specific files to install, click the **Customize** button. This feature allows you to highlight portions of the program to install in case your hard disk has limited space.)

5. Now PSD will install itself. Follow the on-screen instructions to insert each disk.

6. When the installation procedure is complete, click **Quit** to exit the Installer.

7. Finally, move the Print Shop Deluxe fonts into the System folder so you have access to all the Print Shop Deluxe fonts. Double-click the **Print Shop Deluxe** folder, and then drag the font suitcase (PSDeluxe.suit) out of the Print Shop Deluxe folder and into the System folder. Click OK.

Program Tip Remember to make backup copies of your original program disks and keep them in a safe place.

Installing Add-On Libraries

As if there weren't enough projects to build with your Print Shop Deluxe program, you can also purchase additional graphics libraries that instantly increase the amount of art available. The choices become almost mind-boggling.

Additional graphics libraries and folios are available for all three software programs (Windows, DOS, and Mac). There's also a Print Shop Deluxe Companion program with additional project types that include certificates, envelopes, business cards, and postcards.

To install a graphics collection or folio, follow the same installation steps listed in this appendix. When the installation screen appears, instead of choosing to install the program, choose **Install Graphics Collection** or **Install add-on Graphics Collection**.

Appendix A

Print Shop Deluxe Fonts

Paramount

Paramount Bold

Paramount Italic

SCRiBBLE

Sherwood

Signature

Stagecoach

STANDOUT

STEAMER

Stylus

Subway

Tribune

Tribune Bold

BAZOOKA

Boulder

Calligrapher

Chaucer

FILLMORE

Heather

Jester

Librarian

Moderne

NewZurica

NewZurica Bold

NewZurica Oblique

Palatia

Print Shop Headline Shapes

RECTANGULAR

DOUBLE ARCH UP

DOUBLE ARCH DOWN

ARC UP

ARC DOWN

TOP ARCH

PERSPECTIVE LEFT

FAN

PERSPECTIVE BOTTOM

ANGLE UP

ANGLE DOWN

SLANTED LEFT

BOTTOM ARCH

ROUND TOP

ROUND BOTTOM

SQUEEZE

BALLOON

PERSPECTIVE RIGHT

SLANTED RIGHT

PENNANT RIGHT

PENNANT LEFT

Appendix C

Print Shop Deluxe Graphics

Square Graphics

1st

Adirondack Chair

2nd

American Flag

3rd

Apple Basket

A to Z

Baseball

Basketball

Bunny

Children

Biblical
Angel

Burger

Cruise
Ship

Birthday
Cake

Candy Cane

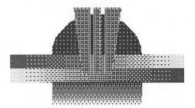
Deco Element

Birthday
Hippo

Celtic
Cross

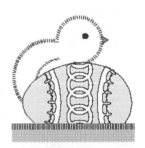
Egg &
Chick

Birthday
Icon

Cherry Pie

Elephant
Forgets

Father Time

Graduation

Ink & Pen

Firecracker

Happy Tooth

International No

Floppy Disk 3.5

Hockey

Kid & Baseball

Floppy Disk 5.25

Holiday Stamp

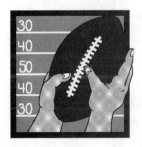

Knowledge

Football

Holly

Leprechaun

Appendix D

Lily
Ornament

Menorah

Owl

Lizards

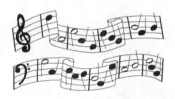
Music

Paintbrush

Lovable
Pup

New Year's
Baby

Party
Couple

Lunch

No Smoking

Pets

Math

Ornament

Pumpkin

 Pushpin

 Sale

 Starfish

 Red Cross

 Soccer

 Stork & Bundle

 Restaurant Icon

 Spaceship

 Swans

 Running

 Speech Bubble

 Teddy

 Running Computer

 Star of David

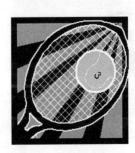 Tennis

Appendix D

Thought Bubble

Volleyball

World

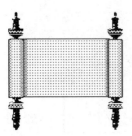

Torah

Wildflowers

Graphic Patterns

Tropical Drinks

Wine & Bread

ABC's

Valentine

Witch & Moon

Balloons

Victorian Biker

Woman in Hat

Bats & Pumpkins

*Cake
Slices*

Gifts

Red Balloons

Christmas Trees

*Leaves &
Acorns*

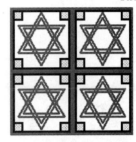

*Star of
David*

*Clips &
Tacks*

*Lips!
Lips!*

*Three-D
Shapes*

Cross

New Year

Turkey

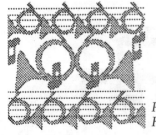

*French
Horns*

Ornaments

Appendix D

Calendar Graphics

Briefcase

Due

Athletic
Shoes

Car Trip

Exclamation

Balloon

Child
Playing

Flag

Birthday
Cake

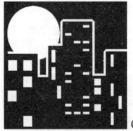

Cityscape

Heart

Book

Closed

House

Lunch

Music

Television

Mail

Phone

Ticket

Medical Symbol

Plane

Initial Cap Square Graphics

Meeting

Reminder

Border & Stars

Money

Sunny Day

Decor

Appendix D

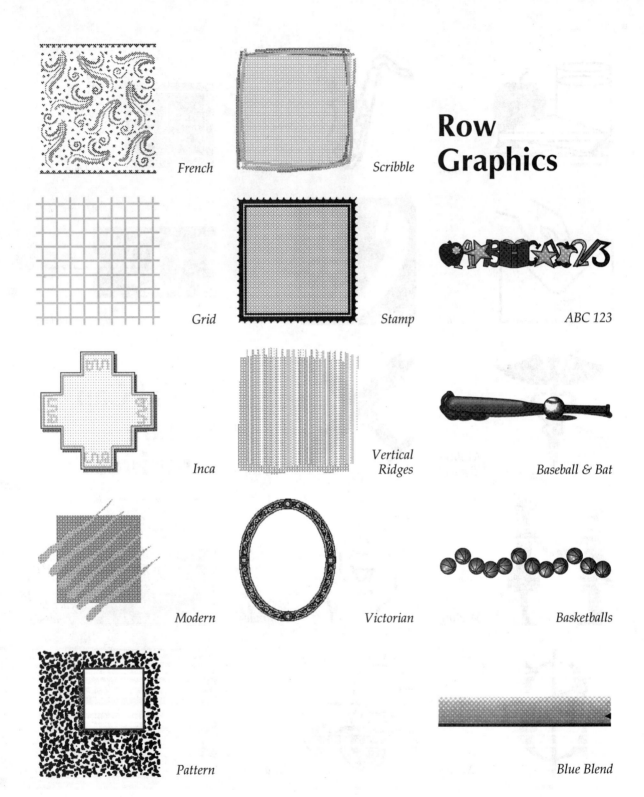

French

Scribble

Row
Graphics

Grid

Stamp

ABC 123

Inca

Vertical
Ridges

Baseball & Bat

Modern

Victorian

Basketballs

Pattern

Blue Blend

Bookworm

Dreidels

Jukebox

Bright Shapes

Football Players

Memo

Chickens

*Haunted
Cemetery*

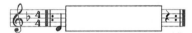

Music

Cupids

Ink Swash

Nativity

Cups & String

Jolly Pumpkins

Noah's Ark

Appendix D

Orange Slices   *Parade*   *Party Snake*

Shell   *Snowman & Hearth*   *Today's Special*

Column Graphics

Balloons   *Bat & Gloves*   *Easter Lilies*

File Cabinet

Halloween Candy

Herbs

Football Player

Hearts

Lightning Bolt

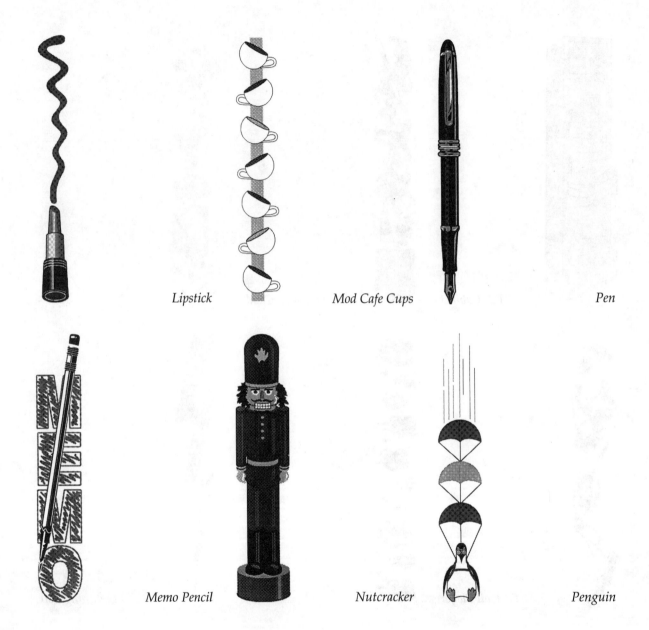

Lipstick

Mod Cafe Cups

Pen

Memo Pencil

Nutcracker

Penguin

Pillar

Restaurant Table

Southwest Strip

Presents

Space Ships

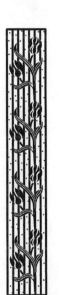

Tulip Ornament

Appendix D

Tall (Portrait) Backdrops

Waiter

Coastal Scene

Baby Animals

Column & Pen

Walking Man

Baby Quilt

Confetti

Bon Voyage

Diner Food

Clown & Hoop

Easter Basket

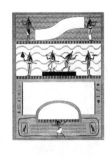
Egyptian Party

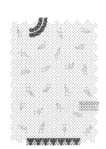
Gradient Cone

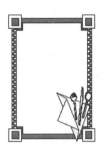
Mod Cafe

Football Field

Haunted House

Notebook

Fruit & Leaves

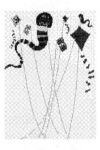
Kites

Ocean & Jungle

Geometric Box

Lilies & Birds

Party Trumpet

Gingerbread Man

Lunch Box

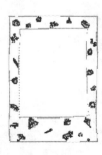
Potpourri

Appendix D

Sand Castle

Volcano

Top Fold Spread Backdrops

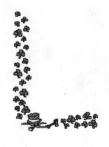

Shamrocks & Hat

Winter Child

Butterfly

Sheep in Field

Winter Snowscape

Celtic

UFO

Woodpecker

Clown & Confetti

Valentine Hearts

Cornflowers

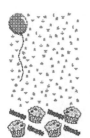

*Cupcakes &
Candy*

Party Horn

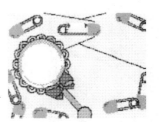

Baby Things

Doves & Mint

Watch & Confetti

Butterflies

Fireworks

Wet Duck

Candy Box

Goofy Stork

Wide (Landscape) Backdrops

Clown with Card

Haunted Tree

American Flag

Crab on Beach

Appendix D

Dance Party

Kids

Summer Sea

Dino Birthday

Party Invitation

Three Wise Men

Dragon

Recipe Card

Tree & Presents

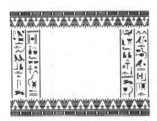

Egyptian

Schoolroom

Tropical Palms

Football Collage

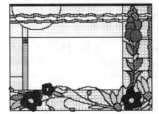

Stained Glass

Side Fold Spread Backdrops

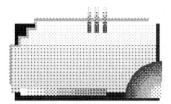

Gradient

Paper Clown

Birthday Cow

Graduation Caps

Pastel Birthday

Birthday Mice

Harvest Maize

Sleeping Bunny

Christmas Sleigh

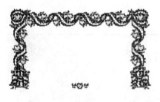

Hearts & Ribbon

Southwest

Fishing

Hourglass

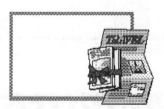

Travel

Appendix D

Witch & Spider

Banner
Backrops

Horizontal

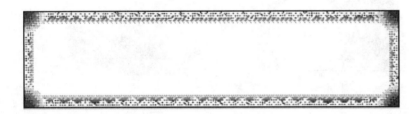

Art Deco

Balloons

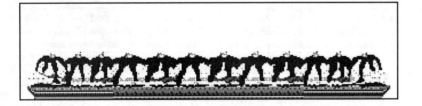

Banana Split

Celebration

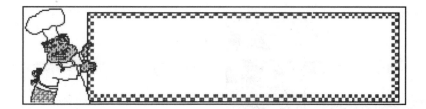

Chef

Christmas Lights

Appendix D

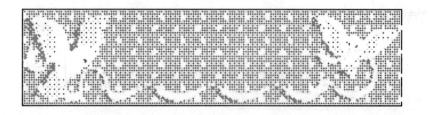

Cupids

Doves & Ribbon

Elephants

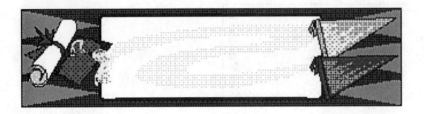

Grad Pennant

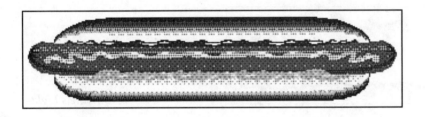

Hot Dog

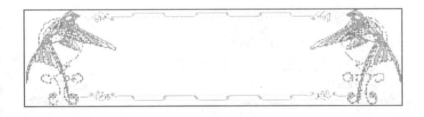

Nouveau Bird

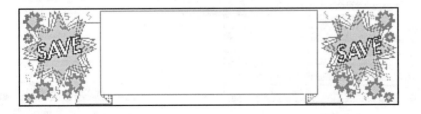

Save

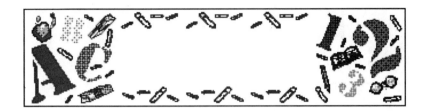

School Jumble

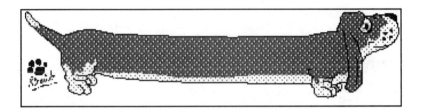

Stretch Dog

Vertical

Christmas Town

Doggone Birthday

Ice Cream Cone

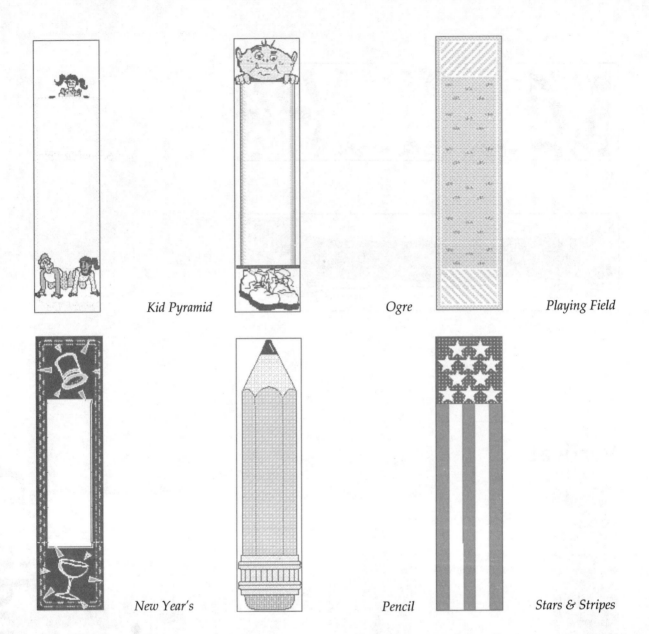

Kid Pyramid

Ogre

Playing Field

New Year's

Pencil

Stars & Stripes

Borders/
Mini-Borders

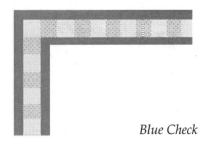

Blue Check

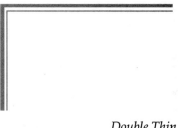

Double Thin

Autumn Leaves

Celtic

Easter Egg

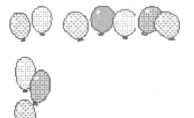

Balloons

Diamond Corners

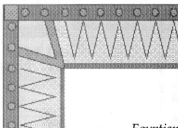

Egyptian

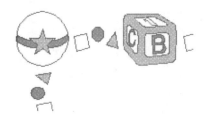

Balls & Blocks

Double Diamond

Eight Point

Bats

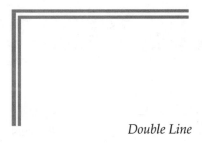

Double Line

Film Loop

Appendix D

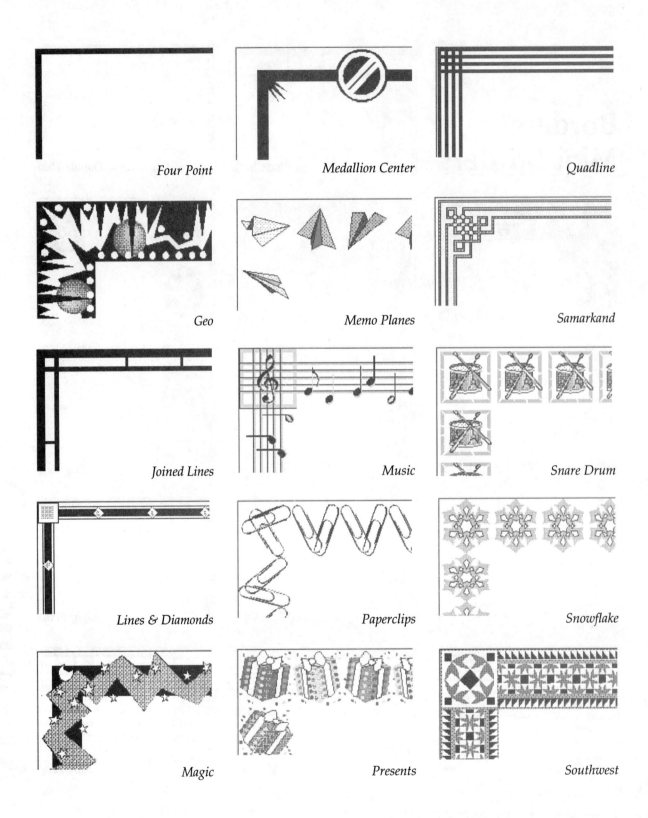

Four Point

Medallion Center

Quadline

Geo

Memo Planes

Samarkand

Joined Lines

Music

Snare Drum

Lines & Diamonds

Paperclips

Snowflake

Magic

Presents

Southwest

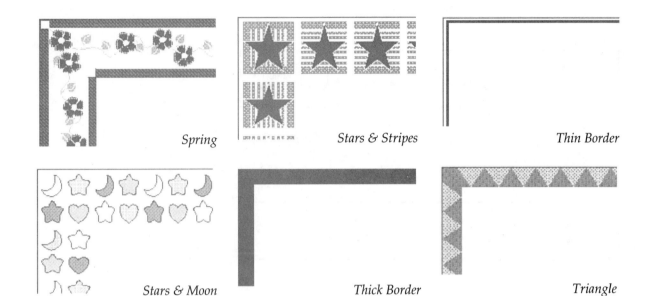

Spring

Stars & Stripes

Thin Border

Stars & Moon

Thick Border

Triangle

Ruled Lines

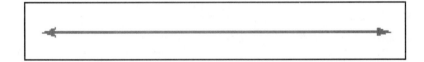

Arrow

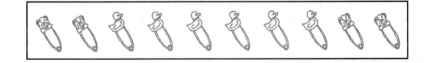

Baby Pins

Birthday Train

Cactus

Cat & Pumpkin

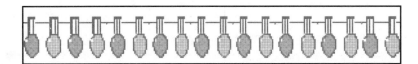

Christmas Lights

Circus Trim

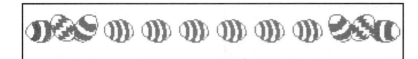

Easter Eggs

Elephants

Flower Vine

Grape Vines

Leaves & Ribbon

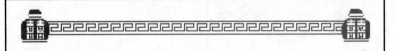

Oriental Pot

Paper Links

Sampler Stitch

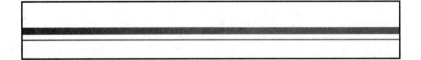

Scotch

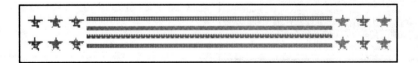

Stars & Stripes

Traditional

Wedding Lace

Witch's Broom

Symbols

3-D graphics, 67
3-D place cards, 94

A

address book, 141
Advent calendar, 85
Amazing Animals graphics
 library, 16
anniversary cards, 20
announcements, 23, 25
Apple Computers, 1
 see also Mac
art, 50
assembling projects, 189-192
assignment sheets, 125
attendance sheet, 130
award certificates, 121
awards, 152

B

baby card, 21
baby showers, 31, 93
baby-sitter instructions, 145
backdrops, 248
 banners, 254
 landscape, 251
 selecting, 189
 side fold spread, 253
 top fold spread, 250
banners
 backdrops, 254
 DOS, 63
 inspirational messages, 107
 Mac, 63
 text blocks, 65
 Windows, 62-63
birthday cards, 12-13
bitmapped files, 216
blank backdrop, 12
blank lines, 19
blocks, 196-197
 calendar blocks, 77, 79
 moving, 202
 resizing, 202
 stretching, 208
 see also headline blocks;
  text blocks
BMP files (Windows), 216

bold text, 93
bookmarks, 158
borders, 214, 259
 deleting, 21
 diamond corners, 24
 graphics, 22
 joined lines, 18
 mini-borders, 20
 Thick border, 19
brochures, 117
bulletin board notices, 106, 122
bumper stickers, 155
business cards, 42
business forms, 39
business projects
 brochure, 117
 bulletin board notice, 106
 coupons, 105
 Employee of the Month
  award, 109
 fax cover sheets, 108
 forms, 102
 mailing labels, 103
 memos, 101
 name tags, 114
 newsletters, 100
 packing list, 116
 reports, 110, 112
 résumé, 111
 time sheets, 115
 transparencies, 113
buttons (pins), 132

C

calendar graphics, 213, 240
calendars, 74-79
canning labels, 162
cards
 folding, 11
 membership cards, 151
 place cards, 94
 postcards, 164
 recipe cards, 139
certificates, 152
charts, 136-137
children's projects, 166-183
child's growth chart, 143
Christmas ornaments, 168
church newsletter, 148
church programs, 149

classroom games, 126
Clear Text option, 203
clicking mouse, 3, 187
clip art, 50
Clipboard (Windows), 50, 216
club & organization projects,
 148-155
collection chart (kids charts),
 182
color, 15, 18
 graphics, 36, 207
 text, 205
Color Control Panel (Tool
 Palette), 212
colored paper, 54
coloring book (kids projects),
 169
Colors option, 202
column graphics, 12, 244
commands, 185
confetti card, 20
copying, 14, 21, 123-124, 209
correcting errors, 201
coupons, 105
cover sheets
 faxes, 108
 reports, 110, 181
crafts
 bookmarks, 158
 decorative paper, 163
 garden labels, 160
 journal, 159
 labels, 161-162
 postcards, 164
cue cards, 128
cursor, 188
customer service response
 cards, 30

D

daily calendar, 80
decorations (parties), 89
decorative paper, 163
 see also wrapping paper
Delete option, 203
Delete tool (Tool Palette), 212
deleting
 borders, 21
 graphics, 209
 text, 203
dialog boxes, 194-196

Index

HURRY, ORDER NOW AND SAVE!

Graphics Collection for just **$29.95 each!**

Graphics Folio for just **$19.95 each!**

60-Day Money-Back Guarantee!

We guarantee you'll be delighted, or we'll refund your full purchase price. If you're not completely satisfied—for any reason—simply return the product(s) to us within 60 days.

Send along a copy of your invoice or packing slip, and we'll promptly refund your money.

Brøderbund®

1-800-521-6263
CALL NOW
REFER TO CODE 288.

Version (Check One)

Product Name	WIN	MS-DOS	MAC	PRICE	TOTAL
The Print Shop® Deluxe Sampler™ Graphics Collection				$29.95	
The Print Shop® Deluxe Business™ Graphics Collection				$29.95	
The Print Shop® Deluxe Comic Characters™				$29.95	
The Print Shop® Deluxe Fabulous Food™				$19.95	
The Print Shop® Deluxe Amazing Animals™				$19.95	
The Print Shop® Deluxe Celebrations Graphics Folio				$19.95	
The Print Shop® Deluxe Sports Graphics Folio				$19.95	
The Print Shop® Deluxe Christian Graphics Folio				$19.95	
The Print Shop® Deluxe Jewish Graphics Folio				$19.95	
The Print Shop® Deluxe Wildlife Graphics Folio				$19.95	
The Print Shop® Deluxe Dynamic Dinos™ Folio				$19.95	
The Print Shop® Deluxe Cats -n- Dogs Graphics Folio				$19.95	
The Print Shop® Deluxe Food and Dining Graphics Folio				$19.95	
				Subtotal	
				Shipping & Handling	$4.00
				Sales Tax*	
				Grand Total	

*Local sales tax must be applied in the following states: AZ, CA, GA, IL, MA, MN, NJ, OH, PA and TX.

Name

Address

City _____ State _____ Zip _____

Daytime Phone Number

Type of payment: ☐ Check/Money Order (U.S. $ only, please) ☐ VISA
☐ MasterCard ☐ American Express ☐ Discover

Account Number

Expiration Date

Signature _____ (required for credit card orders)

Make checks payable to Braderbund Software. Mail to:
Braderbund Software-Direct®,
P.O. Box 6125
Novato, CA 94948-6125

Credit card holders call:
(800) 521-6263.
Refer to code 288.

Monday - Friday, 7:00A.M. - 5:00 P.M., PST